DOWN AND OUT

Poverty and exclusion in Australia

Peter Saunders

First published in Great Britain in 2011 by

The Policy Press
University of Bristol
Fourth Floor
Beacon House
Queen's Road
Bristol BS8 1QU
UK
t: +44 (0)117 331 4054
f: +44 (0)117 331 4093
tpp-info@bristol.ac.uk
www.policypress.co.uk

North American office:
The Policy Press
c/o International Specialized Books Services (ISBS)
920 NE 58th Avenue, Suite 300
Portland, OR 97213-3786, USA
t: +1 503 287 3093
f: +1 503 280 8832
info@isbs.com

British Library Cataloguing in Publication Data
A catalogue record for this book is available from the British Library.

Library of Congress Cataloging-in-Publication Data
A catalog record for this book has been requested.

ISBN 978 1 84742 838 7 (paperback)
ISBN 978 1 84742 839 4 (hardcover)

Cover design by The Policy Press
Front cover: photograph kindly supplied by www.alamy.com
Printed and bound in Great Britain by Hobbs, Southampton
The Policy Press uses environmentally responsible print partners

FSC
www.fsc.org
MIX
Paper from
responsible sources
FSC® C020438

Contents

List of tables and figures

Tables

Figures

Acknowledgments

As with much of my previous research, this book is the product of a team effort. I have been fortunate to work with an excellent team of researchers, and in the collegial academic environment of the Social Policy Research Centre (SPRC). I want to thank in particular Yuvisthi Naidoo and Melissa Wong who undertook the bulk of the statistical analysis of the survey data with dedication and professionalism. I would never have been able to complete the task without their technical expertise (and patience!). Anna Zhu also assisted with some parts of the statistical analysis, and I benefited from several general discussions with my colleagues Bruce Bradbury, Gerry Redmond and Roger Patulny. However, the kind of research reported here requires much more than statistical expertise and many others have also played a critical role. At SPRC, I would like to acknowledge the contributions of Kelly Sutherland and Melissa Griffith, both of whom showed amazing organisational skills and first-rate technical capacity. Sally Doran acted as facilitator of the focus groups that provided the platform on which many of the indicators were built. The work on poverty discussed in Chapters Two and Three draws on a project undertaken with my colleagues Trish Hill and Bruce Bradbury, and I thank both of them for that productive collaboration and their contribution to it. Trish, in particular, dealt patiently with my numerous subsequent queries about the estimates and was able to track down details of what we had done many months after she must have thought that the project was long finished.

The bulk of the funding for the research was provided by the Australian Research Council (ARC) under project grants DP0452562 and LP0560797. The Left Out and Missing Out Project described in Chapter Four would not have been possible without the support and advice of my collaborators – Peter Davidson (Australian Council of Social Service, ACOSS), Janet Taylor (the Brotherhood of St Laurence), Anne Hampshire (Mission Australia) and Sue King and John Bellamy (Anglicare, Diocese of Sydney). Their enthusiasm, wisdom and contribution made a reality of grounding the research in the experience of disadvantaged Australians in two ways: first, they assisted with the development of the research instruments and ensured that the topics covered were relevant and incorporated appropriately; second, Janet, Anne, Sue and their teams set up the focus group interviews and conducted the welfare service client survey that were crucial in ensuring that the research tapped into the knowledge and insights of those at the poverty coalface.

I would also like to take this opportunity to thank the participants in the following seminars and conferences for their valuable feedback and suggestions for improvement: Australian National University Centre for Aboriginal Economic Policy Research; Chinese University of Hong Kong; La Trobe University School of Social Work; Macquarie University School of Sociology; University of Melbourne McCaughey Centre; University of New South Wales Social Policy Research Centre; University of Wollongong School of Economics; Beijing Normal University Institute of Public Policy and Social Development;

Oslo University College School of Social Studies; University of Turku School of Social Policy; University of Umea Department of Sociology; the Australian Bureau of Statistics; the Australian Capital Territory Community Inclusion Board; the Australian Institute of Family Studies; the Australian Institute of Health and Welfare; the Australian Social Inclusion Board; the Department of Families, Housing, Community Services and Indigenous Affairs; the South Australian Social Inclusion Unit; the Australian Council of Social Service (ACOSS); the Brotherhood of St Laurence; Catholic Social Services; Centacare, Tasmania; Legal Aid New South Wales; Mission Australia; the Social Determinants of Health Action Group; the China Research Centre on Ageing; The New Zealand Treasury; and the Norwegian Institute for Social and Labour Research.

Finally I would like to thank my partner, Janet Chan, for her support, advice and encouragement. Her scholarship, integrity and professionalism set standards that I can admire but only strive to attain.

List of abbreviations

ABS	Australian Bureau of Statistics
ACOSS	Australian Council of Social Service
ACT	Australian Capital Territory
ALP	Australian Labor Party
ARC	Australian Research Council
ASIB	Australian Social Inclusion Board
AuSSA	Australian Survey of Social Attitudes
BHPS	British Household Panel Survey
CARC	Community Affairs References Committee (Senate)
CASE	Centre for the Analysis of Social Exclusion
CESC	Coping with Economic and Social Change (Survey)
CPI	consumer price index
CUPSE	Community Understanding of Poverty and Social Exclusion (Survey)
DSS	Department of Social Security
DWP	Department for Work and Pensions
ELSI	Economic Living Standards Index
ESRC	Economic and Social Research Council
ESRI	Economic and Social Research Institute
EU	European Union
EU-SILC	European Union Survey of Income and Living Conditions
FAHCSIA	Department of Families, Housing, Community Services and Indigenous Affairs
GSS	General Social Survey
HDI	Human Development Index
HES	Household Expenditure Survey
HILDA	Household, Income and Labour Dynamics in Australia (Survey)
ICSEA	Index of Community Socio-Educational Advantage
ILO	International Labour Organization
LIS	Luxembourg Income Study
LR	likelihood ratio
LSE	London School of Economics (and Political Science)
MAP	Measures of Australia's Progress
NGO	non-governmental organisation
OECD	Organisation for Economic Co-operation and Development
ONS	Office for National Statistics
OLS	ordinary least squares (regression analysis)
PSE	Poverty and Social Exclusion (Survey)
SIH	Survey of Income and Housing
SPRC	Social Policy Research Centre
UNDP	United Nations Development Programme
UNICEF	United Nations Children's Fund

ONE

Introduction and overview

Dimensions of social disadvantage

This book is about three of the main forms of social disadvantage – poverty, deprivation and exclusion. It discusses what these terms mean, how we think about them, how we measure them, how they relate to each other and what needs to be done about them. It draws on international (mainly European) ideas and policy debates and although the evidence presented is Australian, the arguments, findings and their interpretation apply more generally.

Its starting point is poverty, since this is the aspect of disadvantage that has attracted most attention. However, poverty is only one dimension of disadvantage, and deprivation and social exclusion have emerged as concepts that can enrich our understanding of poverty, including how it is linked to other forms of disadvantage. Deprivation is an important marker of poverty, but it is possible to be deprived but not poor, or to be poor but not deprived. The lack of resources that reflects poverty can also result in exclusion, but this is not inevitable and factors other than lack of income can produce exclusion, so that one can be poor but not excluded, or excluded but not poor.

In order to understand the nature of social disadvantage in modern societies like Australia, it is necessary to explore the similarities and differences between poverty, deprivation and exclusion and identify the factors that connect them together in some circumstances, but not in others. Where these problems co-exist, they can produce cumulative disadvantage, but addressing this issue requires a clear understanding of the complex relationships that create and sustain the different forms of social disadvantage. This complexity must be recognised, both in how social disadvantage is identified and studied and in the solutions that are devised to address it. How a society chooses to define, study and debate issues of poverty and disadvantage provides an important insight into what its citizens value and how that gets translated into government action through the political system. Combating social disadvantage involves giving meaning to its various dimensions in ways that generate concepts that can be measured and once measured, monitored and varied.

Aside from questions of definition and measurement, it has become clear that there are other important signposts of disadvantage that can exert a major impact on the life chances and opportunities available to individuals. These factors are often most vividly exposed in countries that face far harsher conditions than those existing in affluent countries like Australia. Thus, at the beginning of their book *Disadvantage*, Jonathan Wolff and Avner de-Shalit (2007) discuss the case of Leah (or Lucky), a single parent born in North Africa now living in the south of Israel who lacks education and employable skills and struggles with deep depression to give meaning to a harsh and miserable life dominated by men.

After describing Leah's/Lucky's history and circumstances, they note that:

> It is currently very common to think of disadvantage in terms of poverty, and poverty in terms of low income. Obviously there are very good reasons for this, in that income allows one access to a great deal of what matters in life, and is also relatively easy to measure. However, when we think of cases like that of Leah/Lucky, the immediate problems she faces are not confined to lack of money ... her disadvantage is multi-faceted [and] plural in nature. Clearly, providing Leah with more money, and boosting her purchasing power, would have a number of positive effects ... money is an extremely valuable means to other things that make life go well. Yet it is limited too ... *redistribution of money cannot in itself end oppressive social structures.* (Wolff and de-Shalit, 2007, pp 4-5; emphasis added)

Although Leah's/Lucky's problems reflect her specific circumstances, the underlying causes – lack of adequate education, exposure to discrimination, lack of voice in events that affect her, induced depression, unwise choices and bad luck – are common causes of disadvantage for many people, not only those in developing countries, but also in modernized economies like Australia. Unless these causes are identified and their ongoing effects addressed, there will be little prospect of relieving the disadvantages experienced by people like Leah/Lucky and preventing it from being transmitted to future generations.

This suggests that although income will often present a useful starting point from which to identify who is most at risk of disadvantage, it is also important to examine how other factors impact on the likelihood that low income will result in poverty and other forms of disadvantage. Cycles of poverty that result from an inadequate education that restricts employment prospects and constrains earnings will not be prevented by income transfers alone, but also require efforts to raise human capital in ways that can provide the foundation for economic independence and improved social status.

The geographical fragmentation that is a direct consequence of the ebb and flow of the economic forces unleashed by globalisation has meant that one of the most important determinants of social disadvantage is location. This is true not only internationally (witness the problems confronting Leah/Lucky) but increasingly also nationally, as the economic fortunes of different regions within countries diverge (Vinson, 2004). Increasingly, where one lives can have a powerful impact on access to employment, on the ability of a given level of income to support a particular standard of living and on the availability and effectiveness of services to address disadvantage (Fincher and Wulff, 1998).

As Tony Vinson has argued in the Australian context:

> ... when social disadvantage becomes entrenched within a limited number of localities the restorative potential of standard services in spheres like education and health can diminish. *A disabling social climate can develop that is more than the sum of individual and household disadvantages* and the prospect is increased of disadvantage being passed from one generation to the next. (Vinson, 2007, p ix; emphasis added)

Locations, like individuals, differ along a spectrum of disadvantage that reflects differences in local labour markets (and hence job opportunities), the availability and adequacy of local services, social and community facilities and the strength of informal networks that provide support to individuals and families in times of need or crisis. Unless research has the capacity to capture these effects, it will be incapable of identifying all of the factors that contribute to poverty, resulting in a biased view that covers only a limited range of risks.

Vinson (2007, p 1) defines social disadvantage as 'a range of difficulties that block life opportunities and which prevent people from participating fully in society'. This definition highlights the idea that underlying the creation and perpetuation of disadvantage are factors and forces that are often external to those affected by it. The relational aspect of disadvantage that is a consequence of external actions that can be avoided is also emphasised by Wolff and de-Shalit, who argue that:

> By designating those who lack access to some goods ... "disadvantaged" we immediately locate these people in relation to others ... we also hint that by lacking or losing such access their disadvantage may well have been created by others, or, if not, is at least tolerated by them ... their situation is not an inevitable outcome of some "law of nature" ... but rather has to do with the social and political institutions in which they happen to live. (Wolff and de-Shalit, 2007, p 7)

Although these authors use different conceptual frameworks to identify disadvantage, they each seek to locate and analyse it in a broader social context. Although they agree that poverty is one of the factors that contributes to disadvantage, its root causes extend beyond lack of money and need to be identified and addressed separately.

One reason why poverty has exerted such a strong influence on past studies of social disadvantage is the emphasis given to the 'moral imperative' view that poverty is an unacceptable circumstance that once identified, should be eradicated (Piachaud, 1988). As Ringen (2007) has recently noted, this view places poverty on a pedestal above all other social problems, where the emphasis is on prevention, control and containment rather than elimination. Ringen notes that:

> [W]e would not say of social inequality that is should be eradicated. Inequality, if there is too much of it, should be reduced or modified.... But not so poverty. It is an unqualified bad of the worst kind. It is (next to slavery) the ultimate social ill. Therefore it should not just be reduced

or modified or brought under control; it should be eradicated.... The conditions we justly call poverty are not simply unfair or unfortunate; they are unacceptable. (Ringen, 2007, p 112)

The moral imperative that underpins this position places great emphasis on being able to agree on an operational definition of poverty and to accurately identify its existence. However, it has become clear that there is no universally agreed way of identifying poverty, making the goal of elimination unachievable. The high ideals that underlie the moral imperative view of poverty wither when confronted with the mundane realities of measurement.

The 'poverty wars' debate is in large part a reflection of the heavy moral and ideological baggage that has been attached to the concept of poverty and how it is measured (Saunders, 2005a). Studies of statistical poverty that compare incomes as reported in social surveys with a poverty line set by researchers have failed to deliver the robustness, accuracy and scientific indisputability that is required to support the moral imperative position.

This criticism applies equally to other approaches, none of which have the capacity to produce the certainty that the moral imperative position demands. This does not mean that the goal of poverty eradication must be abandoned, but that the tools used to monitor and assess progress must be acknowledged as being limited, with all the imperfections and uncertainties that this implies. The limitations of conventional poverty measures have been highlighted by analysts working with the Organisation for Economic Co-operation and Development (OECD), who have argued that:

> Income measures do not provide a full picture of "command over resources": they neglect individuals' ability to borrow, to draw from accumulated savings, and to benefit from help provided by family or friends, as well as consumption of public services such as education, health and housing. (Boarini and d'Ercole, 2006, p 10)

These arguments should have cast doubt on the wisdom and practical relevance of the moral imperative position. Instead, they have led to rejection of the conventional means of measuring poverty, leaving the problem largely intact while abandoning the measures that are a crucial part of the solution. Measurement has a role to play, but applying current analytical tools to existing data will not generate estimates that can support the normative demands of the moral imperative position. Instead, there is a need to recognise the limitations of existing measures and supplement them in ways that are capable of providing new insights into the nature of poverty in order to guide the task of reducing it.

These weaknesses in the conventional framework have resulted in a fundamental re-think of how to approach the issue of poverty measurement. Two developments have been particularly important. The first reflects a shift away from the use of 'measures' – with all that these imply in terms of scientific objectivity, quantification and precision – towards greater reliance on using 'indicators' that help to set out the broad parameters of the problem without claiming to be definitive. Indicators are particularly valuable as signposts of complex issues like multi-dimensional disadvantage, where measurement is often not only impractical, but also inappropriate.

The use of indicators has implications for the approach used to document and quantify the scope of the problem. Thus, for example:

> It is not necessarily the case that indicators can be treated like numbers by being added together, averaged or otherwise subjected to calculation. Numbers are ordinal (two is greater than one) and aggregative (two plus two is four). Many social problems, however, are incommensurate – neither ordinal not aggregative. Housing is not self-evidently more or less important than education, and a person with three problems is not necessarily worse off than someone with one. (Spicker, 2004, p 434)

The use of indicators not only highlights the difficulties of measurement, but also reinforces the multi-dimensional nature of social disadvantage (see Alber et al, 2007). Indicators also draw attention to the difficulty involved in establishing directions of change and comparing the circumstances of different groups. This in turn implies that a single policy response will often be inadequate, and that coordinated action across several areas will generally be required.

An important insight that underlies the second, more conceptual shift in recent thinking about poverty is what Ringen (1987, 1988) refers to as the distinction between direct and indirect indicators of poverty (see also Halleröd, 1994, 1995). Income is an indirect indicator, based on the premise that when it is low (relative to needs) it is unlikely to be adequate to support an acceptable standard of living. However, low income will not always translate into poverty, because those affected may have access to other resources (for example, accumulated wealth), or may have low needs that can still be met adequately from a low income. Under the indirect approach, the existence of poverty is thus *presumed* to be a consequence of low income, rather than being actually *demonstrated* to exist when income is low.

In contrast, the direct approach to poverty measurement examines living standards themselves (not just the resources that support them) to establish whether or not they are synonymous with poverty. As Ringen (1987) explains, establishing that income is low is not sufficient to prove that poverty exists. Instead:

> To ascertain poverty we need to identify directly the consequences we normally expect to follow from low income…. We need to establish not only that people live as if they were poor but that they do so because they do not have the means to avoid it. (Ringen, 1987, p 162)

This approach puts the primary emphasis on showing that the living conditions actually experienced are unacceptably low and thus that poverty exists, rather than assuming that poverty is the inevitable consequence of having a low income (Mayer and Jencks, 1988). Ringen's definition also highlights the idea that poverty is an *enforced* circumstance, one that those affected are unable to avoid. Hence the use of the term 'deprivation', which captures the notion of enforcement. This is an important feature, but one that presents a challenge when it comes to establishing that those identified as poor 'do not have the means to avoid it' – in part because of the ambiguity that attaches to the word 'means' in this context.

Under the direct approach, income is no longer used to identify poverty. Instead, the focus is shifted onto establishing whether living standard *outcomes* signify that poverty exists – an approach that is better able to identify the locational, contextual and other factors that contribute to poverty. Furthermore, because the direct approach involves establishing that poor outcomes actually exist, the focus is shifted away from examining what poverty means to those who measure it, towards an understanding of what poverty means to those who actually experience it.

Implications for research methods

This reorientation in thinking provides the basis for developing a more credible approach to poverty measurement, but it is not without its own problems. One of these relates to the difficulty involved in establishing that 'people live as if they were poor'; another concerns what it means to say that the conditions in which they live are unacceptable and unavoidable. These issues raise similar problems to those surrounding the setting of a poverty line, in this case multiplied across the many dimensions of living standards. One way of addressing them involves examining community views about what are the necessary or essential ingredients of an acceptable standard of living. If this approach can produce a coherent response, it provides a way of specifying what constitutes an acceptable standard of living (defined in terms of the items needed to sustain it) that is grounded in existing community norms, expectations and practices, giving greater credibility to the findings.

An important feature of this approach is that it can be applied to societies that differ markedly in terms of their economic prosperity and cultural values, yet still produce a list of items that are necessary to achieve an acceptable standard of living in that society. The items identified as necessary or essential will differ from place to place (and over time as living standards and community norms change) making them contextually specific, even though the basic approach has universal application. This implies that, in principle at least, the method can be used to determine what Leah/Lucky needs to live a life free from poverty in her country, just as it can be used to identify how much is needed to avoid poverty in contemporary Australia.

This feature allows the approach to be used to conduct comparative studies of countries that differ substantially in terms of their development and culture. However, this potential will only be realised if the methods are applied consistently using data that are genuinely comparable in different countries. We are currently a long way from attaining that ideal. The OECD has recently argued for greater standardisation of deprivation data, noting that:

> Achieving such standardization in statistical sources is an investment worth doing in the light of the importance for social policy of measuring material deprivation accurately. (OECD, 2008, p 194)

Those countries that have applied the approach have tended to use a similar list of variables, facilitating cross-country comparisons, as illustrated most convincingly by the European Union (EU)-sponsored Survey of Income and Living Conditions (EU-SILC) that is already generating comparative data. The Australian data described later have many similarities with these data, making it possible to include it in the EU comparisons that are already underway (see Whelan et al, 2008; Australian Social Inclusion Board (ASIB), 2009a; 2009b).

A further problem relates to whether it can be assumed that the specification of an acceptable standard of living is any less susceptible to the measurement problems that have bedeviled the use of poverty lines. Strictly speaking, the answer is probably no, although it is important to note that indicators of deprivation are generally used to help identify who is in poverty and how much income is needed to avoid it, not to provide definitive measures of poverty directly (Berthoud et al, 2004). Again, the use of indicators implies a more nuanced and less dogmatic assessment, making the debate over statistical measurement and accuracy less relevant.

This shift of emphasis does not negate the need to strive for accuracy in the reported data and to check the robustness of the indicators used, since this will enhance their relevance, robustness and credibility. While these issues must be addressed, the key point is that the direct approach locates the identification of poverty within a living standards framework that is focused on outcomes achieved rather than income available. If it is accepted that poverty is not always a consequence of low income, then it follows that alternative ways of identifying poverty are needed. The living standards approach provides a lens through which to examine people's lives, focusing on what they do and do not have, can and cannot afford, do and do not do, and do or do not feel. By concentrating on what Sen (1992) refers to as the level of functioning, the identification of poverty is linked more directly to what is actually achieved (or not) rather than on what a given level of income can (or cannot) buy.

One important issue that is highlighted in Sen's work relates to the role of agency – the ability of individuals to set and pursue their own goals – and the importance of choice in facilitating the freedom to act. An essential feature of poverty is that it restricts the ability to achieve goals that individuals themselves have reason to value – what Sen refers to as their capabilities. However, it is also important to establish that what is identified as poverty reflects enforcement rather than choice, or to show that those identified as poor 'do not have the means to avoid it'.

As Giddens has noted, those who choose to live a particular lifestyle – no matter how unacceptable others may regard it – are exercising a choice and cannot therefore be identified as poor.

> Equality and inequality revolve around self-realization. Apart from where people lack even the minimal requirements for physical survival, the same is true of poverty. What matters isn't economic deprivation as such, *but the consequences of such deprivation for individual's well-being.* People who choose to live frugally are in quite a different position from those whose existence is blighted by unwanted poverty. (Giddens, 2000, p 88; emphasis added)

Establishing whether observed living standards reflect enforcement or choice presents another formidable challenge for the new poverty research. The methods used to distinguish between choice and constraint are not ideal and have been subject to extensive criticism, although Giddens' suggested examination of the consequences for well-being provides a promising avenue that is explored in detail in later chapters. The difficulty in isolating the role of choice and constraint can be seen as a weakness of the approach, although it is important to note that it has been effectively ignored by the conventional income approach, where it is assumed that low income automatically acts as a binding constraint on what can be achieved.

In order that these shifts in how poverty is conceived and identified generate new insights into the nature of poverty, it is necessary to determine what is acceptable in the different dimensions of living standards. This has important consequences for how poverty research should be designed and conducted. Comparing incomes with a poverty line may provide the starting point from which to identify who is *at risk* of experiencing poverty, but it must be accompanied by additional evidence showing that this risk translates into an unacceptable standard of living. The use of indicators reinforces the idea that these causal links are not always present, but if a range of indicators all point in the same direction, the probability that this is the case will be greater.

Implicit in these arguments is the view that estimates of poverty defined in terms of low income still have an important role to play in helping to understand the broader picture of social disadvantage. Despite the measurement problems and data limitations, income remains a major determinant of most people's standard of living, with important flow-on effects in other areas of disadvantage, including material deprivation and social exclusion. Income is also an important marker of social status and well-being, while income differences attract considerable public interest, and income redistribution is one of government's principal means of tackling poverty and achieving greater equality.

For all of these reasons, it is important to monitor the income dimension of poverty, but to bear in mind that these estimates need to be placed in the broader context that shapes the contours of social disadvantage. To have an income below the poverty line is to be at risk of poverty and even if other factors prevent this risk from translating into reality, minimising the risk is an important policy objective in its own right.

Engaging with the community

One way of undertaking a broader examination of poverty would be to delve into the details of people's lives in order to establish whether they are achieving a standard of living that is consistent with community standards of acceptability. The findings could then be used to highlight who is missing out, on what, and thus to help identify what forms of additional assistance are required. However, such an approach would be extremely intrusive and it would be difficult to separate the complex links between needs and expectations, resource constraints and preferences that determine the actual choices made (or not made).

An alternative approach is needed that taps into actual experience in a way that respects people's right to privacy, but gives them a voice in identifying the role of constraint and choice in observed consumption patterns, and in judgements about whether or not they are acceptable. In pursuing this idea, poverty is conceived not as a statistical label attached on the basis of arbitrary classifications based on income, but as a description that captures people's aspirations and agency (Lister, 2004).

This shift involves treating those who are the focus of poverty research not as passive subjects to be studied, but as active participants in the research process. How far this process of involvement is taken depends on the goals of the research. If, as here, the main focus is on developing new indicators and applying these to identify the nature and extent of social disadvantage, the involvement should include participating in developing indicators that build on the insights, knowledge and experiences of those living at the coalface of poverty. In other cases, where the focus is on designing action to combat poverty, the scope for active participation will be greater and the underlying imperatives more compelling (Lister, 2004, Chapter 6).

The narrower approach taken here builds on earlier studies that have broadened our understanding of poverty through in-depth study of the lives, experiences and attitudes of those living in, or surrounded by it (for example, Peel, 2003). The approach developed later does not seek to represent the hopes, achievements and disappointments of its subjects in any detail, but uses their views to shape the data collected and indicators developed. This requires the active participation of those with first-hand knowledge about the experience of poverty, including how it constrains the ability to sustain a decent and acceptable standard of living.

Past experience indicates that those people who are experiencing poverty are often unlikely to respond to surveys that are sent to members of the general population. If the bias that results from this under-representation is to be avoided, special efforts are required to ensure greater participation by those likely to be most disadvantaged. These problems can be overcome through working in partnership with community sector agencies whose job it is to deal directly with poverty and its consequences on a daily basis. Those who work to alleviate the harmful effects of poverty can provide an important bridge between those who study it and those who experience it, in the process contributing their own knowledge and insights. This involvement has played an important role in shaping the scope of the research, how it was conducted and how its findings have been assembled and disseminated.

Poverty and deprivation

The remainder of this book is structured around the concepts of poverty, deprivation and social exclusion. Some of the limitations of conventional poverty measures have already been canvassed. The concepts of deprivation and exclusion have emerged and evolved in response to the limitations of income-based poverty measures, although they achieve this in different ways. They are similar in that each seeks to provide a broader perspective on the nature of social disadvantage that pays greater attention to the factors that create, and the outcomes associated with, poverty; they also both adopt a multi-dimensional perspective that locates poverty within a broader living standards framework. They seek to identify what is an unacceptable standard of living by using community views to specify the items and activities ('having and doing') that are regarded as normal or customary in a particular society at a particular point in time.

There are, however, important differences between the ideas underlying the two concepts and how they have been used to better understand poverty and social disadvantage. These will become apparent in the detailed discussion that follows, although it is useful to note at the outset that whereas deprivation has been used to operationalise the definition of poverty by giving concrete meaning to what constitutes an unavoidable and unacceptable standard of living, social exclusion has provided an alternative paradigm that focuses on how relationships, institutions, patterns of behaviour and other factors (including a lack of resources) prevent people from participating fully in the life of their community. Thus while the deprivation approach seeks to overcome the limitations of poverty line studies, social exclusion seeks to offer a broader framework for addressing issues of disadvantage and non-participation.

The deprivation approach has mainly been used to better identify who is in poverty and, in some applications, to help identify an income level that could be used as a poverty line (measured in terms of income). Following its initial development by British sociologist Peter Townsend (1979), the methods used to identify deprivation have been refined in a series of (mainly British) studies (Mack and Lansley, 1985; Gordon and Pantazis, 1997a, 1997b; Callan and Nolan, 1993; Nolan and Whelan, 1996; Pantazis et al, 2006a). These refinements have been accompanied by applications of the deprivation approach to measure child poverty in the UK (Adelman et al, 2003) and to measure deprivation generally in other European countries (Kangas and Ritakallio, 1998; Whelan et al, 2003; Muffels and Fourage, 2004; Halleröd et al, 2006; Whelan and Maître, 2009; Whelan and Nolan, 2009) and have culminated in the inclusion of the questions needed to identify deprivation in the EU-SILC mentioned earlier.

The methodological and empirical improvements generated by these studies have resulted in the deprivation approach becoming part of mainstream poverty research, particularly in Europe (Townsend, 1987). It has been used to supplement low income in the battery of measures used by the British and Irish governments to track movements in poverty in order to assess whether official poverty reduction targets are being met (Department for Work and Pensions (DWP), 2002, 2003a; Office for Social Inclusion, 2004). The same broad approach has also been applied in countries as diverse as Hong Kong (Chow, 1983; Hong Kong Council of Social Service, 2010), Japan (Abe, 2006) and South Africa (Noble et al, 2007; Wright, 2008; Barnes, 2009) and forms the basis of the Economic Living Standards Index (ELSI) developed by the Ministry for Social Development in New Zealand (Jensen et al, 2002, 2003; Krishnan et al, 2002; Perry, 2009).

The increased use of indicators of material deprivation has been described as having 'swept the social policy world as a complement, or even as an alternative, to household income as the primary measure of living standards' (Berthoud and Bryan, 2008, p 14). Confirming this trend, the OECD has argued in its influential report on trends in income inequality and poverty that conventional (income-based) poverty rates should be complemented by deprivation measures because:

> Measures of material deprivation point to the importance of looking at factors that go beyond the income and earnings capacity of people, to other constituents of an acceptable standard of living. (OECD, 2008, p 194)

The attention being paid to deprivation by national governments and international agencies like the OECD suggests that deprivation research has the capacity to provide a better understanding of social disadvantage and to produce a more informed policy response to poverty.

Social exclusion

Social exclusion has emerged as a major organising theme of social policy in an increasing array of countries and has influenced how issues are conceived, debated, researched and addressed. Its modern usage began in France in the 1970s, where it was used to capture the idea that certain groups were marginalised, alienated and effectively excluded from the French social protection system (Paugam, 1995, 1996; Whiteford, 2001). Béland (2007) notes that despite its initial popularity among academics in France, the impact of the exclusion paradigm on policy has been greatest in the UK. There, it was identified in the mid-1990s as one of the thematic priorities of Britain's Economic and Social Research Council (ESRC, 1997) and has since exerted a powerful influence on the formulation of British social policy under the Labour governments of Tony Blair and Gordon Brown.

The National Action Plans released by these governments identify a suite of indicators of exclusion and inclusion, report trends and compare the UK with other EU countries (for example, DWP, 2006). The importance of policies that promote social inclusion and social cohesion has also grown in the EU, where the development of indicators of exclusion has re-invigorated the social indicators movement more generally (Atkinson et al, 2002; OECD, 2010). Interest in the concept among European policy makers culminated in an agreed set of indicators (the 'Laeken indicators', see Dennis and Guio, 2003) that are produced and published in each country and used to monitor progress. The significance of these developments was reflected in the 'Lisbon Agenda' that places social exclusion at the centre of the European social policy agenda (Atkinson, 2007).

In Australia, promoting social inclusion was identified as a central part of the policy platform that the Australian Labor Party (ALP) took to the 2007 federal election. Following its election victory, the government established a Social Inclusion Unit in the Department of Prime Minister and Cabinet and appointed a Social Inclusion Board to provide advice on how to take the new policy agenda forward. Recent reports set out the principles underlying the government's social inclusion agenda, identify policy priorities and present a compendium of social inclusion indicators that can be used to assess Australia's performance and compare outcomes with those achieved in a range of EU countries (Australian Government, 2008, 2009; ASIB, 2009a, 2009b). These developments illustrate that, like in the UK, social exclusion and social inclusion have emerged in Australia as essentially political constructs. This feature has implications for how research is conducted and used, as will be discussed in more detail later.

In contrast to the research on deprivation, where the focus has been on addressing the deficiencies of the income poverty approach, social exclusion has been adopted as an overarching framework for identifying and addressing a range of social problems, one of which is poverty. Definitions abound, but most emphasise that exclusion is the end result of a set of processes that prevent people from participating in different forms of economic, social and political activity. Poverty that results from low income is one among many factors that impede or prevent participation, but its effects are often combined with other factors such as discrimination, fear, low education, geographic isolation and lack of information or access to key services. The effects of exclusion can be wide (affecting large groups of people in specific ways), deep (affecting smaller groups in multiple ways), or concentrated (affecting those living in specific localities) (Hayes et al, 2008).

The adoption of a policy framework designed to promote social inclusion suggests a more remedial, action-oriented focus for government action that focuses on the multi-dimensional, often cumulative, causes and manifestations of social disadvantage. Simplistic solutions have not worked because they have not recognised the underlying complexities; instead, 'joined-up' responses are required to address the many causes in a concerted and integrated manner. Implicit in this approach is the idea that coordination will generate greater returns in terms of policy outcomes than isolated initiatives introduced independently. Thus, for example, providing increased income to the poor will only be effective in the longer term if it is accompanied by other measures that address the many other problems faced by those below the poverty line – poor education, lack of relevant skills, limited access to transportation and other basic services, unsafe and threatening social environments, and so on.

The emergence of studies of deprivation and exclusion not only reflects the inherent strengths of both concepts, but also the fact that studies have shown that those identified as poor on the basis of their income are not the same as those identified as deprived or excluded (Perry, 2002; Bradshaw and Finch, 2003; Hills, 2004). As a recent review of literature in the field has noted:

> In the poverty context, it has been argued forcefully that low income may fail in practice to distinguish those experiencing distinctively high levels of deprivation or exclusion, and studies using direct measures of deprivation for a range of countries have lent some support to this assertion. (Nolan and Marx, 2009, p 319)

This claim is supported by research which finds that 'deprivation is a much stronger factor in distinguishing the economically vulnerable from the non-vulnerable' (Whelan and Maître, 2008, p 212), and that this effect is apparent in both affluent and less-affluent EU countries.

The lack of overlap (or mis-match) between the different indicators in part reflects the fact that the standard of living is determined by a number of factors other than income that are captured in different ways in indicators of deprivation and exclusion (Perry, 2002, Figure 1). It also reflects the underlying dynamics that link changes in people's income to changes in their standard of living and hence to the deprivation and/or exclusion actually experienced (Gordon, 2006). This implies that the incidence of deprivation and exclusion should be identified separately from poverty, in order to compare overall magnitudes and incidence patterns and to determine the degree of overlap or mis-match between them. These results can also be used to develop compound indicators that combine elements of the different approaches.

In terms of policy impact, it can be argued that research on deprivation and exclusion/inclusion have had more of an impact over the last decade than poverty research managed to achieve over the previous half-century. This is not so much because the new approaches provide better concepts or indicators, but because they recognise the complex nature of social disadvantage and do not seek to reduce it to a single (monetary) dimension. They also avoid the normative strictures of the moral imperative position that governments are understandably reluctant to acknowledge, given the frailties of poverty measures.

Deprivation and exclusion represent the modern faces of social disadvantage, although the direct links to low income are often tenuous. Each reflects the constraining influence of inadequate resources, while recognising that individuals are also constrained by structural forces and prevailing attitudes and practices in ways that require a broader policy response. Even so, they have the potential to illuminate aspects of poverty that, together with other factors, can explain why some people are denied the opportunities and experiences that enrich the lives of others.

Outline of the book

The structure of this book reflects the concepts and arguments identified in this discussion. The focus of the next two chapters is on the strengths and limitations of the conventional income approach to poverty measurement. Because of its importance, both as a benchmark against which to compare alternative approaches and as a focus of policy interest and action, a natural place to start is with studies that estimate poverty by comparing income with a poverty line.

Chapter Two presents conventional poverty estimates for Australia to show its magnitude and how its incidence varies across socioeconomic groups and has changed over time. Estimates of Australian poverty are then compared with estimates for other OECD countries, as a way of highlighting what is different about Australia and, in a rudimentary way, to reflect on how these differences relate to different welfare state regimes and policy approaches. Chapter Three extends the analysis of income poverty by combining income-based estimates with other (primarily economic) information that is designed to establish whether those with incomes below the poverty line are indeed poor. The analysis represents a first step along the path from an indirect (income-based) approach to a more direct approach that seeks to incorporate information about the living standards actually achieved, and opens up several issues and methods that are taken up in later chapters.

Chapter Four describes the research that forms the basis of the empirical material presented in later chapters. The Left Out and Missing Out Project was built on a unique partnership between researchers, policy analysts and practitioners that developed a set of indicators of disadvantage that reflect and embody the insights of those experiencing poverty. It facilitated the collection of the data required to produce these indicators in a way that draws on the views of low-income Australians who are forced to rely on the support and assistance provided by community sector (welfare) agencies. Key features of the project are described and some of the background data produced from the Community Understanding of Poverty and Social Exclusion (CUPSE) Survey (originally conducted in 2006) are used to set the scene for later chapters.

Chapter Five summarises the key features of the deprivation approach, including the role of community input, and explains how the CUPSE data were used to identify those items regarded as essential ('the essentials of life') in contemporary Australia. These items are identified and analysed to determine the underlying needs that they are intended to fulfil and how they relate to each other. The findings are examined to identify differences in the responses held by different groups in the community and to establish whether or not a consensus exists about the identification of essential items. The results provide a fascinating insight into the modern Australian psyche, at least as it is reflected in what the majority regard as essential – things that no one in Australia should have to go without.

Chapter Six compares alternative approaches to the measurement of deprivation and examines how they differ and the merits of each. Estimates of the overall incidence and structure of deprivation are presented and examined statistically to see if it is possible to identify a small number of items ('basic deprivation') that can capture the essence of the problem. The use of alternative weighting schemes is examined to assess the sensitivity of the estimates to the methods used to derive them. Finally, the estimates are used to examine and compare the adequacy of the Australian age pension and other income support payments as a way of highlighting the valuable role that deprivation research can play in informing policy in the vexed and challenging area of income support adequacy.

Chapter Seven brings together the analysis presented in Chapters Two and Six to examine the relationship between deprivation and poverty in more depth. The two concepts are compared in terms of how well each is able to identify those who are most disadvantaged. The relationship of poverty and deprivation to several indicators of well-being is then used to assess how well each indicator captures a situation that is harmful to those who experience it. They are then shown to differ empirically by examining the overlap between them: who is poor but not deprived, who is deprived but not poor, and who is both deprived and poor. This third (overlap) category forms the basis for the measure of consistent poverty that is explained and applied for the first time in Australia using the CUPSE data.

The concept of social exclusion is given a thorough examination in Chapter Eight, which explains how it relates to other major policy themes, including poverty and inequality. What is unique about social exclusion is discussed, along with its salience to current and emerging policy priorities. The different dimensions (or domains) of exclusion are identified and the role of social exclusion/inclusion in informing social policy is examined, before the discussion focuses on the emergence and evolution of the social inclusion policy agenda in Australia.

Chapter Nine presents new results on the incidence of three dimensions of exclusion in Australia: disengagement; exclusion from basic services (public and private); and economic exclusion. The profile of exclusion is then examined more systematically, focusing on the role of socioeconomic factors such as gender, age, family type and economic status. Attention then focuses on the incidence of multiple exclusion (within and across domains) and the characteristics of those in deep (multi-dimensional) exclusion. The incidence of exclusion among groups known to be susceptible to poverty is explored as a way of demonstrating that poverty and exclusion are different, and this is confirmed using overlap analysis. Finally, the links between exclusion and perceptions of well-being are examined as a way of confirming that exclusion is an enforced condition that has negative consequences for well-being.

The main implications of the findings for research and policy are examined in Chapter Ten, where it is argued that better data are needed to gain a more complete understanding of the nature of deprivation and exclusion, how they relate to poverty and what this implies for policies designed to address social disadvantage. The data generated by quantitative surveys must be complemented by the information gathered in qualitative research that explores the processes, attitudes and behaviours that give rise to different forms of disadvantage and shapes the underlying dynamics, within and across generations. Discussion then focuses on the role of dissemination, a much-neglected topic that can play an important role in determining whether or not research has an impact. It is argued that more effort is needed to bridge the gulf that currently exists between researchers and policy makers and that better dissemination has a critical role to play in achieving this goal.

The analysis and results presented throughout the book are designed to illustrate how social science research and the evidence it produces can be used to inform social policy development. Conducting the kind of research reported here is an integral part of this process, but effective dissemination of the core messages is also imperative. The strength of the deprivation and exclusion paradigms is that they draw on community understanding of what is needed by all members of society to function fully and effectively as citizens, and this gives them both scientific validity and political credibility. The voices of those who are experiencing poverty are built into the instruments used to identify and measure the different forms of social disadvantage. This makes for a compelling message that those with the power to bring about change should listen and pay heed to.

TWO

Income poverty

Introduction

Two of the principal aims of poverty research are to identify who is poor and to quantify the extent of poverty – in total and among specific groups. These tasks are important because they establish the scope of the problem, highlight where action is needed to address it and can be used to assess the impact of those actions. The estimates provide the basis for examining the association between poverty and such factors as age, family structure, labour force status, health or disability status, migrant status and location. These associations point to some of the causes of poverty, as well as some of its consequences, but these important topics require additional research.

A key component of any poverty study is a poverty line. This provides a benchmark that is used to identify who is poor according to whether income is below or above the line. Government concern about the accuracy and usefulness of poverty lines has not prevented community sector agencies from using them – and the poverty rates derived from them – to draw attention to the issue of poverty and pressure governments to do more about it. In 2007, for example, a consortium of community sector agencies released the report *A fair go for all Australians: International comparisons 2007* that provided details of poverty in Australia and highlighted the failings of successive governments to address poverty effectively (ACOSS, 2007a).

In an update of those findings, it was noted that:

> [T]he ideal of a fair society is not one that can be achieved through the existing policy settings. While 22 out of 30 OECD nations have implemented national social inclusion or poverty strategies to share the social and economic benefits of the nation, Australia has no coordinated response to disadvantage. Given the persistence of joblessness, poor health and other forms of disadvantage for some Australians, such a strategy is needed to bring people in from the margins of society and provide a tool to strengthen communities for the future. (ACOSS, 2007b, p 1)

One of Australia's oldest welfare agencies, the Brotherhood of St Laurence, was established during the Great Depression with the goal of ending social injustice by fighting for an Australia free of poverty. It conducts and sponsors research on poverty and disadvantage with a view to developing new measures that can inform and assist in these tasks. Yet as its executive director has noted, 'our society is still producing a hard core of people in persistent poverty, and we need to direct much of our effort to helping them lift themselves out of it' (Nicholson, 2005, p 1). This concern was reinforced in a report released by The Salvation Army (2010) that pointed out that its service centres were seeing 'the need deepen and the level of disadvantage increase' (p 3). It called for a national child poverty strategy 'to ensure all children thrive academically and emotionally', linked to broader efforts to reduce the growing numbers of working poor.

Research on poverty trends commissioned by another leading agency, The Smith Family, caught the imagination of the public by showing that poverty remained widespread at the end of the 1990s following a decade when the Australian economy grew strongly and average living standards rose sharply (Harding and Szukalska, 2000; Harding et al, 2001). That research identified a growing number of 'unlucky Australians' who had missed out on the benefits flowing from economic growth, prompting the agency's research manager to ask, 'Why, in an otherwise rich country with many opportunities, are so many people experiencing financial disadvantage?' (Simons, 2000, p v). Concern over the growing number of Australians in poverty also prompted the St Vincent de Paul Society to express concern that the growing gap between rich and poor has the potential to produce 'the emergence of two nations with conflicting aspirations and cultures' (McCarthy and Wicks, 2001, p i).

The voices of concern emanating from community agencies working directly on poverty issues stand in stark contrast with the virtual silence from within official government circles, where 'the p-word' was effectively banished from the official language used by ministers in the Howard government that ruled between 1996 and 2007.

The latest official view of Australian poverty is contained in the report *A hand up not a hand out: Renewing the fight against poverty*, which was released following an Inquiry into Poverty and Financial Hardship conducted by the Senate Community Affairs References Committee (CARC, 2004). The Senate report drew on information contained in 259 written submissions, 23 pieces of additional information and hearings with over 240 witnesses and its 95 recommendations were based on the claim that 'current levels of poverty in Australia are unacceptable and unsustainable'. The government ignored them.

A dissenting view, signed by two Liberal senators on the Committee, claimed (incorrectly) that 'no government in the world has ever accepted a figure on the poverty line' and asserted (incoherently) that 'setting targets have [sic] no real benefit, they are a poor measure and are misleading and measuring poverty through "income" has found to be inaccurate' (CARC, 2004, p 447). The divergence of views expressed by those involved in the Inquiry reflects deep-seated political disagreement about how to define and measure poverty, particularly against a background of rapidly rising real incomes, and the implications for government action. Senators split along party lines, with some regarding poverty as a major social problem that can be addressed if informed by research, and others seeing it as a controversial and contested issue that is fundamentally ideological.

It was not until the ALP government took office in 1997 that there was official recognition that poverty exists and presents a challenge for policy that cannot be solved by economic growth alone. Growth provides the extra resources needed to address the problem, but those resources must be redistributed to those affected by poverty because this will not occur automatically through an (unspecified) 'trickle down' process. Participants in the 2020 Summit established to generate policy ideas and priorities for the new government emphasised that poverty was a 'first order issue' that needed to be addressed by setting poverty reduction targets and monitoring progress towards their achievement (Department of Prime Minister and Cabinet, 2008a, 2008b).

The wavering fortunes of poverty on the Australian policy agenda are a direct consequence of the 'poverty wars' debate that split sections of the research community at the turn of the century, undermining public confidence in the poverty statistics and providing the government with an excuse for its lack of action in the area (Saunders, 2005a). Those engaged in the debate were also aware of the limitations of the measures used and concerned about their lack of purchase with policy makers, as well as with voters (Whiteford, 1997). By casting doubt on the poverty line and the estimates based on it, conservative forces exploited the lack of agreement among researchers about where to set the line, undermining the reliability of *any* attempt to estimate poverty. This scepticism was exploited by a government that was keen to see public attention focused on the incomes that were increasing rather than on the misfortunes of those who were being left behind. Meanwhile, the public became confused and alienated by the whole debate.

Concern over the reliability of poverty estimates was reinforced by the fact that most Australian poverty research relied on the Henderson poverty line developed by the Poverty Commission in the 1970s, which had its roots in the notion of a basic wage that was embedded in the Harvester (wage) Judgment of 1907 (see Saunders, 2005b). By the end of the 20th century, the Henderson line was over three decades old and well past its use by date. Other countries (mainly in Europe) were using a more explicitly relative measure – in most cases set at either 50% or 60% of median income – yet these did not have the ability, encapsulated in the Henderson–Harvester tradition, of locating the measurement of poverty within a framework shaped by Australian historical experience, values and institutions (including its characterisation as a 'wage earners' welfare state'; see Castles, 1985, 1994).

However, if the limitations of the Henderson poverty measure were to be addressed by a new poverty line, the critics could be relied on to assemble the same battery of arguments to cast doubt on the new measure. What was needed was not a new poverty line, but a whole new approach to thinking about poverty that was capable of:

• developing a range of new indicators of poverty and disadvantage that draw on recent international research in the field;

- ensuring that these indicators embody Australian attitudes about the nature of poverty and reflect the views of those affected by it; and
- exploring what the new indicators imply about the size and nature of poverty and social disadvantage in Australia, and about the actions needed to address them.

Of particular salience was the need to locate the new indicators within a specifically Australian understanding of the experience of poverty and disadvantage and to ensure that they reflect the views and experiences of those whose circumstances, needs and aspirations they seek to capture.

Equally important was the need to develop indicators that have the credibility and acceptance that make them valuable not only as a research tool that reveals knowledge about the nature of poverty, but also as a vehicle for disseminating information about poverty and mobilising support for action to address it. Ringen has emphasised the importance of this latter feature, arguing that:

> To succeed in the job of informing society it is not enough to uncover a problem, what is uncovered must be believed – and it must be believed in particular by those who may have an interest in disbelieving it and the power to suppress or brush aside unpleasant information.… The way to do this is obviously first to avoid anything that could cause the message to be seen as biased but also … to avoid anything that could cause it to appear exaggerated. (Ringen, 2007, p 133)

The failure of existing Australian poverty studies to avoid problems of perceived bias and exaggeration was seized on by the poverty line sceptics, who exploited these failings to discredit not only the estimates of poverty but also the concept itself (Saunders and Tsumori, 2002). These limitations gained broader acceptance through a series of well-orchestrated media campaigns funded by those with a vested interest in maintaining the existing income disparities. There is, however, substance in some of the problems identified and these needed to be addressed in order to restore in the minds of policy makers and the public the notion that poverty represents an abject failure of policy and is not just a statistical artefact. This involves rethinking not just how poverty is conceptualised and relates to other forms of social disadvantage, but also how the poverty statistics are produced, presented and interpreted.

What poverty means

Although researchers have been debating the definition of poverty for centuries, there is a good understanding of what the term means among members of the general population. Ensuring that the definition of poverty is consistent with community understanding of its meaning is one way of building confidence in the methods used to identify poverty and adding credibility to the estimates produced. Poverty is a commonly used word and even though most people would not be able to provide a formal definition, this does not mean that they lack an understanding of what the term is intended to capture. The problem for researchers involves translating this implicit understanding into an operational definition that does justice to the underlying idea.

Table 2.1 summarises the responses to a survey question that asked samples of Australians what they understood by the word 'poverty'. With the exception of the 2010 survey, respondents were first asked how strongly they agreed with each of the separate definitions shown, before being asked to nominate the single definition that *best* captured their understanding of the term. This two-stage process was designed to elicit a more considered response to what is a complex, multi-faceted concept.

Two findings emerge from the resulting responses: first, the majority of Australians (around three quarters of those surveyed) see poverty either in terms of not having enough to buy basic necessities, or as being a situation of constant struggle to balance financial resources against needs. The first conception describes what poverty actually is, while the second focuses on its experience and consequences, but both share the idea that poverty exists when resources are not enough to buy basic items. These understandings receive far greater support than those that define poverty as not being able to make ends meet or not being able to live decently, or in more explicitly relative terms, as having less than other people or not having what others take for granted.

The second feature of these results is the remarkable stability over a decade and a half in the breakdown of views about the meaning of poverty. In conjunction with the findings themselves, this suggests that views about poverty are not only widely shared, but deeply embedded and resistant to change – even in the face of widespread economic and social change. The results also indicate that generally

Table 2.1: Overall descriptions of poverty (%)

Question: Overall which of these statements *best* describes what being in poverty means to you?	Social security clients, 1995	Adult Australians		
		1999	2006	2010
Not having enough to buy basics like food, housing and clothing	43.0	44.9	44.1	43.1
Having to struggle to survive each and every day	27.1	33.0	31.1	31.3
Not having enough money to make ends meet	12.6	10.8	14.4	8.0
Not having enough to be able to live decently	8.8	6.7	6.3	9.3
Not having enough to buy what most others take for granted	–	2.8	2.8	6.1
Having a lot less than everyone else	1.8	–	–	–
Not being able to afford any of the good things in life	6.9	2.1	1.4	2.3
Sample size[a]	1,117	2,212	2,354	2,356

Note: [a] Excludes multiple responses and 'don't knows'.

Sources: Surveys conducted by the Social Policy Research Centre (SPRC), including the CUPSE Survey.

held views about the meaning of poverty are shared by those who are themselves at greatest risk of poverty (those receiving a social security benefit, who were sampled in 1995). These ideas align with the key features of a broad consensus view of poverty that has emerged in the research community over the last two decades.

It is important, however, to emphasise that the fact that poverty is seen as being unable to buy basic necessities does not mean that how it is operationalised (when setting a poverty line) will remain invariant to changes in the overall standard of living. People's conceptions of which items are basic will vary to reflect not only changes in their own circumstances but also changes in average living standards in their community. The former proposition is confirmed by studies showing that people's perceptions of minimum income levels are positively related to their own income (Saunders and Matheson, 1992), while the latter proposition has been confirmed by studies showing that when people are asked how much income a given family needs in order to make ends meet, the average response varies in line with changes in average community incomes (Rainwater, 1974; Saunders and Bradbury, 1991).

Notwithstanding these refinements, the results in Table 2.1 show that there is a common understanding of what poverty means among members of the community. The challenge is to embody that understanding in a measure that can be used to estimate poverty and to track changes. Despite the difficulties involved, there will always be pressure to produce a single ('headline') poverty measure that summarises the extent of the problem in a way that can be readily transmitted and understood. Getting the poverty message across to the community is an important step in highlighting the problem and mobilising the support needed to address it.

This does not mean, however, that the headline measure cannot be complemented by other indicators that capture different dimensions of the problem (measures of the severity of poverty, or the impact of housing costs, for example) or that capture other aspects of disadvantage such as deprivation, social exclusion or the level of functioning among specific groups. These concepts enrich our understanding of poverty, but they do not reduce the need to define and measure it in a way that everyone understands – an enforced lack of the resources required to buy the items that satisfy basic needs to an acceptable standard.

Measuring poverty

One of the problems facing any single poverty measure is that too much is demanded of it. It is expected to provide a basis for measuring and comparing poverty, for identifying the nature and causes of change, for assessing the adequacy of income support payments and for examining the impact of public policies on poverty. The measure must not only be applicable to all groups and capable of being adjusted to reflect changing circumstances, but must also be credible, in the sense that it reflects judgements and assumptions that are widely shared or endorsed, albeit indirectly and implicitly. More than one measure may be needed to reflect different judgements about what poverty means, and to provide a sensitivity check on how poverty varies when different assumptions are made when measuring it.

However, it is also important to distinguish between the concept or definition of poverty and how it is measured. There is no shortage of definitions of poverty. They reflect the ideas and insights of some of the most eminent and influential social scientists including Adam Smith, William Beveridge, Peter Townsend and Amartya Sen. These definitions capture two central features of poverty: first, that poverty is a situation in which resources are not adequate to meet *basic needs* to an acceptable degree; and second, that any definition of poverty must in some way embody *community perceptions* of what it means to be poor. The items required to meet basic needs are generally referred to as necessities (or essentials – the terms are used interchangeably here), but how they are identified will vary to reflect differences in community standards.

The founding father of modern economics, Adam Smith, argued in *The Wealth of Nations* that necessities should include 'whatever the custom renders it indecent for creditable people, even of the lowest order, to be without'. Over two centuries later, Townsend re-iterated the same idea, arguing that the necessities that apply to individuals must reflect 'the living conditions and amenities which are customary, or at least widely encouraged or approved, in the societies to which they belong'. It is also captured in Sen's definition of poverty as reflecting 'the failure of basic capabilities to reach certain minimally acceptable levels'.

These ideas have been translated into a specific definition by the Irish Combat Poverty Agency (2004):

> People are living in poverty if their income and resources (material, cultural and social) are so *inadequate* as to preclude them from having a standard of living which is regarded as *acceptable* by Irish society generally. (Combat Poverty Agency, 2004, p 1; emphasis added)

This definition makes explicit the idea that poverty reflects a lack of income, and thus should be measured using an income metric, although it leaves unresolved the meanings to be attached to the two key highlighted words 'inadequate' and 'acceptable'.

Much of the poverty literature has involved giving a precise meaning to the terms 'inadequate' and 'unacceptable' by specifying a poverty line that corresponds to the income that is adequate enough to allow a given household or family, in a given place, at a given time, to achieve an acceptable standard of living. Clearly, however, concrete specifications of what is 'adequate' and 'acceptable' require judgements to be made, and this will make them subject to debate and thus contestable.

One approach would be to examine how living conditions vary as income declines, holding other things constant, in order to establish at what point they become unacceptable. In general, however, this has not happened. Instead, the poverty line has been used not only to *measure* poverty, but also to capture the key features of the *concept* of poverty. In practice, this has meant that poverty has been transformed from a situation characterised by unacceptable living standards to one that is equated with having a low income. In the process, the whole question of what constitutes an unacceptable standard of living – the key feature that underpins the moral imperative view of poverty – has been replaced by the more mundane (but less challenging) task of comparing incomes with a poverty line.

One argument in favour of maintaining a focus on the income dimension of poverty has been that people have a right to a minimum level of income since this is the major source of material well-being in modern market economies (Atkinson, 1989). However, even this view can be challenged on the grounds that material well-being depends on access to overall economic resources not just to income, and account thus also needs to be taken of such factors as wealth and indebtedness. It may make sense as a goal of policy to ensure that everyone has access to a minimum level of income that they can allocate at their own discretion. However, this does not imply that when measuring poverty one should focus only on the level of income and ignore the standard of living, since it is the latter that will determine whether or not one is poor, not the former.

This broader perspective has been taken by the European Community Commission, which has defined poverty in the following terms:

> The poor shall be taken to mean persons, families and groups of persons whose resources (material, cultural and social) are so limited as to exclude them from the minimum acceptable way of life in the Member State in which they live. (cited in Nolan and Marx, 2009, p 316)

This approach extends the scope and meaning of resources beyond income, while recognising the relative nature of poverty by emphasising that poverty exists when living conditions (or one's 'way of life') are deemed unacceptable by the standards of one's community. The definition also incorporates the language of exclusion – a term that the Commission has done much to bring to the forefront of the social policy debate in Europe. It leaves open important questions about what is meant by an acceptable way of life and who is to decide, but the logic of the approach requires that these issues have to be addressed before it is possible to identify who is in poverty.

This discussion implies that in order to fully understand the nature of poverty and how it relates to other forms of social disadvantage, it is necessary to adopt an approach that is grounded in people's living conditions and lived experiences. Only by observing, or seeking information about, people's actual living conditions will it be possible to establish whether or not they are consistent with prevailing notions of acceptability and thus whether or not poverty exists.

This implies a more complex and far-reaching research agenda than one that focuses on comparing incomes with a poverty line. It involves adopting a perspective that focuses on the *outcomes achieved*, rather than on identifying and measuring the *resources available*, and drawing inferences from them. Such an approach gets the ordering of priorities right from the outset – poverty is bad

—

because it has adverse consequences for those affected, for their families and for the communities in which they live. For children in particular, even a short spell in poverty can leave scars that extend well into adulthood (Brooks-Gunn and Duncan, 1997; Bradbury, 2003). Low income may be a factor that increases the *risk* of poverty, but the link is not inevitable and the existence of poverty must be established in other ways. This shift in emphasis provides the impetus to look beyond measurement to experiences and impacts. This in turn allows the focus to shift away from the statistics that describe poverty to its effects on people's living conditions and opportunities.

Poverty line studies

There are two ways of implementing the definitions of poverty proposed by the Irish Combat Poverty Agency and the European Commission. The first involves conducting *poverty line studies* that compare people's actual income with an income benchmark (or poverty line) that is assumed to reflect how much is needed to support an acceptable standard of living. The second approach involves conducting *living standard studies* that examine people's standard of living in order to assess whether or not it meets prevailing standards of acceptability. The rest of this chapter discusses poverty line studies, while the living standards approach forms the basis of the material presented in later chapters. Both approaches require an acceptable standard of living to be specified, although because poverty line studies assume a direct link between income and the standard of living, this link is embodied in the poverty line itself.

When the poverty line expressed in monetary terms is set at an arbitrary level (for example, as a percentage of median income), no attempt is made to give meaning to what is acceptable, casting doubt on the relevance of the whole approach – at least as a way of identifying poverty. The definitions presented earlier imply that the terms 'inadequate' and 'unacceptable' are central to what is meant by poverty, yet the use of median income-based poverty lines avoids this reality.

There is also something tautological in defining poverty as a lack of income, identifying it by comparing income with a poverty line and concluding that the solution is to provide increased income to those identified as poor. Such an approach gives too much emphasis to income and too little to the factors that prevent some from generating an income, and others from being able to satisfy their needs or spending it wisely once they have it. It also fails to engage with the important issues highlighted in the above discussion and does not examine whether and how (or even if) low income translates into a low standard of living.

Further compounding the limitations of the income approach to poverty measurement is the fact that the methods used to set a poverty line have been challenged, as has the reliability and accuracy of information on income reported in social surveys. Although much of the attention in the literature has focused on the problems surrounding the setting of the poverty line, problems with the accuracy of the income statistics themselves will also affect the reliability of poverty estimates. A 5% error in reported income will have the same impact on the poverty rate as a 5% error in where the poverty line is set. Although these practical issues are important (and are discussed further later), the key conceptual point is that while income is an important determinant of the standard of living, other factors are also relevant and poverty research must seek to identify these and understand their importance.

Even if there was agreement on where to set the poverty line, relying on income alone to ascertain whether or not someone is poor is subject to many limitations. These have cast a shadow over conventional poverty line studies, yet despite these problems such studies play an important role in identifying poverty and comparing its incidence across groups, over time and between countries. This information provides the starting point from which to examine the causes of poverty and the impact of anti-poverty policies.

This still leaves open the task of how to set the poverty line, for which a number of approaches have been proposed (see Callan and Nolan, 1991; Hills, 2004, Chapter 3). The budget standards approach estimates how much income is needed to buy a specified basket of goods by identifying the items in the basket and costing them (Bradshaw, 1993; Saunders, 1999). The consensual approach derives a poverty line from people's views on how much income they need to make ends meet (Saunders and Matheson, 1992; Van den Bosch, 2001). The 'official' approach sets the poverty threshold at the level of social security payments (which are assumed to reflect an endorsed or 'official' minimum income standard). Finally, the relative income approach sets the poverty line at a given percentage of mean or median income.

Each approach has its strengths and weaknesses. The budget standards approach conforms with an everyday understanding of how family finances operate, but is complex and time-consuming to apply and can lead to endless debate about which items to include and how to cost them. The use of responses to 'making ends meet' questions that form the basis of the subjective approach has been shown to produce results that vary wildly (see Saunders, 2003a). Moreover, the use of such a poverty line can create an incentive for people to understate their ability to make ends meet in the knowledge that this would result in a higher poverty line and greater pressure to raise benefits.

There is also evidence that many people with modest to high incomes report finding it difficult to make ends meet (Hamilton and Denniss, 2005, Chapter 4), raising doubts about whether the responses can be used to set a poverty line. A poverty line set at the level of social security payments is straightforward to apply, but cannot be used to assess the adequacy of those payments and leads to the counter-intuitive implication that governments can reduce poverty by cutting benefits. Relative income cut-offs provide a valuable point of comparison with community standards within and between countries, but bear no obvious relation to the acceptability of living standards and thus do not capture this key feature of the concept of poverty.

Empirically, the poverty lines produced using each method differ substantially, providing no clear basis for deciding where the correct figure lies. This may be because the relationship between income and poverty status may not be strong enough for income to be a *measure* of poverty, only an *indicator* – albeit a rather good one – as Spicker (2004) has suggested. Increasingly, poverty line studies have used the relative income approach because of its ease of application and transparency. By setting the poverty line at a given percentage of median (or mean) income, the approach identifies as poor those whose incomes are so far below the norm that they are unlikely to be able to participate in customary activities and otherwise achieve an acceptable standard of living. It is straightforward to vary the level at which the cut-off is set and to check what difference it makes to the estimates. The relative income approach is also well suited to drawing cross-country comparisons of poverty because it uses the same relative income benchmark in each country and avoids the problems involved in converting national poverty lines to a common currency.

Relative income poverty lines are now widely used by international agencies like the OECD (see OECD, 2008; Förster and d'Ercole, 2005) and in international research projects like the Luxembourg Income Study (LIS, see Smeeding, 2004, 2006). There is much to be gained from individual countries applying the same benchmark when producing national poverty estimates and many Australian researchers now use a poverty line set at 50% of median income (Harding et al, 2001; Saunders and Bradbury, 2006; Wilkins, 2008; Saunders and Hill, 2008). This approach has also been used to estimate poverty by government agencies including the Australian Institute of Health and Welfare (AIHW, 2007), the Department of Families, Housing, Community Services and Indigenous Affairs (Harmer, 2009) and the Australian Social Inclusion Board (ASIB, 2009a).

Some academic studies present estimates based on poverty lines set at both 50% and 60% of median income in order to assess how sensitive the estimates are to where the poverty line is set. As will be shown later, this has the effect of increasing estimated poverty considerably in Australia because the level of social security payments for some groups (for example, age pensioners) falls between 50% and 60% of median income, leading to a bunching of incomes in this range (see Tanton et al, 2009). What can look like a large change in the poverty rate may thus actually reflect a large number of households moving from a few dollars on one side of the poverty line to a few dollars the other side of it when the line itself is shifted. The higher cut-off (set at 60% of the median) is one of the Laeken indicators and is the benchmark most commonly used when studying poverty in EU countries (Guio, 2005; Whelan and Maître, 2008), and this benchmark is included in the compendium of social inclusion indicators developed by the Australian Social Inclusion Board (ASIB, 2009a).

When estimating poverty, it is necessary to adjust household income to reflect differences in household size (and hence in household needs) in order to achieve comparability between households that differ in size and composition. An income that may be adequate to sustain an acceptable standard of living for a single person may not do so for a couple with two children, for example. This adjustment is applied using an equivalence scale, which captures the relative needs of different households. The scale applies a weighting factor to each household member (other than the first adult, or head of household, who is assigned a weight of one) that reflects each member's needs expressed as a proportion of the needs of the household head.

The weights are less than one for two reasons: first, because of economies of scale in household consumption (two adults can watch the same television, they do not need two sets); and because the consumption needs of children are lower than those of adults. One commonly used equivalence scale (the so-called 'modified' OECD scale) assigns a score of 1.0 to the first adult in the household, 0.5 to each subsequent adult and 0.3 to each child (where children are defined as those aged under 18). This scale assumes that children's needs are equivalent to one fifth of the needs of an adult couple, and implies, for example, that the total needs of the four individuals in a two-child couple are just over twice as high ($1.0 + 0.5 + \{2 \times 0.3\} = 2.1$) as the needs of a single adult living alone.

As with the poverty line itself, there are many different equivalence scales to choose from, but no agreement on which is best, while the different methods used to estimate the scales produce different results (Buhmann et al, 1988). However, the choice of equivalence scale is important because it will have a major bearing on the relative poverty risks facing different groups and will thus influence views about the adequacy and acceptability of the living standards of each group. Most scales only take account of differences in household size and composition, yet other factors such as the presence of disability, location and ethnicity can also affect the ability of a given income to support a specific standard of living. The resulting differences in poverty risks are concealed if these factors are not included in the equivalence adjustment and this can make a substantial difference, for example in the case of the needs associated with disability (Saunders, 2007).

The above discussion has been conducted in terms of an income poverty line, with the implication that poverty status should be determined on the basis of income alone. There are sound reasons for continuing with this approach, since income is the main economic resource available to most people and the provision of income support is an important policy goal. Moreover, government policies are often compared and assessed in media accounts that identify 'winners and losers' in terms of their impact on the incomes of different families. However, the existence of non-monetary forms of income means that money income has become a less reliable measure of the standard of living and thus a more imperfect indicator of whether or not poverty exists.

Examples of in-kind income that give rise to such concerns are public income provided to individuals and families in the form of education and health care services (the social wage), non-market income (imputed rent from owner-occupied housing), indirect income (employer-provided subsidies for housing or health care) and deferred income (accrued pension rights). These forms of non-cash income meet specific needs, contribute to living standards and thus weaken the link between money income and the standard of living. This suggests that they should either be included in a broader definition of income, or that the poverty line should be modified to reflect their existence.

One such adjustment that has a long history in Australian poverty research relates to the benefits associated with home ownership. Unlike renters, homeowners do not have to pay rent and thus face lower housing costs over the longer-term, making it easier to support a specific standard of living from a given level of income. This factor has been incorporated into poverty studies by estimating poverty both before and after deducting housing costs, where the latter reveal lower rates among homeowners (Commission of Inquiry into Poverty, 1975; Bradbury et al, 1986). Adjusting for the impact of non-cash income is more difficult in other areas because of the problems involved in valuing the benefits received, and in deciding whether or how to vary the equivalence scale adjustment to reflect the idea that the benefits that result from non-cash income meet specific needs.

Finally, there is the accuracy of the income statistics themselves. The Australian Bureau of Statistics (ABS) has expressed concern over the quality of the incomes reported in their surveys by households at the bottom of the income distribution (see Chapter Three). This concern is based on evidence suggesting that the standard of living of these households is higher (possibly much higher) than the income figures themselves suggest (ABS, 2002a, 2003). As a consequence, the ABS has excluded households with incomes in the lowest decile from the 'headline indicator' of financial hardship included in its flagship publication *Measures of Australia's Progress 2010* (see, for example, ABS, 2010), although the detailed analysis undertaken by Saunders and Bradbury (2006) suggests that the problem applies to only a small percentage of households (far fewer than the 10% in the lowest decile). The ABS has been taking steps (described in ABS, 2007b, 2009b; and Pietsch et al, 2006) to address the concerns it has identified. This has resulted in improvements in data quality – but at a cost in terms of making it more difficult to estimate how poverty has changed over time.

Some households have been removed from the data when estimating poverty because of concerns that their reported incomes are unlikely to accurately represent their standard of living. Two groups that have been identified as falling into this category are the self-employed and young adults (juveniles) who are still living with their parents. These groups were excluded from the original 1960s study of poverty in Melbourne (Henderson et al, 1970) and by the Poverty Commission, leading many subsequent academic studies to follow suit (for example, Saunders and Matheson, 1991). The rationale for excluding these groups was not based on concern over the reliability of the data on reported income, but on the difficulty of separating personal and business income (in the case of the self-employed) or on the grounds that income was likely to be supplemented from unidentified sources (mainly from parents, in the case of juveniles).

Aside from the quality of the income data, there are also important questions about the period over which income is measured. Traditionally, Australian poverty studies have used either current (weekly) income or recent (annual) income, the difference showing up in different poverty rates because short-run income fluctuations tend to even out over a longer time period. Some economists have taken this observation to its logical extreme, arguing that it is lifetime (or permanent) income that determines the level of household consumption and since this is what determines the standard of living actually achieved, poverty should be estimated using permanent (lifetime) income rather than weekly or annual income.

Additional important issues relate to the duration and dynamics of poverty. These features can only be captured using longitudinal (panel) data to estimate the length of spells spent below the poverty line, which groups experience the most persistent poverty and the factors that trigger movements into and out of poverty. The dynamics of poverty has been attracting increasing interest internationally (see OECD, 2008, Chapter 6) and has been the subject of several Australian studies based on data collected in the Household, Income and Labour Dynamics in Australia (HILDA) Survey (see Wooden and Watson, 2002). In one study, Headey et al (2005) show (using a poverty line set at 50% of median income) that although the annual poverty rate varied between 12% and 14% between 2000-01 and 2002-03, only 7% of households were poor in two out of those three years, while just over 4% were poor in all three years. These estimates suggest that a good deal of poverty is transitory, although the authors also note that many of those who escape poverty remain only marginally above the poverty line and thus face 'some significant risk of slipping back into poverty' (Headey et al, 2005, p 550; see also Buddelmeyer and Verick, 2008).

Although the HILDA Survey is shedding new light on an important aspect of poverty, it will be some time before the forces that drive the dynamics of poverty are fully understood. Research conducted to date has also opened up a new perspective on the issues of definition and measurement reviewed above. Is it appropriate, for example, to apply the same poverty line (for example, expressed as a percentage of median income) that is used in static (single year) studies when estimating the persistence of poverty over several years? Can it be assumed that the needs of households whose composition changes (because of marital separation or death, for example) are the same as those of households with unchanged composition, or does some account need to be taken of the impact on needs of the event that caused the change when applying the equivalence scale adjustment?

This discussion has highlighted some of the limitations of the methods applied in poverty line studies, including the techniques employed and the data on which they are based. It suggests that whenever possible, estimated poverty rates should be subject to sensitivity analysis in order to provide an indication of their robustness.

Despite all of the problems, it would be a mistake to discard income-based poverty estimates entirely. It is important to recognise that estimated poverty rates are just that – estimates – but that they provide an important initial insight into the *poverty risks* facing different groups, how these vary and are changing over time. But further evidence is needed to establish whether or not these risks translate into a standard of living that fails to meet community standards of acceptability.

Overall, it is difficult to dispute the view, based on evidence for a broad range of countries, that, 'it is hazardous to draw strong conclusions about whether a household is poor from current income alone' (Whelan and Maître, 2008, p 208).

Poverty in Australia

It was noted earlier that most international poverty studies now use poverty lines set at 50% and 60% of median equivalent disposable household income and this approach is applied here to estimate poverty in Australia. The estimates refer to 2005-06 (for consistency with the survey data presented later), when the values of these poverty lines for a single adult living alone were:

- $281 per week for the 50% of median income poverty line
- $337 per week for the 60% of median income poverty line

The modified OECD equivalence scale can be used to calculate the poverty lines for other household types. Thus, for example, the equivalence factor for a household consisting of a couple with two children is equal to 2.1, so that the 50% of the median poverty line for this household is equal to $281 \times 2.1 = \$590.1$.

The unit of analysis (within which income is assumed to be shared according to need among all members) is the household, and person weights are applied when estimating poverty rates for the population or sub-groups within it. This means that the poverty rates express the percentage of individuals living in households with incomes below the poverty line. However, although the household is the unit used to *estimate* poverty, the findings are *presented* on a family basis, where a family is defined as related individuals living together (single people, married couples, couples with children and lone parents with children), with children aged 15 and over treated for equivalence purposes as adults in this case. Those households that contain unrelated individuals living together (group households) and co-habiting family members that do not fit the above categories (for example, adult siblings living together, or three-generation family households) are aggregated into the 'other households' category. The source of data for the estimates is the ABS Survey of Income and Housing (SIH) but no attempt has been made (nor could it be) to adjust the reported data to reflect the changes in survey methodology referred to earlier. Further details of the methods used to generate the estimates are provided in Saunders et al (2007a).

Application of these methods to the 2005-06 SIH data produces the poverty estimates shown in Table 2.2. They indicate that more than 2.2 million Australians were living in households with incomes below the 50% of median income poverty threshold, resulting in an overall poverty rate of 11.1%. These households contain over 410,000 children, or more than one in ten of all Australian children. Among adults, the risk of poverty rises sharply among those aged 65 and over, who face a poverty rate of 24% – almost three times the rate for single adults aged under 65 and more than twice the national figure. When the poverty line is increased

Table 2.2: Overall poverty rates and numbers in 2005-06

	Poverty rate (%)	Number (000s)
Poverty line set at 50% of median income		
Adults	11.3	1,798.0
Over 65 years	23.9	597.4
Under 65 years	8.9	1,200.5
Children	10.7	411.6
Persons	11.1	2,209.6
Poverty line set at 60% of median income		
Adults	19.4	3,103.4
Over 65 years	45.2	1,128.0
Under 65 years	14.7	1,975.3
Children	19.5	753.7
Persons	19.4	3,857.1

Source: Saunders et al (2007, Tables B.3 and B.4)

from 50% to 60% of median income, the poverty rate almost doubles, from 11.1% to 19.4%, and the relative risk facing both children and older people increases relative to the average. At this higher level, close to one half of all older people and almost one fifth of all children are living in households below the poverty line.

The estimates in Table 2.2 are close to those produced by the Department of Families, Housing, Community Services and Indigenous Affairs (Harmer, 2008, Chart 9), the Australian Institute of Health and Welfare (AIHW, 2007, Table 8.15) and the Australian Social Inclusion Board (ASIB, 2009a, Table 5). The fact that these agencies have published the estimates and drawn conclusions (albeit guardedly) about the implications for policy is indicative of the value of poverty research. The Australian Institute of Health and Welfare report notes that the measures focus attention on 'people or households whose incomes are relatively low, compared with the overall population, and who may therefore experience comparatively low material living standards than society's norm' (AIHW, 2007, p 376). This somewhat guarded assessment supports the view that additional evidence may be needed before those with incomes below the poverty line can be identified as poor.

The poverty rates in Table 2.2 take no account of the depth of poverty – the distance between how much income people have and how much income they need. The Australian Social Inclusion Board's compendium of social inclusion indicators contains information on the average poverty gap, defined as the difference between actual income and the poverty line, averaged across all households with incomes below the line. In 2005-06, the average poverty gap was $38.0 using the 50% of median poverty line and $64.1 using the higher (60% of median income) threshold. The estimates are equivalent to 13.6% and 19.1% of national median income, respectively. They provide a lower bound on the extent of income redistribution required to raise everyone's income up to the poverty threshold – to achieve the moral imperative target to eradicate poverty entirely.

In order to get a better understanding of who is at greatest risk of poverty and to begin to identify the factors that contribute to that risk, it is necessary to disaggregate the estimates. This is done in Table 2.3 for classifications based on family type, age, labour force status, number of earners and state of residence. These are only a selection of the many breakdowns that are possible and each sheds light on different dimensions of the poverty landscape and raises different issues about cause and effect. Table 2.3 helps to identify four important factors that affect the risk of poverty: household structure (and the adequacy of government income support provided to different families), age (and lifecycle variations in income and need), engagement with the labour market (and the impact of joblessness), and (to a limited extent) location. The ability to examine this last issue is restricted because detailed information on location has been suppressed in the microdata to protect the confidentiality of the survey respondents.

The estimates also capture different elements of the overall picture and reflect the underlying patterns that link the different categories. Thus, for example, most lone parents in Australia are female so there is an important gender dimension implicit in the lone parent poverty rates. Poverty is lower among couples than among lone parents mainly because unlike lone parents, couples can both become earners and the second set of earnings can have a marked poverty-reducing impact. The estimates embody these effects but do not indicate how changes in specific characteristics affect the risk of poverty when other factors are held constant. The marginal impact of identified factors on the risk of poverty (odds ratios) can be estimated using regression analysis to isolate, for example, the impact of lone parenthood on poverty from the impact of being a female-headed household (see Wilkins, 2008).

Turning to the results themselves, Table 2.3 indicates that poverty risks are highest among single people (older and working-age) and lone-parent families, particularly those with more than one child. Children in lone-parent families with no or one sibling are three times more likely to be poor than similar children in couple families using the lower poverty line, and this differential increases to four when the higher poverty line is used. Children in larger families (with four or more children) also face a high risk of poverty, irrespective of whether they live with one or both parents.

The poverty profile follows a U-shaped pattern with age, declining in middle age before rising sharply among those aged 65 and over, particularly among single older people. Close to half of those in this latter group are in poverty and even though this is tempered by the fact that many age pensioners have an income that is only marginally below the poverty line, the equivalised median income of older people in Australia is below the average for people aged over 65 in all EU countries, and well below that in countries such as Denmark, Finland, Sweden and the UK (ASIB, 2009a, Figure 9).

Table 2.3 reveals that joblessness is an important cause of poverty, with poverty rates of 40% or more in jobless households and households headed by someone who is unemployed. Having at least one earner reduces the risk of poverty

Table 2.3: Poverty rates in 2005-06 by family type, age, labour force status, number of earners and state of residence

	50% median	60% median
Family type		
Single older person	46.9	65.9
Older couple	17.8	43.8
Single working-age	24.8	30.0
Working-age couple	6.5	11.2
Couple with children		
1 child	5.1	8.6
2 children	6.6	10.7
3 children	7.0	14.9
4+ children	16.3	27.4
All couples with children	7.0	11.8
Lone-parent family		
1 child	16.7	33.4
2 children	21.4	41.3
3 children	21.5	58.6
All lone-parent families	16.4	33.4
Mixed family households	3.2	9.7
Age of oldest member		
Under 25	11.0	20.6
25-44	9.5	16.0
45-54	7.3	12.7
55-64	11.7	18.2
65 and over	20.1	38.1
Labour force status of oldest member		
Employed full time	1.4	3.0
Employed part time	5.2	13.0
Self-employed	13.5	20.3
Unemployed	44.7	64.8
Not in the labour force	25.7	44.9
Number of earners		
No earners	39.9	65.5
One earner	6.9	14.5
Two or more earners	1.9	3.6
State/territory		
New South Wales	11.3	19.3
Victoria	12.0	20.3
Queensland	10.6	19.8
South Australia	12.3	20.7
Western Australia	9.5	17.3
Tasmania	13.0	24.3
Northern Territory/ACT	5.1	9.1
All families	**11.1**	**19.4**

Source: Saunders et al (2007, Appendix B)

—

considerably, but full-time employment is needed before the risk falls towards zero. Poverty is also above-average among self-employed households, although these estimates should be treated with caution because of the problems involved in measuring income for this group discussed earlier. (This issue is returned to in the following chapter.)

Table 2.3 also indicates that poverty varies across Australia, from below 10% in Western Australia to 12% in Victoria and South Australia, and 13% in Tasmania. These differences reflect a number of factors including differences in the age and family structures of the population in each state, as well as differences in economic performance and labour market strength. Some of the state differences remain after adjusting for such factors as age and family composition, country of birth and educational attainment, although the overall state effects are outweighed by the (negative) impact on poverty associated with residing in the state capital city (Wilkins, 2008, Table 5).

The estimates in Tables 2.2 and 2.3 provide useful information on where poverty risks are greatest and thus yield valuable insights into (some of) the underlying causes of poverty. It is clear that lone parenthood and joblessness (which often go together) increase the risk of poverty, while the fact that poverty risks are higher among older people, lone-parent families and among families with larger numbers of children (whether couples or lone parents) points to inadequacies in the income support provisions for these groups. The sensitivity of the estimates to a shift in the poverty line from 50% to 60% of median income highlights the importance of deciding which income benchmark to use when measuring poverty in a country like Australia, because of the flat-rate, income-tested nature of its social security system. Despite their limitations, poverty estimates provide an important departure point for further analysis of the nature, causes and consequences of poverty.

Recent changes in poverty risks

The complexities involved in estimating poverty at a point in time increase when estimating how poverty has changed over time because it then becomes important to ensure that the data are comparable for different periods. It has already been noted that the ABS has been seeking to improve the quality of its household income data and this has meant that the more recent income data is not comparable with that for earlier years. Because of this, estimates of poverty trends in Australia should always be treated with caution. Despite these statistical imperfections, the general public and policy makers are interested in knowing how poverty is changing as well as how much poverty exists at a particular point in time – in part because it is difficult to judge whether to be concerned about the 11% poverty rate shown in Table 2.2 without knowing how it compares with what existed in the past.

Changes in the ABS data used to estimate poverty will have an impact on the results, but it is difficult (probably impossible) to untangle how much of the observed change in estimated poverty is real and how much is a consequence of the changes in the underlying data. Comparisons with poverty trends estimated using the HILDA data provide an indication of the impact of the data improvements introduced by the ABS, but any conclusions must be heavily qualified because so many other factors are also changing. Even without these complications, problems arise when deciding whether and how to vary the poverty line over time. If it is linked to median income, then the poverty line will change automatically as median income changes, but this has been criticised on the grounds that it implies that poverty is a 'moving target' that becomes difficult to reduce – particularly when incomes are rising rapidly.

One response to such criticism involves estimating poverty using a poverty line that is adjusted only to reflect changes in consumer prices, which then becomes anchored in a particular year and poverty is estimated using that fixed benchmark. Governments prefer this latter approach because it is better equipped to show progress, although relative poverty lines (adjusted in line with income growth) are also important because they capture how well the poor are sharing in the increased prosperity associated with economic growth.

Using a poverty line set at 50% of mean (average) income, Harding and Szukalska (2000, Table 1) estimate that the Australian poverty rate declined from 14.6% in 1982 to 13.3% in 1999. King (1998, Figure 4.1) applied the (somewhat higher) poverty line developed by the Poverty Commission (which is linked to movements in average after-tax household income adjusted for changes in population size) and found that poverty increased from 12.5% in 1972 to 16.7% in 1996. Applying the same basic approach, Saunders (1994, Table 9.2) estimates that poverty increased from 10.7% to 16.7% between 1981–82 and 1989–90. Together, these estimates suggest that poverty in Australia fell in the mid- to late-1970s, began to rise around the end of that decade (although it is not possible to identify the actual turning point as there are no data available covering the period between 1974 and 1982), and continued on an upward trend through the 1980s.

Harding et al (2001, Table 16) apply a range of poverty lines and find that they all indicate that poverty increased between 1990 and 1999, although the extent of the rise varies considerably. Using a poverty line set at 50% of median income and the modified OECD equivalence scale described earlier, they estimate that poverty increased slightly, from 9.8% in 1990 to 10.1% in 2000. The most comprehensive study of changes in Australian poverty has been undertaken by Wilkins (2008), who examines annual income data from all of the 11 ABS income surveys undertaken between 1982 and 2003 after making adjustments to increase their comparability (although not adjusting for the changes in survey methodology described earlier). Using a poverty line set at 50% of median income and the modified OECD equivalence adjustment, he finds that poverty rose from 11.1% in 1981–82 to 12.9% in 2002–03 and that this rise is statistically significant. The increase was steady between 1982 and 1995, declined over the next two years, before increasing steeply between 1997 and 2003. The overall trend is similar when the higher 60% of median income poverty line is used. These estimates confirm that there was little overall change in poverty over the 1990s as a whole, but that year-to-year changes varied over the decade.

It is difficult to combine these different estimates into a single coherent picture, although the overall picture is one of a modest decline in poverty after the Poverty Commission reported in the mid-1970s, followed by a steady increase through the 1980s and into the first half of the 1990s. Sometime between 1990 and 1995 poverty started to fall, but it then increased up to 2002-03 (shown by Wilkins) and continued to increase between 2003-04 and 2005-06 (Saunders et al, 2007a, Table 22). Estimates based on data from the HILDA Survey show a sharp increase in the poverty rate from 11.9% to 13.5% between 2006 and 2007 that more than offset the steady decline that occurred between 2001 and 2006 (Wilkins et al, 2010, Table 7.1).

This latter figure is slightly above the rate of 12.5% in 1972 estimated by the Poverty Commission, and indicates that little progress has been made in reducing poverty over the intervening quarter of a century. Even though most (possibly all) of those who were poor in 2007 will have been better off in absolute (purchasing power) terms than those who were poor in 1975, the fact that their relative position had not improved overall is indicative of a failure to implement the redistributive policies required to make in-roads into poverty reduction.

How does Australia compare internationally?

The problems involved in developing a consistent set of data on household incomes to estimate changes in poverty *within* any country are minor when compared to those involved in producing the data needed to compare poverty rates *between* different countries. Each country uses different methods to collect information on household incomes and the underlying definitions can differ in ways that may have a major impact on the results. For example, differences in whether adults living together are automatically regarded as married, or the age at which children are treated as adults in the data will affect poverty rates, while variations in the scope of income itself (for example, whether or not near-cash provisions like food stamps or employer-provided benefits are included as part of income) will have a more general impact. Unless these differences are identified and removed (or minimised) by adopting a common definitional framework, they will exert an unknown impact on the observed differences in national poverty rates and distort the cross-national comparisons.

The demand for comparable microdata on economic well-being and inequality resulted in the establishment of the LIS in the early 1980s. The goal of the LIS project is to develop a comparative household income microdata base by adjusting national data sets to conform to a standardised conceptual and definitional template that supports cross-country comparisons of poverty, economic inequality and living standards (Smeeding, 2004). The LIS project began in 1983 with seven countries but now includes five waves of data for 25 countries spanning two decades.

The project has set 'new standards for all comparative research' (Atkinson, 2004, p 166), and the LIS data have been used by international agencies to study differences in income distribution (Atkinson et al, 1995) child poverty (UNICEF, 2000), and have informed work conducted by the World Bank, the International Labour Organization (ILO) and the United Nations Development Programme (UNDP). They have also formed the basis of a large number of independent academic studies (see Smeeding et al, 1990; Gottschalk and Smeeding, 2000; Förster and Vleminckx, 2004; Kenworthy, 2004) that have greatly advanced understanding of the extent and causes of international differences in economic inequality and poverty.

Comparative data on specific aspects of poverty can also be generated from national statistics by ensuring that they conform to an agreed template. This methodology was originally developed by the OECD to study differences in the impact of taxes and benefits on average production workers in different countries, but has since been applied to generate comparisons of different aspects of poverty and income inequality (Förster and Pearson, 2002; Whiteford and Adema, 2007; OECD, 2008, Chapter 5). This ('model family') approach has also been widely used to compare national systems of family benefits and to estimate their impact on child poverty and the well-being of children (Bradshaw and Finch, 2002; Bradshaw et al, 2006). The approach has the advantage that because only a limited number of variables needs to be rendered comparable, it is easier to implement and is thus capable of generating more up-to-date information than the LIS, where the process of data standardisation is complex and lengthy. Against this, the model family methodology does not provide the flexibility that the household-level LIS data gives to individual researchers to set the scope and parameters of their investigations.

The OECD has recently examined how close the poverty rates estimated using their agreed 'template' approach are to those derived from the LIS data (see Whiteford and Adema, 2007, Table 1; OECD, 2008, Table 5.A2.1). The basic income concept and the equivalence scale used are the same in both cases, and the resulting poverty rates are similar – generally within one percentage point of each other. The two main differences occur in Germany and the UK, where the overall poverty rate differs by four percentage points in both cases and where child poverty rates differ by an even larger amount. Part of the explanation may be due to the fact that the LIS estimates are five years earlier than the OECD estimates, and this gap (covering the period between 1999 and 2005) was one in which child poverty was declining rapidly in the UK following the government's child poverty reduction pledge (see Couch et al, 2010).

Because the OECD estimates are more recent, they form the basis of the cross-country comparisons shown in Table 2.4. There is considerable national diversity in the overall poverty rate, which varies from a low of 5% in Denmark and Sweden to 17% in the US and 18% in Turkey. Australia's poverty rate of 12% is close to the national figure reported for 2005-06 in Table 2.2, and is around two percentage points above the OECD average. This implies that Australia ranks

Table 2.4: Poverty rates in OECD countries, mid-2000s

Country	Overall poverty rate:		Specific poverty rate:		
			People of working age (18-64)	Children (0-17)	People of retirement age (65+)
	50% median	60% median			
Australia	12	20	10	12	27
Austria	7	13	7	6	7
Belgium	9	16	7	10	13
Canada	12	19	10	15	4
Czech Republic	6	11	5	10	2
Denmark	5	12	5	3	10
Finland	7	15	7	4	13
France	7	14	7	8	4
Germany	11	17	8	16	10
Greece	13	20	9	13	23
Hungary	7	12	7	9	5
Ireland	15	23	12	16	31
Italy	11	20	10	16	13
Japan	15	21	12	14	22
Luxembourg	8	13	8	12	3
Netherlands	8	14	7	12	2
New Zealand	11	23	11	15	2
Norway	7	12	7	5	9
Poland	15	21	14	22	5
Slovak Republic	8	14	8	11	6
Spain	14	21	11	17	17
Sweden	5	11	5	4	8
Switzerland	7	12	7	9	18
Turkey	18	24	14	25	15
UK	8	16	7	10	10
US	17	24	15	21	24
OECD average	10.1	16.8	8.8	12.1	11.7

Source: OECD (2008, Tables 5.A2.1, 5.1, 5.2 and 5.3)

equal 18th (with Canada) out of the 26 countries included in the analysis in terms of its overall poverty rate.

The countries with higher poverty rates than Australia include several with lower levels of national income (Greece, Ireland, Poland, Spain and Turkey) but also two of the OECD leaders in terms of economic prosperity (Japan and the US). This observation suggests that there is no simple cross-country relationship between the level of national income and national poverty rates: increased national income increases the potential to reduce poverty, but that potential will not be realised unless policies are put in place to achieve it.

The breakdown of poverty rates into those affecting three key social groups – people of working age (18-64 years), children (under 18) and people of retirement age (65 and over) – also reveal some interesting national differences. The first point to note is that in every country except Austria, the poverty rate among either children or older people exceeds that among the working-age population. Countries are divided equally into those where child poverty is highest and those where poverty among older people is highest and only in Spain and the UK are child and older person poverty rates the same. Cross–country variations in poverty rates are also far higher among children and older people than among those of working age. This suggests that income support policies that operate through social security systems exert a greater impact on poverty among vulnerable groups than policies that maintain employment levels and reduce unemployment among working-age families generally.

Countries that have the lowest overall poverty rate also tend to exhibit the smallest variation in poverty rates across the three groups, suggesting that in these instances, anti–poverty policies have been not only successful but also broad in their impact. In contrast, when overall poverty is high, there is greater variation in poverty rates among the three groups, suggesting that while policy has been weak overall, resources have been targeted to achieve specific poverty outcomes.

The Australian poverty rate is similar to the OECD average in the case of both children and working-age households, although the older person poverty rate of 27% is well above the OECD average of around 11%. These results imply that older Australians face a greater risk of poverty than their counterparts in most other OECD countries. Australia does better when it comes to child poverty and this is in part a reflection of its high level of spending on child benefits (OECD, 2007a). However, the generosity of family benefits is only one factor that determines the child poverty rate, which also depends on employment rates among parents, the mix between couple and lone-parent families, and between single-earner and dual-earner families, and the dispersion of wages (see Bradbury and Jäntti, 1999; Whiteford and Adema, 2007). For these reasons, it is more difficult to attribute the country variations in child poverty shown in Table 2.4 to differences in national social security policies than is the case for older people, where pension policies exert a greater impact on incomes (although this does not always translate into large poverty-reducing effects).

Importantly, the variation in national poverty rates displayed in Table 2.4 indicates that Australia's failure to reduce its poverty rate between 1972 and 2007 was not a consequence of how poverty is measured. Even when the poverty line is fixed to average (or median) income, it is possible to introduce policies that reduce poverty. Each country can thus choose its own poverty rate and that choice reveals much about national priorities and community values.

Summary

The methods discussed and results presented in this chapter are based on an approach that defines and identifies poverty in a single (income) dimension. Although this approach has many limitations, the results highlight the valuable

—

role that conventional poverty research can play in contributing to an initial understanding of the nature of the problem. Commonly used definitions of poverty and public opinion surveys reveal a clear and consistent understanding of poverty as a situation where economic resources are not adequate to meet basic needs. One way of establishing whether resources are adequate involves comparing income with a needs-based adequacy benchmark or poverty line.

The results presented in Tables 2.2, 2.3 and 2.4 show how poverty line studies are capable of generating valuable information about the size and distribution of poverty risks among the population. These estimates are suggestive of some of the factors that contribute to poverty, but these conclusions are tentative for two reasons: first, because the estimates need to be validated against living standards before it can be concluded that those with incomes below a poverty line are living in poverty; and second, because it is not possible to identify causal factors simply by estimating the extent of a problem.

The conceptual and methodological weaknesses of the income approach are likely to be broadly similar across all OECD countries and are thus unlikely to create major distortions in cross-country comparisons of poverty rates. In this context, the country differences shown in Table 2.4 are of particular significance because they confirm that what countries experience and do – the factors that shape and help ameliorate poverty – vary in ways that affect observed outcomes. Again, the results highlight that the conventional approach, whatever its limitations, provides an important first step on the road to better understanding. Poverty research has an important role to play as part of the broader task of identifying social disadvantage, and income-based poverty line studies provide valuable information on which other approaches can build.

THREE

Beyond low income: economic resources, financial hardship and poverty

Introduction

The poverty line studies described in the previous chapter represent a first step in the process of identifying who is at risk of experiencing poverty. However, they need to be accompanied by other evidence demonstrating that this risk cannot be avoided and translates into an unacceptable standard of living to confirm that poverty exists. This will involve drawing on data that tap more directly into the circumstances of those at risk and interpreting these data in ways that overcome the limitations of income-based studies. Applying this approach will introduce new controversies and potential areas of disagreement over the precise form that these methods should take.

This chapter explores one approach that uses data on household spending patterns, wealth holdings and the incidence of financial hardship to refine income-based poverty estimates. The use of broader measures of economic resources than just income and the idea that the existence of poverty must be demonstrated using evidence on living standard outcomes are features of the deprivation approach discussed in the next chapter. Their use in this chapter illustrates the potential of the underlying ideas to extend and improve poverty line studies, but the precise methods adopted are indicative and the estimates presented are best regarded as experimental.

It is more than a century since Seebohm Rowntree undertook the first poverty line study in York, England (see Rowntree, 1901; Bradshaw and Sainsbury, 1999). Since that pioneering study, two main approaches have been developed to improve the methods used to identify poverty. The first draws on information on economic resources other than income to establish whether those identified as poor have the capacity to satisfy their needs by drawing on these resources. Those with access to such resources can (if they are adequate) be regarded as having the option not to be poor, and can thus be removed from the poverty counts. The second approach draws on outcome data to validate the implicit assumption that low income translates into an unacceptable standard of living. Those whose living standards do not appear to be unacceptable can also be regarded as not poor and removed from the numbers in poverty. These two refinements will be referred to as *the resource exclusions approach* and *the validation approach*, respectively.

Although both approaches have the effect of reducing the numbers identified as poor, they achieve this differently: resource exclusion studies achieve the reduction by removing those with access to additional resources which suggest that they have the capacity to avoid poverty; validation studies achieve the reduction by removing those with incomes below the poverty line who do not appear to be experiencing a poverty-level standard of living. The resulting reduction in the numbers identified as poor does not mean that poverty is any less of a problem, but rather that a stricter definition has been used to identify its core.

Both approaches draw on information other than income, but each involves modifying poverty line studies in ways that are better able to capture the realities of poverty (both as it is defined, and as it is experienced) while taking low income as the point of departure. In so doing, they recognise the primary role that income plays in putting people at risk of poverty, while acknowledging that other evidence is needed to confirm that this risk translates into an unavoidable outcome.

Australian poverty researchers have long recognised that factors other than income are relevant to the poverty status of some groups. The most well known example relates to those identified as self-employed, which Table 2.3 (Chapter Two) indicates face an above-average poverty rate. However, concern over the difficulty of distinguishing between personal and business income for the self-employed and their ability to offset business costs against income (leading in some instances to negative income) has led to a questioning of whether reported income can be used to assess the poverty status of this group (Bradbury, 1996; Eardley and Bradbury, 1997). The response, adopted by the Poverty Commission and subsequently by many Australian poverty researchers, has been to remove the self-employed from the analysis altogether when estimating poverty (Commission of Inquiry into Poverty, 1975, Chapter 3; Saunders and Matheson, 1991).

The impact on the poverty rate of removing the self-employed is complex and ambiguous. First, it depends on how the poverty rate among the self-employed compares with the poverty rate among other households. If the self-employed have a higher poverty rate, their removal will, other things constant, lead to a reduction in measured poverty. However, their removal may also cause the value of median income to change, leading to a change in the poverty line, and this will have further flow-on effects on measured poverty. If most of the self-employed have incomes that are above the median, then the exclusion of all self-employed households will reduce the median and result in a lower poverty line and a reduced poverty rate. In contrast, if the self-employed are concentrated below the median of the income distribution, their removal will increase the median, leading to a higher poverty line. This may or may not lead to more poverty, depending on how many other (not self-employed) households now fall below the higher line, but even if the median is unchanged, the poverty rate is still likely to change when the self-employed are removed. The net effect on the poverty rate thus depends on a number of separate effects and cannot be determined unambiguously.

Another problem with this approach is that by removing all households who are self-employed, it is no longer possible to examine the extent of poverty among this group, or to compare it with the poverty rates of other groups. It is likely that some, possibly many, of those who report their labour force status as self-employed are genuinely poor. The need to examine this issue is all the more important because the self-employed make an important contribution to the economy and represent a large and growing proportion of the workforce. This suggests that a more differentiated treatment of the self-employed may be preferable, and this idea is explored later.

The resource exclusions approach

A number of recent Australian studies have supplemented income using information on other dimensions of economic resources in order to generate more comprehensive indicators that can form the basis of improved estimates of poverty (and living standards more generally). These developments have been made possible by the improvements in the quality of the ABS survey data mentioned earlier and in the scope of the Household Expenditure Survey (HES) data and by new data made available in some waves of the HILDA Survey. The approach has been endorsed by the Australian Treasury, which has undertaken work designed to develop 'a wellbeing framework to underpin analysis and advice across a full range of our public policy responsibilities' (Parkinson, 2004, p 1). One dimension of well-being identified in the Treasury framework is the level (and distribution) of *consumption possibilities* that refers to 'people's command over resources to obtain goods and services to satisfy their needs and wants' (Parkinson, 2004, p 8).

The concept of consumption possibilities has been examined by the ABS, who note that it can be used to supplement or replace income when examining issues of poverty and economic hardship:

> The use of consumption possibilities to identify economic hardship is a conceptual move away from previous efforts which used income alone as the basis for identifying economic hardship. This shift has been influenced, in part, by the fact that income is not a good predictor of living standard outcomes…. ABS Income and Expenditure Survey data [suggest that] some of the households in the bottom income deciles may not be experiencing economic hardship or that they may be financing their consumption from assets, debt or from some sort of transfers. This situation underlines the role of wealth as an important component of consumption and well-being, and the need to go beyond income alone as a determinant of economic well-being and economic hardship. (ABS, 2009a, p 2)

Households with low consumption possibilities will be at risk of poverty because:

> … consumption possibilities are defined as the capacity (or capability) of people to satisfy their needs and wants for goods and services…. People with low consumption possibilities have less capacity (or

capability) to undertake consumption and to cope with unexpected costs. They are therefore considered to be at greater risk of experiencing economic hardship. (Billing et al, 2010, p 4)

A similar approach has been developed by researchers at the Melbourne Institute of Applied Economic and Social Research using data from the HILDA Survey. Headey (2006), for example, draws on information on income and wealth to produce indicators of economic capability as one of four dimensions of capability using the framework developed by Sen (1999). He argues that a dynamic, multi-dimensional approach is more likely to attract the attention of policy makers than one based on identifying disadvantage using a (static) uni-dimensional, income-based poverty line. He also shows that a capabilities approach is better able to explain the variability in indicators of financial stress, self-rated health and life satisfaction than one based on the use of a poverty line (Headey, 2006, Table 20). Headey does not reject the use of income poverty lines altogether, since they are used to generate indicators of low economic functioning in the form of both static poverty rates and estimates of the persistence of poverty (Headey, 2006, Table 6).

The idea that wealth ownership is an important component of economic resources and a determinant of economic capacity has been applied by the ABS (2007a) and Billing et al (2010) to identify households with 'low economic resources' or 'low consumption possibilities' as those at the lower end of the distributions of both income and wealth. A similar approach has been incorporated into other studies of poverty and disadvantage conducted at the Melbourne Institute. Thus, Scutella et al (2008) have developed a multi-dimensional indicator of social exclusion that includes both a poverty line (set at 60% of median income) and a wealth line (set at 60% of median net wealth) as indicators of exclusion from material or economic resources. In an extension of the approach, Hahn and Wilkins (2008), in a report commissioned by the Australian Fair Pay Commission, have examined the incidence of poverty and low pay using a range of indicators of poverty, including one based on income alone (below 60% of the median) and others that also include relative levels of wealth (below 60% of the median) and consumption (below 60% of the median). The thresholds are also varied from 60% to 75% to assess the sensitivity of the results to such variation.

Using the 60% threshold, they find that the proportion of all employees who are poor declines from 6.8% when an income threshold alone is used, to 4.6% when it is combined with a wealth threshold, and to 2.9% when it is further combined with a consumption threshold (Hahn and Wilkins, 2008, Table 15). These results imply that less than half of those identified as poor on the basis of income alone remain poor once account is taken of their wealth and consumption spending. Headey (2007) has also estimated poverty using HILDA data on expenditure and wealth as well as income. His results confirm that conventional poverty rates decline sharply (but not uniformly across all household types) once account is taken of the expenditure level of the household, and that a further slight decline occurs when account is also taken of household wealth.

The use of information on consumption expenditure to supplement income when estimating poverty has also been examined by Saunders (1997, 2003b) using data from the ABS HES. This variant of the approach utilises information on the *difference* between income and expenditure rather than applying separate benchmarks for each, as is done in the Melbourne Institute and ABS studies described above. The advantage of using the *balance* between income and spending to better identify who is in poverty is that this difference reflects the ability of households to live within their means and is thus an important indicator of whether or not they are 'struggling to make ends meet' and hence likely to be poor. Application of the approach indicates that in 1993-94, just over 20% of households had incomes below an income poverty line, but less than half of these (8% of all households) had both incomes and expenditures below the same line. Furthermore, if those in the latter group who were spending less than their income are also removed (on the grounds that the implied saving suggests that the household is not poor), the poverty rate declines even further, to less than 3% (Saunders, 2003b, Figure 1 and Table 4.1).

The impact on poverty of applying a resource exclusions approach is now examined using data from the combined household income and expenditure survey conducted by the ABS in 2003-04 (ABS, 2006a, 2007b). That survey also collected comprehensive information on the wealth holdings of Australian households, making it even better suited to the task. The combined survey was conducted over the course of the year, and the incomes reported in different quarters have been adjusted in line with quarterly movements in the consumer price index (CPI) to make them consistent across the year.

The analysis begins by estimating a set of benchmark poverty rates using poverty lines set at 50% and 60% of median income. These estimates are based on comparing the price-adjusted incomes in each quarter with a poverty line expressed relative to median price-adjusted income across all four quarters (further details are provided in Saunders et al, 2007a, Section 3; and Saunders and Hill, 2008). The resulting poverty rates, shown in Table 3.1, represent a point of departure for both the resource exclusions and validation approaches and allow the impact on poverty of these modifications to be established. (It should be noted

Table 3.1: Benchmark poverty rates for 2003-04

	Number (000s)	Poverty rate (%)
Poverty line set at 50% of median income		
Adults	1,569.7	10.1
Children	365.3	9.4
Persons	1,935.0	9.9
Poverty line set at 60% of median income		
Adults	3,073.5	19.7
Children	785.6	20.2
Persons	3,859.0	19.8

Source: Saunders et al (2007, Tables S.1 and S.2)

that these estimates are not comparable with those for 2005–06 shown in Table 2.2, because they are based on the larger HES sample, not just the component of that sample that also responded to the SIH.)

In order to assess the impact on poverty of applying a resource exclusions approach, the removal of households from the poverty counts (with consequent implications for estimated poverty rates) has not been allowed to affect the median income estimates on which the poverty lines are based. This makes it possible to assess the impact of the different exclusions on poverty using a fixed poverty line benchmark. In practice, the median will only be unchanged if the households that are removed fall equally below and above the median of the distribution as a whole, and the evidence presented below indicates that the medians of the pre- and post-removal distributions are in fact very similar.

Thus far, the discussion has focused on those households like the self-employed where there are concerns about the relevance of reported income for poverty analysis. However, the earlier discussion of data reliability and the role of income as a determinant of the standard of living implies that other factors can also influence whether or not the conventional methods used to estimate poverty are capable of producing accurate results. In addition to containing detailed information on income, expenditure and wealth, the 2003-04 HES also includes evidence on the incidence of different forms of financial stress. This allows the data on consumption spending, wealth and financial stress to be used to refine the income-based poverty estimates by applying the ideas that underpin the consumption possibilities concept described earlier.

The basic idea underlying the approach is that where households with low income can be shown to either have access to other forms of economic resources (as evidenced in their level of spending or ownership of wealth), or do not exhibit the characteristics that are expected to be associated with poverty (as reflected in an absence of reported financial stress), then there is a case for removing (or excluding) them from the poverty counts. In practical terms, the approach has not involved removing households from the analysis altogether (as is done in many Australian poverty studies). Instead, it has involved changing the status of the relevant households from poor to not poor. In effect, this treats their initial identification as poor (based on income alone) as a 'false positive' because additional information suggests that they have access to the resources needed to escape poverty, or because they do not face the financial stress that is expected to result from being poor.

Although the precise methods used to adjust the benchmark poverty estimates can be challenged, the approach is designed to illustrate how additional data can be used to better identify who cannot avoid and is actually experiencing poverty, and to gauge the impact that this has on estimated poverty rates. The goal is therefore to illustrate the potential impact of the approach, rather than produce definitive findings, and the methods described below can be easily adjusted to examine how robust the results are to such variation. This section examines the impact of the adjustments that relate to access to economic resources, while those

—

that relate to the incidence of financial stress are considered under the validation approach discussed in the next section.

The following economic resource adjustments have been made progressively to the benchmark (full sample) poverty estimates shown in Table 3.1:

1. Removal of all households with zero or negative income
2. Removal of households who report their labour force status as self-employed
3. Removal of households below the poverty line with 'unusually' high reported expenditure given their incomes
4. Removal of households with incomes below the poverty line who have high wealth holdings

The first two steps in this process exclude those households where there is greatest concern that income may be under-reported or reflect business losses among self-employed households. The latter two steps combine information on expenditure and wealth with that on income to provide a more comprehensive assessment of the economic resources available to households that can be used to better establish whether or not the household is poor.

Removing households with zero or negative income and the self-employed

The removal of households who report zero or negative income and those who are self-employed were applied together, in part because there is considerable overlap between the two groups. As Table 3.2 indicates, although relatively few households report zero or negative income (less than half of one per cent of all households), over one in seven (15.3%) are affected by the self-employed exclusion. In terms of the *numbers affected*, the removal of self-employed households is thus of far greater significance than the exclusion of those who report zero or negative

Table 3.2: Impact on poverty rates of excluding households with zero or negative income and self-employed households (weighted)

	Number of households affected (000s)	Median income ($)	Poverty rate based on median of whole sample:		Poverty rate based on median adjusted for the exclusions:	
			50% median	60% median	50% median	60% median
Whole sample	7,736	497.4	9.9	19.8	–	–
Exclude zero or negative income	33	498.4	9.7	19.6	9.9	19.7
Exclude zero or negative income and self-employed households	1,187	491.1	9.8	20.4	9.0	19.6

Source: Saunders and Hill (2008, Table 3)

income. Furthermore, around half of the very small numbers who report zero or negative income are also affected by the removal of the self-employed.

The second column of Table 3.2 shows that the two exclusions together reduce median income by just over $6 a week (1.1%). The fact that median income declines when the self-employed are removed (it obviously increases when those with zero or negative income are removed) indicates that the majority of the self-employed have incomes in the upper half of the income distribution, although the magnitude of the change suggests that many of the self-employed also have incomes below the median. The estimates in the four right-hand side columns of Table 3.2 indicate how the poverty rates change when the different adjustments are applied, using poverty lines set at 50% and 60% of the overall (pre-adjustment) median of the distribution.

Many households are affected when the self-employed are removed, and this has a larger (absolute) impact on the poverty rate when the median is unchanged than the removal of households with zero or negative income (particularly at the higher poverty line). Although all of those with zero or negative income are by definition below the poverty line, only some of those who are self-employed will be and their incomes more diverse, but the numbers in the latter category are much larger. The impact of the self-employed adjustment is greater when the poverty line is set at 60% of the median (irrespective of whether or not the median is adjusted to reflect the removal). The fact that the poverty rate rises when the self-employed are removed indicates (using a fixed poverty line) that their poverty rate is lower than that of all other (not self-employed) households. This means that the risk of poverty is lower among self-employed households in general, but it does not follow that no self-employed households are poor, as is shown later.

Exclusions based on expenditure

Since the concern about the reliability of the income data for low-income households relates to the *balance* between income and expenditure, the *ratio* of expenditure to income has been used as the basis for removing households from the poverty counts. Headey (2007) excludes those who are income poor (defined as having an income below 50% of the median) who do not also have expenditure (described as consumption by Headey) that is below 50% of median expenditure. Although there are good reasons why households with low incomes may be forced to incur debt in order to meet their needs (and thus have an expenditure to income ratio that exceeds one), when this ratio is very high it raises doubts about relying on income alone to indicate the current living standard of the household and hence to determine whether or not it is poor.

The HES expenditure variable used in this analysis includes the amounts spent on all goods and services, but excludes expenditure on income tax, principal repayments on mortgages, superannuation and life insurance because these represent different forms of saving. No attempt was made to take account of any 'lumpy' expenditure on consumer durables and other major items that may

—

have been purchased during the survey period. One consequence is that some households that have a high ratio of expenditure to income because they happened to purchase a large item in the survey period are removed (and hence treated as false positives). However, the exclusion adjustment is only applied to households with incomes below the poverty line, and it makes sense to remove from the poverty count those in this situation who can afford to incur large one-off expenditures.

Since it is necessary to set a threshold for the expenditure to income ratio before the exclusion can be applied, the distributions of two expenditure to income ratios for all households with incomes below the poverty line was examined. The first is the ratio of total expenditure to disposable income, while the second is the ratio of equivalised total expenditure to the 50% of median income poverty line (which is also, by definition, equivalised). Examination of the distribution of the first ratio revealed that there are a small number of households with high spending to income ratios that reflect a low level of reported income rather than a high level of total expenditure. The second ratio overcomes this problem by expressing expenditure as a ratio of the poverty line for each household type, and its value at the top of the distribution declines by a factor of around 10 relative to the first ratio.

The distribution of the second expenditure to income ratio for households with incomes below the (50% of median income) poverty line is shown in Figure 3.1. It is clear that a large proportion of households with incomes below the poverty line report levels of expenditure that exceed the income required to reach the poverty line (that is, have a spending to income ratio that exceeds one). This implies that the actual standard of living of these households is likely to be above

Figure 3.1: Distribution of the ratio of equivalised household expenditure to the poverty line (50% of median income)

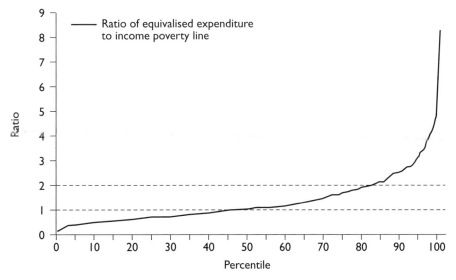

Source: Saunders et al (2007, Figure 1)

the poverty line, even though they may be incurring debt and may not be able to sustain this standard indefinitely. This finding is not very sensitive to whether or not households with zero or negative income and the self-employed are excluded from the sample, or to whether the poverty line is set at 50% or 60% of median income. For illustrative purposes, the threshold value of the ratio was set equal to two, resulting in the removal of around one fifth of income-poor households from the poverty estimates, with the poverty rate declining from around 10% to just over 8% (see Table 3.3).

Exclusions based on household wealth

The important role that wealth plays in combating poverty has been examined in studies that focus on the role of housing wealth in protecting older Australians from poverty (Bradbury et al, 1986; King, 1998). Although it provides valuable information, this approach ignores the role of wealth held in forms other than occupied housing in protecting low-income households at all stages of the life cycle from poverty. To explore this issue further, the wealth holdings of households with incomes below the poverty line were examined. (An alternative approach would involve supplementing the income measure so that it better captures income from the ownership of all forms of wealth, although imputing income to housing and other forms of wealth is a complex exercise.)

Two wealth variables were examined: total household net wealth and net wealth minus owner-occupied housing wealth. Figure 3.2 shows the distributions of these two measures of wealth for individuals in households with incomes below

Figure 3.2: Distributions of net wealth and net wealth minus owner-occupied housing wealth for households under the poverty line (50% of median income)

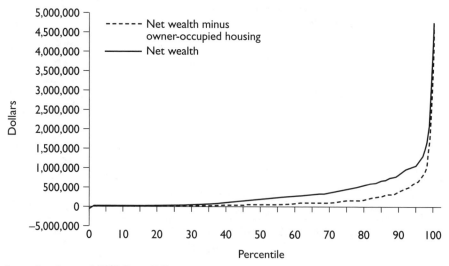

Source: Saunders et al (2007, Figure D.1)

the 50% of median income poverty line. Both distributions are very similar, as they are if the higher poverty line is used.

Figure 3.2 indicates that while most households below the poverty line have low wealth holdings, a not insignificant proportion of them have considerable wealth, even after deducting net housing wealth (see also Marks, 2007). The value of both wealth measures increases rapidly among the wealthiest fifth of households with incomes below the poverty line. It accelerates among the wealthiest 10% of these households, which includes a small number of extremely wealthy households. By way of illustration of the impact of these findings, if a wealth threshold of $500,000 is applied, it would result in the exclusion of between 7% and 23% of income-poor households, depending on whether or not net housing wealth is included.

Although a case can be made for applying the more comprehensive (inclusive of housing) wealth measure, the illiquid nature of housing wealth compared with other assets raises problematic issues in the context of poverty measurement, where the low housing costs associated with home ownership have particular significance. For this reason, a wealth threshold based on non-housing wealth has been used to explore the impact of wealth holdings on measured poverty. For illustrative purposes, the removal based on wealth was applied to households with non-housing wealth that exceeds the levels at which the prevailing (March to June 2004) pensions assets test starts to reduce benefit entitlement, that is, at a level of $149,500 for a single person or $212,500 for a couple. (The value of owner-occupied housing is not taken into account when the pensions assets test is applied.) Use of the pension assets test thresholds grounds the approach in what can be regarded as an official assessment of what is a reasonable level of wealth for low-income Australians.

The impact of the wealth adjustment on the number of households below the poverty line is shown in Table 3.3. The estimates indicate that for the original poverty measures, depending on where the poverty line is set, between 16% and 18% of income-poor households have wealth that is above the pension assets test thresholds. The fact that the proportion of low-income households with high wealth is lower at the higher poverty line reflects the fact that many of the extra households identified as poor when the poverty line is moved from 50% to 60% of the median are in receipt of a social security payment and thus by definition

Table 3.3: Percentage of poor households with wealth above the pension assets test limits, 2003-04 (weighted)

	Poverty line	
Poverty definition	50% of median income	60% of median income
No exclusions	18.3	16.0
Exclusion 1: households with zero/negative income and/or self-employed	15.0	13.3
Exclusion 2: exclusion 1 plus households with equivalised expenditure more than median income	11.2	9.7

have low net wealth. When households with zero or negative income or who are self-employed are excluded, the proportion affected by the wealth exclusion declines to between 13% and 15%, while if households with high expenditures (as defined earlier) are also excluded, the percentage with high wealth declines further, to between 10% and 11% of those defined as poor on the basis of income alone.

Impact on poverty rates

It has already been noted that the removal of households with zero or negative income and those who are self-employed has conventionally involved removing these households from the analysis altogether. This approach has been justified on the grounds that reported income does not provide an accurate picture of the standard of living of these households, so that their complete removal from the analysis is justified. When it comes to applying the expenditure-based and wealth-based exclusions, however, the issue is complicated by the fact that the methods used depend on arbitrarily selected thresholds, and a decision must be made about whether to remove only those households who exceed these thresholds with incomes below the poverty line, or to remove all households above the threshold, irrespective of their income-based poverty status.

Of these two options, the first is problematic because it can result in the removal of a large number of households, reducing sample size and lowering the efficiency of the estimates. This problem is avoided if only those households with incomes below the poverty line are removed and, as noted earlier, this approach treats those households who are identified as poor on the basis of income alone as 'false positives' when account is taken of additional information on their expenditure or wealth. It should be noted that the false positives approach results in an automatic reduction in the poverty rate (since the numerator is reduced but the denominator is unchanged).

The impact of both approaches on estimated poverty rates is shown in Table 3.4. The results show, for each poverty line, the progressive impact of treating the exclusions as 'false positives' (that is, assuming that the households affected are not poor) and of discarding the excluded cases altogether (that is, removing the households affected from the sample entirely) – except in the case of the first step, where only the latter approach is applied for consistency with other Australian poverty studies, as explained earlier.

The removals based on expenditure and wealth have a substantial impact on the poverty rates estimated using either poverty line, although it is difficult to compare the magnitude of the effects because they depend on the order in which the different adjustments are applied. The *combined* impact of all three adjustments under the 'false positives' treatment of the latter two adjustments results in a reduction in the percentage of households with incomes below the two poverty lines by 2.7 and 4.0 percentage points, respectively. Both declines are smaller if the identified cases are removed altogether, although the differences are not great. These effects are much smaller than those found by Hahn and Wilkins (2008),

Table 3.4: Cumulative impact of the exclusions on poverty rates in 2003-04 (weighted)

	Poverty line			
	50% of median income		60% of median income	
	'False positives' approach	Exclusions discarded entirely	'False positives' approach	Exclusions discarded entirely
No exclusions (benchmark case)	9.9		19.8	
Exclude self-employed and those with zero/negative income	–	9.8	–	20.4
Exclude those with high expenditures	8.2	8.4	17.5	18.1
Exclude those with high levels of wealth	7.2	7.4	15.8	16.6

Source: Saunders and Hill (2008, Table 7)

although this reflects the different methodologies used to identify households with low economic resources. The approach used here has the advantage that it builds on the conventional approach based on income alone and estimates the impact of modifying that approach.

Although the effects shown in Table 3.4 appear substantial, it is worth noting that the impact of all three exclusions using the 50% of median income poverty line is far smaller than the change in the original (baseline) estimates that results from increasing the poverty line from 50% to 60% of median income. This is illustrated by the fact that the poverty rate using the higher poverty line *after* applying all three adjustments (15.8%) is still well above the benchmark poverty rate using the lower poverty line *before* making any adjustment (9.9%). Another perspective on the results is provided by Saunders and Bradbury (2006, Figure 5), who estimate that the replacement of annual by weekly (current) income leads to a decline in the 2001–02 poverty rate (using the 50% of median income poverty line) from 12.4% to 11.2%. This decline of 1.2 percentage points compares with the 'false positives' decline of 2.7 percentage points shown in Table 3.4.

Of course, the relevance of the alternative approaches used to measure poverty cannot be established on the basis of their impact on the poverty rate. The results presented here are designed to illustrate the conceptual basis underlying different approaches and highlight the choices that are required to make them operational. Overall, it is clear that applying a resource exclusions approach can make a substantial difference to estimated poverty rates, but so do many of the other choices that have to be made when estimating poverty on the basis of income alone. This reinforces the need for sensitivity analysis as a way of checking how the estimates vary with changes in the many assumptions on which they are based.

The validation approach

Unlike the approaches described so far, which seek to remove from the poverty counts those households that have access to economic resources other than income, the validation approach seeks to confirm that those with incomes below the poverty line are experiencing a low standard of living by drawing on evidence on outcomes. The indicators that have been used to validate estimates of income poverty in this way are based on reports of the incidence of financial stress using data from the HES and HILDA Surveys. Implicit in this approach is the idea that evidence of financial stress can be used, in conjunction with other information about household circumstances, to identify hardship or poverty, although this has not always been an explicit goal (Bray, 2001; McColl et al, 2001; Butterworth and Crosier, 2006).

The basic idea that underlies the validation approach is that information on the reported experience of financial stress can be used to confirm that households identified as being in poverty on the basis of their income are experiencing the kinds of financial and budgetary pressures that one would expect to find among those who are poor. Experiencing difficulty making ends meet and struggling to survive have been identified as a commonly accepted understanding of the meaning of poverty (see Table 2.1 in Chapter Two). The use of financial stress data to produce more robust and credible estimates of poverty thus represents an approach to validation that is consistent with widespread understanding of the experience and consequences of poverty.

It can be argued that combining information on income with that on consumption expenditure as discussed earlier can also be interpreted as an application of the validation approach. This is because a low level of consumption is used to validate that low income is associated with an outcome that is synonymous with poverty. There is a degree of truth in this view, although the fact that the variable under consideration is *consumption expenditure* (the amount spent) as opposed to *actual consumption* (the quantity consumed) suggests that a resource interpretation is more appropriate than an outcome interpretation.

Validating poverty using reported financial stress

Several studies have examined the incidence of reported financial stress using information collected for the first time in the HES conducted in 1998-99 (ABS, 2000, 2002b; Bray, 2001; McColl et al, 2001). The data relate to whether or not the household had experienced a range of forms of financial stress over the previous 12 months due to a shortage of money. The ABS financial stress questions cover 13 specific forms of financial stress or hardship, the first seven of which overlap with similar questions included in the HILDA Survey. The financial stress variables that are included in both the HES and HILDA are identified in Table 3.5, which shows changes in the incidence of each indicator over the decade to 2008. The remaining six HES questions relate to activities that the household has not

—

Table 3.5: Recent trends in the incidence of hardship and financial stress (unweighted percentages)

	HES		HILDA	
Indicator	1998-99	2003-04	2004	2008
Due to a shortage of money				
Could not pay gas/electricity/telephone bill	16.6	15.2	14.7	12.1
Could not pay the mortgage/rent on time	n/a	n/a	6.8	6.0
Could not pay registration/insurance on time	6.7	6.1	n/a	n/a
Pawned or sold something	4.3	3.6	4.7	4.0
Went without meals	2.8	2.2	3.8	3.4
Unable to heat home	2.3	2.4	2.7	2.2
Sought assistance from welfare/community organisations	3.5	2.8	3.4	3.1
Sought financial help from friends/family	10.2	10.4	13.9	12.4
Could not afford				
A night out once a fortnight	19.6	18.8	n/a	n/a
A special meal once a week	11.7	11.5	n/a	n/a
A meal with friends or family once a month	5.2	6.0	n/a	n/a
A holiday away for at least one week a year	28.0	25.8	n/a	n/a
Brand new clothes – have to buy second-hand clothes	11.3	10.8	n/a	n/a
Spend time on leisure and hobby activities	9.1	8.8	n/a	n/a

Sources: HES and HILDA Survey, unit record files

Note: n/a = not available.

participated in because they cannot afford it. All 13 HES financial stress indicators form the basis of the analysis that follows.

The estimates in Table 3.5 are unweighted although they differ only slightly if weights are applied – generally by less than one percentage point. Both sets of indicators produce similar incidence rates in the common year (2004), although the HILDA estimates are slightly above those derived from HES. There are, however, large differences in the incidence of each indicator in both surveys, with around 15% not being able to pay household utility bills at some point over the year, around 12% seeking financial help from friends or family members and more than 25% unable to afford a week's holiday away each year. In contrast, far fewer respondents report going without meals or not being able to afford heating in the home. The variation in incidence rates across the different indicators reveals the complex nature of financial stress and how it affects different households – a complexity that cannot be adequately captured in a single poverty rate.

It is of interest to note that the HES questions refer to two factors that are identified as causing financial stress – a shortage of money and a lack of affordability – although the distinction between them is unclear. The phrase 'shortage of money' (which is also used in the HILDA financial stress questions) focuses more narrowly on a lack of available cash resources, whereas a 'lack of affordability' implies a broader and perhaps longer-term assessment of one's economic circumstances. In terms of the events covered, the 'shortage of money' variables refer primarily to the *consequences* of financial stress, whereas the 'lack of affordability' variables refer to actual *activities* (and in one case, clothing) that have had to be foregone. In these instances, respondents are asked to indicate which of the following four reasons explains their lack of participation: not applicable; don't want it; can't afford it; and other reason. Only those who provide the third response are defined here as experiencing financial stress.

Responses to the seven financial stress questions that have been included in the HILDA Survey have been analysed in a series of studies (Butterworth and Crosier, 2006; Breunig and Cobb-Clark, 2006; Headey and Warren, 2007, 2008; Wilkins et al, 2010, Chapter 9). Results from these studies have raised doubts about the interpretation of the financial stress responses to the HILDA Survey and their ability to identify poverty, in part because of reporting differences between different members of the household about the existence of such stress (Breunig et al, 2005; see also Siminski and Yerokhin, 2010). Despite these reservations, measures of multiple stress and multiple hardship derived from the HILDA data have been used in official reports to compare the circumstances of different groups of transfer-reliant households who derive more than half of their income from transfer payments as a way of assessing the adequacy of different social security benefits (see, for example, Harmer, 2008, Chart 10).

These and other studies have found that the incidence of financial stress is not restricted to those in poverty, but extends into the upper reaches of the income distribution (Bray, 2001; Saunders and Adelman, 2006; Marks, 2007). This raises further doubts about the ability of the financial stress data *by itself* to identify poverty and to draw implications about the incidence of hardship and poverty or about income adequacy more generally. This is reflected in the cautious interpretation of what the HILDA financial stress data imply for the adequacy of income support payment levels expressed in a recent official report, where it was argued that: 'While providing some insight into the adequacy of payments, the incidence of poor outcomes reflects a much wider set of factors ... [including] the full range of resources such as wealth and access to services, and personal characteristics, competencies and behaviours' (Harmer, 2008, p 21).

Despite these limitations, examination of the financial stress data *in combination with other indicators* has the potential to broaden our understanding of the nature and consequences of poverty. Although all of the studies cited above have examined the incidence (and multiple incidence) of financial stress, few have examined the use of the financial stress data to validate income-based poverty estimates. The main exception is the study by Bray, which compares the incidence of financial stress among low- and high-income households using a range of definitions of these terms. That analysis was conducted separately on three dimensions of financial stress that factor analysis identified as independent components – referred to by Bray as 'missing out', 'cash flow problems' and 'hardship' (see Bray, 2001, Chapter 3). The results reveal that when low income is defined as having less than 50% of median (equivalised) income, the incidence of at least one form of each of the three dimensions of financial stress among low-income households was 50%, 27% and 15%, respectively. If a multiple definition is used (experiencing at least two indicators in each dimension), the incidence rates declined to 33%, 16% and 8%, respectively (Bray, 2001, Table 18).

The results led Bray to conclude that:

> [T]he measures only identify half the households experiencing multiple hardship, while at the same time classifying as low-income large numbers of households who report no financial stress at all. This is not surprising, as while the incidence of financial stress is related to income levels, and hence income can be considered as a risk factor, it ignores the wider range of circumstances that also comes into play. (Bray, 2001, p 71)

These comments, and the analysis that underpins them, suggest guarded support for the use of financial stress in conjunction with income to produce a better indicator of who is experiencing poverty.

In pursuing this idea, a composite indicator has been developed that covers both low income and the incidence of financial stress. For this purpose, financial stress has been identified using the 13 HES indicators described earlier (see Table 3.5). In order to apply this version of the validation approach, a definition of what constitutes a 'high' level of financial stress is required, and this involves making a judgement about where to set such a threshold. As before, the threshold was set after examining the data and should be regarded as illustrative, although the results are presented in a way that allows the impact of varying the threshold to be assessed.

Figure 3.3 and Table 3.6 compare the distributions of the number of financial stress indicators experienced by households with incomes below and above a poverty line set at 50% of median income. Around one third (37%) of individuals in households with incomes below this poverty line report experiencing none of the financial stress indicators, as do around 58% of households with income above the poverty line. Around one quarter of households with incomes below the poverty line experience four or more stress indicators, although Figure 3.3 indicates that there are also some households with incomes above the poverty line who also experience this degree of multiple stress. Although the numbers are very small, the incidence of more than five indicators of financial stress is similar for households with incomes either side of the 50% of the poverty line.

Table 3.6 indicates that the two distributions of financial stress incidence do not vary much if the poverty line is raised from 50% to 60% of median income. This implies that as income is increased over the range between 50% and 60% of the median, it has little impact on the incidence of financial stress. This contrasts starkly with the earlier finding (see Table 3.1) that the poverty rate is very sensitive to whether the poverty line is set at 50% or 60% of median income. Together, these two pieces of evidence thus reveal that the sharp rise in the numbers in poverty that results when the poverty line is moved from 50% to 60% of median income

Figure 3.3: The distribution of financial stress indicators experienced by households with incomes below and above 50% of median income

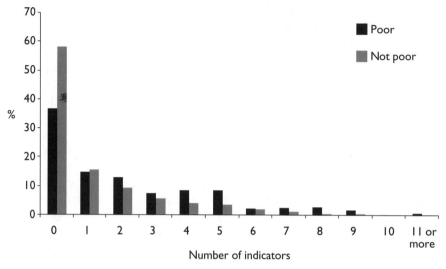

Number of indicators

Table 3.6: Distribution of financial stress indicators for people in households with incomes below alternative poverty lines

	Poverty line	
Number of financial stress indicators	50% median income	60% median income
Zero	37.0	35.7
One	15.0	15.7
Two	13.2	13.1
Three	7.5	8.5
Four or more	27.4	27.0
Total	100.0	100.0

Source: Saunders et al (2007, Table E.2)

is not confirmed by evidence on how financial stress varies over this range. This confirms the earlier suspicions about the sensitivity of results to where the poverty line is set in the Australian context.

If only those households with incomes below the poverty line who also experience at least one form of financial stress are identified as poor, then the poverty rate based on the 50% of median income poverty line would decline from the 9.9% figure shown in Table 3.4 to 6.2% (= 9.9 × {1 – 0.37}). If the poverty line is set at 60% of median income, the decline would be from 19.8% to 12.7%. In both instances, the impact on poverty is larger than that associated with any of the three resource exclusion adjustments shown in Table 3.4.

If a stricter definition of financial stress is employed (for example, one based on experiencing at least two indicators), the decline in poverty would be commensurately greater. If the financial stress validation was applied progressively (that is, after the other exclusions have already been applied, as shown in Table 3.4), the 'false positives' poverty rate (which is clearly appropriate when applying a validation approach) would decline further, from the 7.2% shown in the final row of Table 3.4 to 5.4% using the 50% median poverty line, or from 15.8% to 11.5% using the 60% of median poverty line.

These results imply that attempts to validate income-based poverty rates using information on financial stress can have a large impact on estimated poverty rates – potentially larger than the combined impact associated with excluding households on the basis of reported levels of expenditure and wealth. This is an important finding in the Australian context because the financial stress data are all that are currently available on a regular basis to validate estimates of poverty based on income alone.

One of the motivations for examining the more complex approach to poverty measurement implicit in the use of the indicators discussed above was to overcome the problems associated with estimating poverty for a group like the self-employed where there are major deficiencies in the incomes reported in household surveys. At the same time, it has to be acknowledged that there is interest in better understanding the extent of poverty among the growing numbers of self-employed small business owners, many of whom face difficult challenges keeping their businesses viable while supporting their families. It is therefore important to examine what impact the methods described in this chapter have on the estimated poverty rate among this group.

This issue is explored in Table 3.7, which compares poverty rates by labour force status, using the two alternative poverty lines and different exclusion adjustments. The first set of estimates are based on the full sample (prior to the removal of any households), while the second removes households by applying the consumption, wealth and financial stress adjustments described earlier, but then adds back in all remaining self-employed households. If the three adjustments account for all of the self-employed, then adding them back in will make no difference to the poverty rate, whereas if some of the self-employed are not affected by the adjustments, the poverty rate will change when they are added back into the

Table 3.7: Poverty rates by labour force status – sensitivity analysis

	Poverty rate:			
	50% of median income		60% of median income	
Labour force status	Full sample	Adjusted sample	Full sample	Adjusted sample
Employed full time	1.7	0.4	3.4	1.6
Employed part time	4.5	2.2	10.6	5.4
Self-employed	12.0	4.4	20.4	8.6
Unemployed	40.2	30.1	62.1	51.7
Not in the labour force	20.3	11.9	42.4	28.6
Total	9.9	5.2	19.8	11.4

sample. An increase in the poverty rate in these circumstances will indicate that some of the self-employed remain poor even after taking account not only of their income but also their consumption, wealth and financial stress.

The results reveal that some of the self-employed do indeed fall below the poverty line, even after the three adjustments have been applied. At the lower poverty line, the self-employed poverty rate of 4.4% is twice that for part-time employees and 11 times that for full-time employees. These poverty rate relativities are not greatly different from those that existed in the original data, which implies that poverty is a real risk for the self-employed. The same broad picture is revealed when the higher poverty line is used. These results thus highlight the limitations of the common practice in Australia of excluding the self-employed from poverty line studies because of income measurement problems. Poverty is often a companion of self-employment and although many of the self-employed are not poor, many others are at risk and this needs to be acknowledged when estimating poverty and given attention when designing policies to combat it.

Summary

This material presented in this chapter complements the results reported in the previous chapter by illustrating how information on economic resources and living standard outcomes can be used to better identify whether or not households with low income are indeed poor. The two approaches address this issue in different ways, but their common objective is to identify a sub-set of those with incomes below the poverty line that display the characteristics that are likely to exist if poverty is present. The first approach achieves this by removing from the poverty counts those households where there are doubts about the reliability of reported income, or where reported levels of consumption expenditure or wealth suggest that low income does not have to translate into a standard of living that signifies poverty. The second approach replaces low income as the criteria for identifying poverty with the combination of low income and poor outcomes, as identified by information on financial stress.

If the various adjustments discussed in this chapter are applied, the poverty rate declines from around 10% to between 6% and 7% when the poverty line is set at 50% of median income. If a higher poverty line (set at 60% of the median) is used, the decline is from around 20% to between 13% and 16%. In both cases, therefore, the estimated poverty rate falls substantially, although the decline is nowhere near as large as that involved in shifting the poverty line upwards from 50% to 60% of the median. This illustrates that statistical and technical issues, while important, have less of an impact on estimates of poverty than basic choices about where to set the poverty line.

The specific applications described in this chapter are intended to be illustrative of the potential of the two approaches to better identify poverty in ways that draw on a broader range of indicators of economic resources and financial hardship that are consistent with community understanding of the meaning of poverty.

—

The actual thresholds used in both approaches can be challenged, and should be, but the underlying methodology is capable of producing estimates that are more robust and compelling than those based on income alone. In presenting the results, the aim has been to highlight the underlying ideas that are captured in each approach and show where judgements have to be made in order to make those ideas operational.

It is important to emphasise that the results are not only illustrative but also limited, because they draw on available survey information that is often far removed from the experience of poverty and social disadvantage. Although it seems reasonable to question whether households with incomes below the poverty line who have substantial holdings of wealth are indeed poor, that in itself does little to enrich our understanding of what poverty actually means to those who do experience it. In order to explore this issue, new data are needed that tap directly into that experience in ways that are consistent with community understanding of what is unacceptable. This important insight provides the impetus that has informed the research described in the following three chapters.

FOUR

Experiencing poverty: the voices of poverty and disadvantage

Introduction

The previous two chapters have examined how income data can be used to estimate poverty (or the risk of poverty) and how those estimates can be refined by drawing on other information about the economic resources available to, and the financial pressures faced by, households with incomes below the poverty line. The approaches described produce fewer poor households but also provide more compelling evidence that poverty exists, and thus provide a sharper focus and contribute to a better understanding of the issue. However, their impact is constrained by the fact that the data used do not relate directly to actual living standards, do not embody knowledge about the experience of poverty and do not adequately reflect broader community understanding of the meaning of poverty.

An approach that incorporates these features is required to give greater credibility to the measurement of poverty. This must involve drawing on information that is generated specifically for this purpose rather than by applying arbitrary assumptions to data that have been collected for other purposes. Importantly, the process of producing such information provides an avenue for engaging with those who are most affected by poverty and disadvantage in order to access their knowledge and insights in ways that can inform the development of better research instruments.

It is thus necessary to engage directly with low-income Australians and those at the receiving end of disadvantage. This has involved drawing on the resources, experience and commitment of analysts and practitioners working in several of Australia's leading community sector agencies that provide different forms of assistance to those who are vulnerable and in need. The resulting collaboration provided a means through which the views of clients (and staff) of a selection of the services provided to those in need could be obtained, examined and understood. This produced two major contributions to the research: first, the interviews conducted with groups of welfare service clients were used to guide the development of a questionnaire designed to collect the information needed to identify poverty and other forms of social disadvantage using indicators that are grounded in experience; second, service clients were asked to provide the information needed to quantify their own problems using indicators that were derived from community norms and opinion.

Ensuring that the data reflect the experience of disadvantaged Australians is an important goal because it enhances the relevance of the research and adds credibility to the findings. Ensuring that disadvantaged Australians are adequately represented in the data collected is also critical, because social surveys often achieve a low response rate among those who are most disadvantaged. This is no surprise, since coping with the stresses associated with poverty leaves little time (or energy) to respond to surveys. Despite this, there are obvious problems if a survey that seeks to develop new indicators of disadvantage does not reach those who most directly experience it. The approach described in this chapter addresses these challenges by ensuring that the voices of low-income Australians are incorporated into the research instruments and that their views are captured in the data generated by the research.

The Left Out and Missing Out Project

A partnership between poverty researchers, policy analysts and welfare practitioners provided the broad intellectual insight and practical know-how needed to design and conduct a study capable of achieving the above objectives. Funding was provided for two related projects by the Australian Research Council. The first focused on generating a new conceptual framework for identifying poverty and disadvantage that provides an Australian perspective on research that has been progressing internationally. The second, the Left Out and Missing Out Project, was undertaken in collaboration with research and policy analysts from the Australian Council of Social Service, Mission Australia, the Brotherhood of St Laurence and Anglicare (Diocese of Sydney). These agencies provided the cash and in-kind support needed to refine the ideas developed in the first project and their service staff facilitated access to service clients, whose views helped to shape the issues examined and influenced the methods used to examine them.

The research was conducted in two stages. In stage 1, a series of focus groups with service clients and agency staff discussed how low-income people experience, perceive and respond to different forms of economic adversity and social disadvantage. The discussions began by asking participants to describe what they thought was needed to achieve a decent standard of living, and to identify what they saw as the key pathways into poverty and the barriers that prevent people from re-integrating into mainstream economic and social activities. The results are described in detail by Saunders and Sutherland (2006), and only those points that had a bearing on stage 2 of the research (described later) are summarised here.

The aim of the discussions was partly to test the validity and applicability of the view, expressed by the Senate poverty inquiry referred to in Chapter Two that poverty is:

> ... fundamentally about a lack of access to the opportunities most people take for granted [including] food, shelter, income, jobs

education, health services, childcare, transport and safe places for living
and recreation. (CARC, 2004, p 3)

They were also designed to see if those on the receiving end of disadvantage agreed
that the term poverty refers to 'a concept of deprivation, lack of opportunity to
participate fully in society, of social isolation and exclusion' (CARC, 2004, p 3).

The use of focus groups with low-income and disadvantaged Australians to
help identify the dimensions of disadvantage was part of a deliberate strategy to
build on the experiences and insights of those in poverty. Focus group discussions
were conducted between May and July 2005, and involved 10 meetings in New
South Wales and Victoria with service users who had a high risk of exposure to
exclusion and deprivation. Three additional focus groups were conducted with
service providers and other agency staff, although these produced similar findings
to those reported below and are not discussed separately; details are provided in
Saunders and Sutherland (2006).

The characteristics and circumstances of the focus group participants reflected
the nature of the services through which they were recruited: public housing
tenants; long-term unemployed people; lone parents undergoing training; homeless
adults; unemployed young people; Year 9 Indigenous students; young people in
crisis accommodation; new migrants/refugees; and emergency relief clients. They
were recruited through and by service providers using a deliberately purposive
sampling approach, since it was imperative that they were able to communicate
their ideas within a group environment that shared experiences and identified
common problems.

No attempt was made to achieve a representative sample, the focus being on
involving those who were best able to communicate their knowledge in a focus
group format, not on achieving statistical robustness. Even so, the focus group
interviews played a key role in grounding the research in the experience of low
income and disadvantage. For this reason, the information gathered was critical
to the successful implementation of a strategy designed to overcome some of the
limitations of existing poverty measurement studies.

A total of 71 service clients participated in the discussions, with groups varying
in size from 3 to 10 participants, and each discussion running for approximately
one-and-a-half hours. Almost half (45%) of the participants were aged 25 or
under, half were single, and although almost two thirds (64%) had completed
Year 10 schooling or less, almost two fifths (39%) had some form of post-school
qualification or training. In terms of family composition there was greater diversity:
the majority (58%) had no children, while almost one fifth (18%) had four or
more children. Not surprisingly, very few (6%) were in paid work, and almost
one third (31%) were unemployed, a similar percentage were studying and over
three quarters had a Centrelink (welfare) payment as their main source of income.

Participants in each focus group were asked to share their knowledge, opinions
and experiences in response to two key questions:

What constitutes a decent standard of living in Australia today?

Who is missing out (or excluded) in these areas, and why is this happening?

As anticipated, although these questions are articulated in general terms, the initial focus of the discussions on what was needed in *general* to have a decent life evolved into a discussion of the *specific* problems facing the participants themselves. The discussion was thus able to tap into individual experience in a way that did not threaten the participants, or expose them to any further stigma.

In order to help structure the discussions, they were originally organised around a series of standard of living domains that had been identified in other living standard studies. These initial domains were:

- Housing
- Location
- Health and health care
- Employment
- Education
- Care and support
- Social and civic engagement
- Financial resources

The scope of these domains was subsequently varied to reflect the comments provided by the focus group participants, and these revised groupings provided a better representation of the connections and linkages around which people structure their lives. Transport, for example, emerged from the discussions as being a major barrier to participation and engagement for many and was thus given an increased presence in the listing. Some reorganisation of the original domains was also made to better capture the ways in which items were seen as interconnected aspects of people's lives. Thus, housing and location were grouped together, as were education and employment, since many comments indicated that these are closely related spheres of experience and activity.

After this initial discussion, the focus group participants were asked to comment on the relevance and usefulness of some of the questions that have been used in existing surveys to identify who is missing out, experiencing hardship or living in poverty – the financial stress questions discussed in the previous chapter. Four key questions were selected from among the HES financial stress questions, covering the necessity and affordability of food, clothing, holidays and financial resources. Participants were asked to draw on their own experience and comment on how useful these questions were in identifying who was experiencing hardship, and were invited to provide any further suggestions for questions they thought could be useful in finding out whether or not people were disadvantaged.

The voices of disadvantage

In order for the focus group discussions to serve their expected role, it was important to ensure that the participants were indeed experiencing poverty. This was evident in many of the statements made about their circumstances and the difficulties they had bridging the gap between resources and needs on a daily basis. The impact that a shortage of money had on the ability of participants to achieve a decent standard of living was a constant theme throughout the discussions. Many argued forcefully that a lack of financial resources reduced their choices and opportunities in life and led to a range of interconnecting problems including poor housing, limited access to health services, poor nutrition, reduced social participation, poorer educational outcomes, low self-esteem and reduced employment opportunities.

Lack of money and the problems to which this gives rise were always at the forefront of people's minds as they struggled to make the limited money available cover what they needed. The following quotes illustrate what struggling to make ends meet means in practice:

'Everything comes down to money ... everything costs.'

'Everything is so expensive, like meat, meat is so expensive and I live by myself and I have to pay child support and buy nappies and food for my daughter when I see her. I get money taken out from my Newstart Allowance [unemployment benefit], now they're talking about putting me on Austudy [student assistance] which is less and I still have to support my daughter and pay my rent and my bills – it's impossible.'

'We barely survive week to week at the moment let alone having anything left over.'

'It's very hard to go out and meet new friends; it's close to impossible 'cause you just can't afford to do things.'

Access to limited financial resources meant that many people had to make difficult choices between items that were seen as essential for a decent life because their money could not be stretched far enough. For some, this meant missing out on food, while for others, it involved missing out on decent housing, or being unable to pay the bills. As some participants put it:

'I think every one of us in here has forgone, usually it's food we forgo – it's the easiest thing to do because we must all pay the rent, that is our first priority, then of course we have to pay the bills like electricity, gas or phone and if we have water, that sort of thing, we must pay that and usually us, ourselves is the last important thing we have to pay for.'

'That's an issue for me at the moment. I mean I'm living in a dump because I can't afford the rent, my daughter and I are sharing a bedroom, it's a one bedroom place because on the Newstart [Allowance] I cannot afford to pay [more] rent.'

'I think the problem with welfare is it doesn't stretch enough and then if something goes wrong it sends you reeling right back so there isn't any margin for you to try and put anything away, you're just barely making ends meet ... well your fridge breaks down, then you can't pay one of your bills, or three or four of your bills, to replace your fridge because you can't live without your fridge.'

Even when their financial resources were stretched to the limit, some still felt that home and contents insurance was important in maintaining an adequate standard of living. As one participant observed:

'The problem is that if you don't have that insurance, in the position we are all in, if you get your stuff stolen then you know you're stuffed – you don't have any way of replacing things.'

Living on the edge instils a keen sense of the financial penalties associated with different courses of action, as was illustrated by the deep knowledge that many had about how their benefits would be affected if their behaviour changed. As one person noted:

'... this is the thing that I don't understand with social security, if you're on Newstart [Allowance] and you're looking for work, you get a certain amount of money plus rental assistance; if you want to study, Austudy is minus the rental assistance. It doesn't make sense to me because you're still paying rent [but] they reduce your pay, they take away your rental assistance and it doesn't make any sense.'

The importance of employment in generating income and status, and giving structure to one's life, emerged in several ways. One participant identified its overall significance with the following words:

'Well, I didn't work till I started working last year in May. I did, you know, part-time work here and there when I was younger, but I had five children so I wasn't working. But now I'm working, I feel like I'm me again rather than just a mum or a wife ... I'm not putting being a mum down at all ... well I mean, money's great, but it was more for my self-esteem because it's a step towards where I wanna be.'

The same point was reinforced by another participant, who noted:

'Oh yeah, your self-esteem, if you have none, it's very hard to get started and you are starting from the bottom at 42 ... I don't want to sit at home with two children either for the rest of my life.'

Gaining access to employment was a particularly acute problem for those with any health problems, many of whom felt that they faced discrimination or were not offered retraining options that were appropriate to their circumstances. As one man put it:

> 'I'm a copper chef by trade which is a year 2 chef, but 'cause of the disability I have I dare not go back there because my body will just not tolerate it. I need, I want retraining, I will never work full-time again because my body is just different to what it was, and education is very important 'cause if you're uneducated, or inexperienced it's another big thing that you can't get a job.'

Lack of employment resulted in a low income, which in turn prevented other actions that might reduce a self-fulfilling sense of despondency and dependency. Healthcare was often not affordable, particularly in relation to dental treatment, which was identified as a particular problem that had flow-on effects in other areas, as the following comments illustrate:

> 'I mean it causes so many problems having bad teeth and stuff and it is treated something like, treated as a luxury. I'm sorry but dentistry in a first world country is not a luxury – it's a necessity.'

> 'I'm on the waiting list so I'll probably be that old when I get my teeth done I won't have any left.'

As one agency staff member observed:

> 'Health impacts on employment ... people will have bad dental health, often their teeth are in such a state they won't access training, they won't access employment, so it has this roll-on effect to all the other areas of their life.'

High healthcare costs meant that difficult choices had to be made about whether or not to take out private health insurance.

> 'It's a catch 22 situation where you can't afford to spare the money to pay the insurance, but you can't afford not to have the insurance in case something goes wrong. But then if you pay that money and nothing goes wrong then you've had to go without that fifty bucks a fortnight that you could have otherwise spent on food.'

> 'My son had epilepsy, he's grown out of it thank God for that, but I just thought to myself thank God I've got my healthcare card to pay for his medication, I would have been absolutely stuffed if I didn't have that card.'

Another area where difficult choices had to be made was in relation to housing, where the costs involved often meant that sacrifices had to be made in other areas. Some opted to pay more in rent than they could really afford because they attached great importance to the role of secure and affordable accommodation in providing a stable foundation to their lives:

> 'I pay more [for rent] because I can't handle that sense of insecurity. I'm up in [suburb] and I feel safe. If I want to go for a walk it's that feeling of being in a place, of not feeling insecure is very important for me and I'm willing to forego other things to feel secure or to not be thinking about it at all … I'll go hungry.'

Those who chose to economise on housing costs or couldn't afford to pay more often ended up in poor quality accommodation that exposed them to health risks and restricted their ability to interact socially.

> 'I'd be happy with a dump so long as I could pay less rent for it, you know a piece of shelter. I guess it's important to have a solid home and something that's stable but also when I weigh it up between do I want a nice looking house or a crappy house, I'd rather pay less, you know if I could pay less money and live in a crappy house I would choose that.'

> 'I'm fed up … of getting cold at night 'cause there's like a cold draft coming in from underneath the door, you know a gap that shouldn't be there or part of a wall that moved, and you can feel that cold if you've got arthritis or something, you know you feel it.'

> 'I've got mushrooms growing in the bathroom, that's been happening for six months, which I have to go in there every day and make sure they're not growing – the house is falling down around me and people wonder why I don't want them to come to my house [it's] 'cause I'm embarrassed by it.'

There was also a strong feeling among participants that the attitudes of staff within support agencies, particularly among those working in public housing agencies and welfare administrations, reinforced stigma and prevented people from accessing the support services they needed. This view was captured by one participant who noted that:

> 'Some government agencies, they don't talk to you they talk down to you.'

Another wryly observed that:

> 'And the Housing Commission people aren't very nice people that work there – they can be very very nasty.'

Being accepted for who you are was also considered key for many of the younger participants, as the following interchange illustrates:

> 'Not so much fitting in but being accepted for who you are.'

'Yeah.'

'You don't have to fit in.'

'Yeah that's it.'

'Just people at least respecting you enough to leave you alone to do what you want.'

'Like a feeling of belonging, like you can be around people that like you for who you are.'

For many there was a sense that they faced multiple problems that were interconnected and had a cumulative detrimental effect on their prospects for breaking the cycle of disadvantage and achieving a decent standard of living. This sense of being overwhelmed was captured by one participant, who noted that:

> 'For instance I can only speak for myself, I'm 48 years old, I have nothing, no car, no qualifications, no recent experience of any work and I have a slight disability … I'm not on disability benefits because I'm not disabled enough, so I have to be on the dole [and] a lot of employers don't want to know you, a heck of a lot don't, and the ones that do – where are they?'

It is clear that participants were struggling to make ends meet, generally out of a welfare income that was inadequate and often incapable of being adjusted appropriately to reflect changes in their circumstances.

Although the numbers involved are relatively small, the information generated by the discussions is rich in both its scope and detail. This is an impressive achievement given the inherent complexity of the notion of a decent standard of living, although it is important to acknowledge that in framing the discussions around the positive idea of what constitutes a decent standard of living, the direct link to notions of poverty and disadvantage may have become somewhat tenuous. Poverty is not the opposite of decency in most characterisations of living standards, although the approach proved to be a valuable way of promoting a wide discussion of the issues without stigmatising those whose views were being sought.

Despite these qualifications, the focus groups were successful in grounding the research in the lives of disadvantaged Australians and in identifying what they thought was needed to attain a decent standard in each of the domains of their lives. Those who participated in the interviews had a keen awareness of what they and their families (particularly, where relevant, their children) had to go without as a result of the circumstances they were in. But many were also wary of setting unrealistic expectations for themselves about what was achievable while acknowledging their own limitations, and were keen to undertake training programmes or otherwise take steps to improve their longer-term prospects.

Housing, as noted, was one area where the most difficult choices often had to be made, because of the cost involved. Although it absorbs a large fraction of total income, housing frequently determines how easily people can access local services, or use public transport, or simply feel safe and secure in their local neighbourhood. Some participants indicated that they spent more than they could afford on their housing in order to provide a secure platform for their lives, choosing to go without in other areas. Others chose to live in sub-standard accommodation in order to give them more choice and flexibility elsewhere in their budgets. Those in public housing often complained about the demeaning treatment they received by those whose job it was to assist them – service agency staff as well as government bureaucrats. Being treated with respect does not form part of any definition of poverty, yet its absence contributed to a loss of dignity and a sense of being excluded that are common companions of poverty.

Overall, the nexus of connections between housing, location and transport emerged as a factor that played a major role in determining the overall standard of living for many, and the choices and sacrifices that had to be made in these areas exerted an influence that spilled over into others. It was far easier to attain a decent standard of living in all of its dimensions on a platform of adequate and well-located housing that facilitates connections into local services and social and community networks.

Access to affordable healthcare was an important issue in its own right, with many participants placing great emphasis on having good access to health services in times of need. These services had to be both close enough to be accessed, and affordable in terms of any out-of-pocket charges. Where services were under-resourced (as in the case of public dental treatment), waiting times were often so long that those without the resources needed to 'jump the queue' missed out altogether. One participant's description of Australia's public dental system as being "like that in a third world country" vividly captured existing under-resourcing and the need for action in this area.

Poor health reduced people's job prospects and many participants displayed a keen awareness of what was needed to increase their likelihood of finding a job in an increasingly competitive labour market. Although relatively few participants actually had a job, most were keen to get into (or back into, or prepare for) the labour market and most saw this as the main gateway out of their current situation. While there was some acknowledgment of the lack of jobs (particularly in rural areas), many saw their own limited education, low skills or disability as the main factors preventing them from being employed.

Views about what was needed to rectify this situation varied greatly between different groups, reflecting the diversity in their circumstances, but most saw a need for improved access to information and to other types of basic living skills, such as proficiency in English language or access to a computer. Those who experienced a disability (however mild) found inadequate recognition among employers of how this constrained them, with many seeing themselves as facing permanent exclusion from the labour market. Education was also seen as another important pathway to better employment prospects, not just formal education, but also the acquisition of life skills in areas such as communication and budgeting, which were important in their own right, but could also add value to the benefits of formal education programmes. However, the cost of formal training often put it beyond the reach of participants.

Many of the younger participants bemoaned the lack of acknowledgment of the specific issues they faced, with many feeling that they were often consulted but rarely listened to. Some lacked the basic information that could help them to survive minor crises and move on in their lives, and there was a worrying sense among some that they were already heading along an inescapable downward trajectory.

So there was a second nexus of factors that went together, in this case encompassing education, employment and financial resources. Many recognised the limitations of their own educational background and wanted to take steps to rectify this, and all placed great emphasis on ensuring that their children received an adequate education. Education – defined broadly to include all advancements in human capital – was an important element of a decent standard of living because it increases the probability of finding a job and this in turn helps build social networks and contributes additional financial resources.

A third nexus of factors that emerged as important covered the issues of care, support and social engagement. The impact of these issues depends critically on how closely people are located to services and to the networks (family or community-based) that provide formal and informal support when needed. Lack of information prevented people from accessing facilities, which were often seen as 'not for people like us'. Many young people in particular saw this as a barrier that prevented them from accessing employment, education, health and housing services. Although there were relatively few comments about the role and importance of civic engagement, it was apparent that some (again especially young people) felt distrustful of bureaucratic structures and isolated from the political and other processes that could allow their voices to be heard.

In reflecting on the discussions, it is apparent that three general themes are of particular importance: first, the experience of disadvantage encompasses many aspects that cannot be meaningfully reduced to a single, monetary dimension: money remains a very important determinant of the ability to achieve a decent standard of living, but it is not all about money, and many other factors, including access to services and information, are also important; second, many low-income Australians are missing out on a decent standard of living (even when that standard is defined modestly) and are constantly faced with difficult choices between the competing demands on their limited economic, personal and social resources; and third, the views of those who are missing out about what is needed to have a decent standard of living are relatively modest, although they include having access to adequate economic resources, to affordable housing in a clean and safe neighbourhood, to good local services, to transportation, to information and advice and being treated with respect and dignity.

These factors mean that the disadvantages faced by low-income people are multi-dimensional and reflect many interconnected factors that can combine to produce cumulative, seemingly intractable problems. This complexity needs to be recognised when designing policies to combat poverty and social disadvantage, and when assessing their impact.

Some of the more specific findings revealed new insights into the nature of disadvantage. Lack of access to dental care was one issue that created considerable suffering over long periods and contributed to low self-esteem and reduced job prospects for those affected. Mental health and other forms of disability also prevented people from overcoming other problems, particularly lack of employment. Lack of access to information, and to care and counselling services, prevented people from participating more fully, economically and socially. The overriding importance of adequate transport in allowing such participation was another factor that was often mentioned as critical.

Reference has already been made to the modest nature of most people's aspirations of what is needed in material terms to achieve a decent standard of living. Many also had a strong sense of the importance of being treated with respect and dignity, particularly by those working in the government agencies that exert enormous control over their daily lives. Others related experiences of disrespectful and demeaning treatment that eroded their sense of identity and compounded the barriers they were trying to overcome.

Some were acutely aware of how their own limitations and past decisions had contributed to their current problems. Those with children were very conscious of the need to ensure that their children avoided these mistakes, yet where they were living and their limited budgets often made it hard to achieve this. Fear of cross-generational poverty, of failing as a parent to provide an adequate future for one's children, although not explicitly mentioned, often seemed just below the surface – particularly for mothers.

Many of the younger people felt that even when they voiced their concerns, they were not listened to. They said that they wanted information about how to cope, but few people were available to listen to what they needed and provide guidance that they could relate to. This perception led to feelings of alienation that exacerbated their problems, giving rise to an age-related aspect of disadvantage more generally.

Few of these findings are new, although the discussions reported here illustrate how different factors connect together, often compounding the challenges required to deal with them. Other studies have examined various kinds of data on actual living standards but rarely do they manage to draw out these interconnections in the ways that emerged from the discussions. Another important difference is that the findings reported here are drawn directly from the accounts of those forced to survive on a low income with the help of welfare agency support. These factors give the findings added relevance and underline the importance of ensuring that they are captured in the instruments used to develop the indicators of disadvantage.

Identifying disadvantage: the survey instrument

It is apparent from even the small number of interviews conducted that the disadvantage faced by low-income people is often multi-dimensional, is characterised by many interconnected factors and is frequently a consequence of deep-seated, long-standing factors. This complexity must be captured in the indicators used to identify disadvantage if they are to adequately represent the problem and inform policy. At a minimum, this involves ensuring that the factors highlighted by the focus group discussions as being of central concern to them must be incorporated into the data collected if the research is to tap into the experiences of disadvantage and respond to the voices that have conveyed its meaning.

In practice this involved using the focus group discussions to identify which items to include in a survey of living standards and to help structure the grouping together of questions so that they are better aligned with the interconnected elements of people's lives. Many of the issues highlighted in the earlier discussion influenced the structure and content of the questionnaire that formed the basis of stage 2 of the research. Specific examples include the insertion of questions relating to the importance of housing and locational issues, of access to dental care and other services when needed, of being treated with respect by others and being accepted for who one is, and modification of the ABS financial stress questions to reflect the focus group comments about their relevance.

The principle aim of stage 2 of the research was to provide a national picture of the extent and nature of poverty and other forms of social disadvantage using concepts and definitions derived from and consistent with, the experience of disadvantage, and with prevailing community understanding of what poverty means. Two separate but related surveys were conducted. The first was conducted on a representative sample of the general population (hereafter the community survey, or sample), and the second a shorter survey of the clients of selected welfare services (hereafter the client survey, or sample). A third survey, which was a repeat of the client survey, was conducted two years later on a larger and more geographically representative range of service clients (hereafter the 2008 client survey, or sample).

These three surveys were designed to achieve a somewhat different purpose. The information collected in the community survey was used to develop a series of indicators of disadvantage on which to build a national picture of the extent and profile of social disadvantage in Australia. The indicators were also used to compare the extent and nature of disadvantage in specific groups using a set of *national*, community-endorsed benchmarks.

The first survey of welfare service clients (conducted in parallel with the community survey) had three main aims: to offset the common tendency for those most at risk of poverty to be under-represented in surveys of the general population; to assess whether and how welfare services clients' understandings of poverty and other forms of disadvantage differ from those of other members of the community; and to allow the extent of disadvantage among welfare service clients to be compared with that in the general community using benchmarks that reflect *community* opinion. Particular attention focused on whether indicators other than those like poverty that are based on income alone provide a different perspective on the nature of social disadvantage, and if so, to identify these differences.

The aim of the second client survey was to provide a more comprehensive national picture of the extent and nature of social disadvantage among the users of welfare services and to assess the extent of any change in disadvantage between 2006 and 2008. This was a period prior to the onset of the global financial crisis in which the Australian economy was growing strongly and during which unemployment declined to a record (post-1973) low level, and the second client survey was designed in part to assess the impact of this increasing prosperity on those who were most disadvantaged. A second goal was to assess whether the findings produced from the earlier client survey were confirmed as an initial check on the robustness of the underlying methodology.

In light of the complex nature of the questionnaire required to elicit the required information, it would have been ideal if all three surveys could have been conducted directly using face-to-face interviews, as these provide an opportunity to clarify any ambiguities and follow up on issues raised where necessary. This approach has been adopted in other countries where similar surveys have attracted financial support from government, and been conducted by, or with assistance from, official government agencies. However, the limited Research Council funds available to this project meant that the cost of conducting direct interviews was prohibitive, so the community survey was conducted by mail. The two client surveys were administered directly by service providers, who approached clients when they accessed services and asked them to complete and return the questionnaire while on the premises (with the assistance of agency staff when requested).

The main survey instrument was the Community Understanding of Poverty and Social Exclusion (CUPSE) Survey, a shorter version of which formed the basis of the two welfare service client surveys. (The questions omitted from the client surveys related to topics that were not the focus of the Left Out and Missing Out Project.) The questions included in both versions of the CUPSE Survey reflected the focus group discussions as explained earlier, but also drew on previous Australian studies of deprivation and hardship, including the Coping with Economic and Social Change (CESC) Survey conducted in 1999 by SPRC (Saunders et al, 2001; Saunders, 2002) and research on deprivation undertaken for the Department of Social Security by Travers and Robertson (1996; see also Travers, 1996).

The survey also reflected the content of overseas studies, including the Breadline Britain Survey originally conducted by Mack and Lansley (1985) and subsequently refined by Gordon and Pantazis (1997a), the Poverty and Social Exclusion (PSE) Survey undertaken by Gordon and Townsend (2000), and the Millennium Survey described and analysed by Pantazis, Gordon and Levitas (2006a). Selected questions from related studies conducted in Ireland (Nolan and Whelan, 1996)

—

and New Zealand (Krishnan et al, 2002) were also modified to suit Australian conditions. The replication of questions included in overseas surveys allows the research methods to be validated against previous research and the findings to be compared with those produced in other countries.

After modifying the survey in response to comments received during an initial pilot, the community survey was mailed out to a random sample of the adult population drawn from the electoral rolls in April 2006. (Voting is compulsory in Australia, so the electoral rolls provide a good coverage of the population above the voting age of 18.) A reminder postcard was sent to all recipients one week later and a replacement survey was sent to those who had not yet replied around three weeks later, following the procedures recommended by Dillman (1978).

The deadline for receipt of responses was set at the end of July, by which time 2,704 completed surveys had been returned. After adjusting for surveys sent back from incorrect addresses, refusals and non-response, this is equivalent to a response rate of just under 47%. The response rate was well below the 62% response achieved by the CESC Survey, which was conducted in 1999, but exceeds the 44% response rate achieved by the other major Australian survey conducted at around the same time – the 2003 Australian Survey of Social Attitudes (AuSSA) (Wilson et al, 2005). Further details of the sampling methods, and a summary and comparisons of the three sample characteristics, are provided in Appendix A of Saunders et al (2007b).

During the three-month window over which the community survey was run, the first client survey was conducted, producing 673 responses. The second client survey was conducted two years later, over a similar three-month window, between May and July 2008. The questionnaire was identical to that used in the original client survey, aside from a small number of minor adjustments to overcome problems with the wording and lay-out of some questions. This latter survey was administered, as before, by the staff of participating services, although this time a larger number of agencies was involved, and the survey was distributed in a larger number of states and territories. It produced 1,237 completed responses – approaching twice the number achieved in 2006.

The composition of the two client samples reflects the nature of the services that participated in each survey, which in turn was dependent on the capacity and willingness of service agency staff to distribute and collect the questionnaires and to assist with their completion if required. Differences in the services that participated in each of the two client surveys affected the composition of the samples recruited, which are thus not comparable with each other, or with the community sample. This means that extreme caution must be applied when drawing comparisons between the community and client samples, or between the two client samples, unless an attempt is made to adjust for these compositional differences. Efforts have been made to adjust for these differences when possible to produce more robust comparisons, but the underlying differences in survey methodology mean that a degree of caution must be applied even when comparing these aspects of the findings.

Overview of sample characteristics

The detailed comparisons reported by Saunders, Naidoo and Griffiths (2007b, Table A.3) indicate that the community sample is broadly representative of the general population. A range of comparisons with official ABS statistics revealed that despite its overall good representation of the population, the following groups were under-represented in the CUPSE community sample: men compared with women; those who have never been married; those who live alone; Indigenous Australians; those with lower levels of education; those in private rental accommodation; and those with incomes between $1,000 and $2,000 a week. Some of these differences are interrelated, while others reflect the difficulty involved in contacting some groups by mail. There is also a tendency for some of the groups that are under-represented to be likely to experience above-average levels of social disadvantage. Overall, however, most of the differences are relatively small and do not give rise to serious concern about the ability of the community sample to generate important and valid insights into the topics investigated.

The one area where the difference between the sample and the adult population was most pronounced is in relation to age structure. As is common for postal surveys, older people (aged 50 and over) tend to be over-represented relative to younger people (aged under 30) among the respondents. This was the case with the community sample, as Figure 4.1 indicates. This age-related bias can affect key aspects of the survey results and in these instances, population-based weights have been applied to the raw data so that the community sample has the same age structure as the adult population as a whole.

Figure 4.1: The age compositions of the CUPSE community sample and the general population

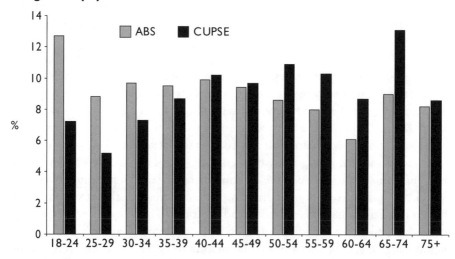

Source: ABS (2006b)

This adjustment was made to ensure that the views contained in the community sample provide a better representation of those held by the general population, particularly in relation to aspects that have an important bearing on the methods used when analysing the survey data. However, weights have not been applied to the sample data more generally, in part because there is no agreement about what weights to use, but also because it is harder to conduct and interpret statistical tests using weighted data. Most of the analysis is thus based on the unweighted (raw) data, although comparisons are also made between the unweighted and weighted estimates where this provides additional insight into the findings. This means that it is important to recognise that the unweighted estimates refer to characteristics of the sample itself, not of the general population, and this needs to be kept in mind.

The disproportionate representation of older people in the community sample contrasts with the two client samples, both of which contain an over-representation of younger people. This reflects the nature of the services that participated in the two client surveys, most of which are targeted at meeting the needs of younger people. This difference in the age composition of the community and 2006 client samples has the potential to distort the comparisons between them, and for this reason the 2006 client sample has been re-weighted to give it the same age structure as the community sample before making these comparisons. This also has relatively little impact on the findings and for this reason most of the results presented later are also based on the original (unweighted) client sample data.

Although the CUPSE data has its limitations, it provides the basis for generating new indicators of social disadvantage that can supplement the available poverty estimates. The community sample allows, for the first time in Australia, a comprehensive national picture of different dimensions of social disadvantage to be assembled that encompasses not only poverty, but also the different forms of deprivation and social exclusion. The two client samples allow the extent of disadvantage among these vulnerable groups to be established using national benchmarks that are embedded in community opinion about what it means to be down and out in contemporary Australian society.

Summary

This chapter has explained how the Left Out and Missing Out Project was designed, focusing on the effort made to ensure that the survey instruments and sample variables reflect the experiences and voices of low-income Australians and incorporate 'international best practice', as reflected in overseas research on poverty and disadvantage. These efforts have helped to improve the quality of the survey data, increasing their relevance and adding to the validity of the findings.

Together, the focus group discussions and the three surveys on which they are in part based represent a landmark contribution to understanding the nature of social disadvantage in Australia. The community sample provides the data needed to produce the first set of national indicators of social disadvantage that reflect community opinion on what is needed to achieve an acceptable standard of living. The two welfare service client samples provide important new data on the circumstances, attitudes and perceptions of disadvantaged people and allow them to be compared with others in the community using indicators that reflect *community* benchmarks.

All surveys have their limitations and this is also true of CUPSE, although this inevitability should not be allowed to detract attention from the strengths of what is a unique and rich set of data on attitudes to, and experiences of, poverty and disadvantage. The effort put into developing a questionnaire capable of shedding new light on these issues will be rewarded if the data are used to deepen our understanding of social disadvantage and promote actions that address it. Better research is an important input into this task, but the real test revolves around whether that research leads not only to better understanding, but also to better outcomes.

FIVE

Identifying the essentials of life

The concept of deprivation

The concept of deprivation has exerted a major influence on poverty research since it was first used to identify poverty over three decades ago by Townsend (1979). Since then, the ideas he developed have had a profound and growing impact on how poverty research is conducted, reducing its dependence on the use of poverty lines. The basic ideas captured in the concept and measurement of deprivation have already been outlined in Chapter One. This chapter provides a more thorough discussion of the concept and presents new evidence on a key ingredient of the approach – the identification of what constitutes the essentials (or necessities) of life that form the basis for identifying deprivation.

Townsend's development of deprivation was motivated by his concern to give a richer and more nuanced empirical meaning to the concept of poverty that encompasses a more direct articulation of what poverty actually involves. This requires specification of the many dimensions in which people's needs remain unfulfilled because of a lack of resources. In what has become its classic modern formulation, Townsend defined poverty in the following way:

> Individuals, families and groups in the population can be said to be in poverty when they lack the resources to obtain the types of diet, participate in the activities and have the living conditions and amenities which are customary, or at least widely encouraged or approved, in the societies to which they belong. Their resources are so seriously below those commanded by the average individual or family that they are, in effect, excluded from ordinary living patterns and activities. (Townsend, 1979, p 31)

The important feature of deprivation embodied in this definition is that it focuses directly on the lack of access to, or participation in, those goods and activities that are necessary for people to function effectively as members of the society in which they are living. Effective functioning is interpreted broadly to cover people's ability to meet their material needs as consumers, workers, family members and citizens. By locating deprivation within a specific social context and adopting a living standards framework, the approach overcomes the limitations involved in deciding whether or not someone is poor on the basis of their income alone.

Importantly, however, deprivation is closely linked to poverty because of its focus on a *lack of resources* (relative to needs) as the underlying cause. But deprivation, like poverty, is a relative concept and can only be identified as a divergence from the average, ordinary or expected living standards that exist in a particular place at a particular point in time. If instances of deprivation can be identified, this can help to establish who is poor and possibly also identify how much income is needed to avoid it. Evidence that deprivation exists is interpreted as indicating that resources are not adequate to meet needs at an acceptable level as defined by the community, but deprivation itself is not assumed to measure poverty, an approach that would place stricter requirements on the robustness of the indicators used to measure deprivation (Berthoud et al, 2004).

The deprivation approach represents an important departure from the poverty line studies described earlier because it focuses on identifying whether people can afford the things that are regarded as essential, not on whether their income is above or below a poverty line. However, deprivation does not avoid all of the measurement problems associated with poverty line studies, and identifying the role of choice in contributing to observed outcomes raises difficult issues that must be resolved before deprivation (like poverty) can be regarded as an enforced or unavoidable situation. In addition, the multi-dimensional nature of deprivation inevitably raises problems about deciding where to set a threshold that separates those who are deprived from those who are not. This can in turn make deprivation estimates appear as arbitrary and hence contested as those produced by poverty line studies.

Furthermore, deprivation may not always co-exist with poverty, particularly if no account is taken of the factors other than income that contribute to economic resources and thus determine the standard of living and hence deprivation (Perry, 2002, Figure 1). Nor is explicit account taken of the delayed or lagged response that links changes in people's income to changes in their standard of living and hence the deprivation actually experienced (Gordon, 2006). A sudden decline in income (because of the loss of a job, for example) will not automatically translate into deprivation because its effects may be cushioned or delayed by drawing on previously accumulated resources to maintain the standard of living. Similarly, those in poverty whose incomes suddenly rise may still experience deprivation for some time while their circumstances adjust to their increased prosperity (Gordon, 2006, pp 41-5).

More fundamentally, the existence of deprivation may reflect factors other than a lack of income, including poor working conditions, inadequate neighbourhood facilities, lack of access to financial credit or appropriate health services, special needs or barriers that prevent people from participating in widely practiced and endorsed community activities. These factors (many of which were mentioned in the focus group discussions reported in the previous chapter) may or may not be a cause or consequence of poverty, and will often be associated with it, but they do not constitute poverty as such. Deprivation and poverty are different, even though evidence that deprivation exists can help to identify how much is needed to avoid poverty.

Applying the deprivation approach

In order to make Townsend's definition of deprivation operational, it is first necessary to identify which goods and activities are 'customary, or at least widely encouraged or approved' in society. It is then necessary to establish who does not have these items and who among them are constrained from acquiring them by a lack of economic resources. In Townsend's own work, he addressed these issues by conducting a survey in which he asked people if they did not have items that were identified as necessities. The list included such things as basic accommodation amenities (an indoor flush toilet, a washbasin, a bath or shower and a gas or electric cooker), an annual holiday away from home, a cooked breakfast most days, a refrigerator, and (for children) a party on their last birthday. People were assigned a score of one for each item that they did not have and these scores were summed to produce an overall index of deprivation.

The methods originally used by Townsend have been subject to extensive criticism on several grounds: first, no attempt was made to establish that the items included in the list of necessities met the criterion of being 'widely encouraged or approved'; second, no attempt was made to distinguish between those who were missing out on the identified items because of a lack of resources, and those who did not have the items because they did not want them; finally, the summed deprivation index used by Townsend assigns at equal weight to each item, whereas it can be argued that some items might have a greater impact on deprivation than others, implying that a more complex weighting scheme is appropriate.

At one level, these criticisms can be regarded as primarily technical issues that can be readily addressed. However, they can also be seen as raising more fundamental challenges to the whole approach, including the problems involved in differentiating between necessary and non-necessary items, not only conceptually, but also being able to implement this distinction in practice using the responses to a survey that asks people what they need and what they have. Evidence from deprivation studies indicates that some people have many items not identified as being necessary, while simultaneously claiming not to be able to afford some of those items identified as necessities (McKay, 2004). This raises questions about the logic of the approach, since one would expect the acquisition of necessities to exercise the first claim on available resources, with anything left over then used to purchase items that are not necessary.

One possible explanation for this apparent paradox is that it reflects adjustment lags, as discussed earlier – the idea that living standards shift only slowly and can thus lag or lead variations in income. Another is that individual views about whether an item is necessary or not may differ from the views held by a majority in the community. It is possible to test this latter idea using the survey responses (see below), but even so, it is likely that choice is a factor that explains the observed patterns of ownership (or participation) of both necessities and non-necessities. On this interpretation, and consistent with basic economic reasoning, what one actually has (or does) is the outcome of decisions that balance preferences (what

---

one would like) against resources (what one can afford). It is important to establish that those identified as deprived have not chosen this outcome, yet unravelling the role of choice and constraint in observed patterns of behaviour (and ownership of items) is difficult because they are intertwined elements of the decision-making processes that drive observed consumption and participation patterns.

The difficulty in identifying the role of choice, combined with individual variations, led Piachaud (1981) to cast doubt on the ability of the deprivation approach to provide the basis for setting a unique poverty line. Reflecting this (widely shared) view, most deprivation studies now focus on examining the deprivation profile and exploring its implications for poverty without using the results to derive a poverty line. This is a sensible response, since part of the justification for (and attractiveness of) the deprivation approach is that it avoids the need to specify a poverty line. The existence of deprivation is itself evidence that living standards are unacceptably low.

The relevance of the deprivation approach to Australian conditions was emphasised almost two decades ago by the Department of Social Security who conducted an internal review of approaches to establishing the adequacy of its payments (DSS, 1995). It concluded that the approach should be included as part of a new research agenda on income support payment adequacy because:

> ... of its strong focus on outcomes, its potential for providing a tool for setting priorities based on empirical evidence of deprivation and because of its emphasis on seeking to build on and refine existing relativities. (DSS, 1995, p 27)

Its recommendations were never implemented, although the Department did fund a small-scale exploratory study that applied the deprivation methodology to examine the adequacy of social security payments. The study involved 110 income support recipients and was conducted by Travers and Robertson (1996), who describe their approach as follows:

> This study follows a tradition of research on standards of living where questions on income are supplemented by questions on how people are actually living in terms of their possessions, housing, transport, social activities, as well as how they themselves view their living standards. One of the primary tasks of the study is to see if relative deprivation in terms of these direct measures follows a similar pattern to deprivation in terms of income. In other words, the study addresses the question: are those who are worst off in terms of income also worst off in terms of housing, transport, social activities, and morale? (Travers and Robertson, 1996, p 1)

One positive feature of the study was its use of focus group discussions to identify which of a set of 37 'basics of life' items the participants had, and their views on how necessary each item was. Participants were first asked to assign a score to each item ranging between zero ('not necessary') and four ('very necessary'), and

—

were then asked to indicate whether they did not have each item because they could not afford it. A weighting scale was applied to these latter items, where the weight reflected the percentage that agreed that the item was necessary. Finally, an index of deprivation was derived by summing the (weighted) number of necessary items that people did not have and could not afford.

The study was limited by the small size of its sample and by the fact that it covered only income support recipients, who were asked to identify which items were necessary. This ran the risk of generating responses that reflect the 'bounded realities' that constrain the lives of those who are poor or disadvantaged so that 'what one conceives of as "necessary" will be influenced by one's knowledge of how others live' (Noble et al, 2007, p 131). In order to avoid such potential contradictions, it is important that necessities are identified by the community as a whole, so that *community benchmarks* can be established about which items are necessary in order to identify and measure deprivation. This approach is likely to produce a different picture from one that identifies the views of specific groups about which items they regard as essential and then uses these *group-specific benchmarks* to identify deprivation in those same groups.

It is the use of community views to identify essential items and hence deprivation that links the concept of deprivation to a definition of poverty based on the idea of unacceptability in living standards. This does, however, raise the question of whether or not there is a sufficient degree of agreement within the community about what is unacceptable, and that such agreement can be identified in surveys of the kind used in deprivation studies. If it is not possible to identify a robust and stable community consensus on what items are essential or necessary, it will not be possible to produce credible estimates of deprivation.

The study conducted by Travers and Robertson broke new ground in Australia, generating results that were of sufficient interest for the authors to recommend that:

> The questionnaire developed and tested in this pilot study be used in a national survey. Ideally, such a survey should not be confined to clients of the DSS [Department of Social Security]. The reason for this is that a survey of DSS clients can tell us only about relative deprivation among clients, that is, whether one group is faring better or worse than another. It does not tell us how DSS clients are faring relative to the population at large. (Travers and Robertson, 1996, p vi)

Unfortunately, these recommendations were never taken up, although the study's findings did influence some of the financial stress questions that were subsequently included in the HES and HILDA Surveys described in Chapter Three and informed the development of New Zealand's ELSI that is referred to in Chapter Six.

To date, no attempt has been made to establish whether or not the Australian community regards the items included in the HES and HILDA financial stress questions as being necessary, although the focus group findings reported in Chapter Four cast some doubt on their general relevance. Because of this, the existing studies that have examined the financial stress data cannot be strictly described as forming part of the literature on deprivation. Thus, although Headey and Warren (2007, p 54) argue that the financial stress data contained in the first four waves of HILDA data can, when combined with income poverty measures, provide 'an improved understanding of who is financially disadvantaged and why', they also acknowledge that financial stress and deprivation are different.

The criticisms levelled at Townsend's original application of the deprivation approach have led to a series of refinements that have produced a more complex and superior method for identifying deprivation. First, the strength of community support for each item being essential is examined directly, with only those items that attract majority support included in the list of necessities. This moves the decision about which items to include out of the hands of the researcher and into the hands of those members of the community who participate in the survey. It gives empirical expression to the need to establish that the items are 'widely encouraged or approved' in society at the time, and does so in a way that conforms to the widely supported use of majority opinion to determine the outcome (Gordon, 2006).

A second development has distinguished between those who do not have the items identified as essential because they cannot afford them and those who do not have the item because they do not want it. Only those in the former group are deprived, since only they face 'an *enforced* lack of socially perceived necessities' (Mack and Lansley, 1985, p 39; emphasis added). Third, alternative weighting schemes have been used to produce a range of indicators of deprivation, with sensitivity analysis conducted to establish how much impact this has on who is identified as deprived and how different groups compare (HallERöd et al, 1997). Studies have examined the use of weights that reflect the percentage of the population that actually have each item (prevalence weighting) and the percentage of the population that regards each item as essential or necessary (preference weighting) (see Van den Bosch, 2001; and Willitts, 2006).

The use of either weighting scheme can be applied to only those items identified as essential, or to all items. The latter approach avoids the (rather arbitrary) distinction between necessary and non-necessary items, since every item is included when measuring deprivation, even though some will appear in the index with a very small weight. This still leaves open the question of whether or not the lack of an item reflects a lack of affordability, but if a prevalence weighting scheme is adopted, it removes the need to ask whether or not each item is essential. Against this, if it can be demonstrated that there is wide support for the identified items being essential, this adds to the ease with which the approach can be understood in the community, thus contributing to its dissemination, and possibly also to its coherence and acceptance.

It seems more compelling to identify someone as deprived if they cannot afford an item that is widely regarded as necessary than if they cannot afford an item that almost everyone else has. As was shown earlier (see Table 2.1 in Chapter Two), community views on the meaning of poverty tend not to favour the use of those

—

approaches that emphasise not having what everyone else has, or takes for granted. This suggests that determining whether or not there is a consensus surrounding the identification of essential items is an important step towards establishing the credibility of the deprivation approach. Reflecting this view, the remainder of this chapter focuses on identifying which items are essential, while the issues involved in identifying deprivation are addressed in Chapter Six.

Identifying the essentials of life

Before one can determine which items people regard as essential, one must decide which items to include in the list from which they are asked to choose. This issue has received inadequate attention in previous deprivation studies, but it is important because people are only asked to indicate whether or not items included on a *specified* list are essential. This means that the pattern of responses could be distorted if the list includes irrelevant items (for example, those that meet higher order or luxury needs) or omits items that are important in meeting basic needs. In principle, this problem can be overcome by giving people the chance to add necessary items that are not on the list, although this option has generally not been available in existing studies. Even so, ensuring that the items in the list cover what people see as important for maintaining an acceptable standard of living is an important determinant of the ability of deprivation studies to tap into people's knowledge about what it means to be poor.

Those who have conducted deprivation studies will argue that the items included draw on evidence about what items meet basic needs and where ownership is most widespread (since necessities should, by definition, be owned by everyone who can afford them), as well as by previous research exploring what those who are poor are forced to go without. This approach has been followed here, in that the selection of which items to include has drawn directly on the evidence provided in interviews with low-income people, which, as indicated in the previous chapter, influenced both the content and structure of the CUPSE questionnaire. This approach links the quantitative results produced by the community-wide survey used to estimate deprivation with qualitative information about the experiences, opinions and aspirations of those living in poverty.

In practice, the number of potential essential items is huge and the initial list should ideally cover as many items as possible to avoid claims that artificial truncation will bias the findings. Against this, there are obvious practical limitations to how many items can be included (particularly in a postal survey) without imposing too high a burden on respondents, resulting in a low response rate. The list can be shortened by omitting items such as sufficient food to avoid starvation, and access to a rudimentary level of shelter and clothing that are widely accepted as essential in wealthy countries like Australia. Since virtually everyone has these items, their presence or absence cannot be used to differentiate between those who are deprived and those who are not.

Having decided on the composition of the list of potential essentials items, the next issue relates to whether and how to establish a threshold to identify which items meet the criteria for being essential. Whether one applies a threshold to distinguish between those items that are essential and those that are not, or applies a prevalence-based weighting scheme to all items, there is obvious value in knowing the strength and diversity of community opinion on which items are essential. It is important to note, however, that the issue at stake here is not the degree to which individuals regard items as essential *for themselves*, but rather the extent to which the items are regarded as essential *for people in general*. Use of the former may indicate the extent to which people's living standards are consistent with their own aspirations, but what determines deprivation is whether their achievements satisfy community norms of acceptability.

This raises potential problems in relation to items that may be relevant only to those with specific needs, or for items that are only needed at particular times or in specific circumstances. In these cases, it may be difficult for people to judge whether an item is essential if it meets a need that falls outside their range of experience. This problem can be avoided by adding the phrase 'access to' before the item, or 'when needed' after it (for example, access to medical treatment when needed) so that it is clear that the circumstance matters in practice, even though the item matters in principle.

A related but somewhat different issue arises in relation to items that meet the needs of those at a particular stage of the life course, such as children. Clearly, an item that is relevant only to children is, strictly speaking, not essential for everyone, since not everyone has children at any particular point in time. In this instance, it can be argued that the approach implicitly assumes that those asked whether child items are essential 'for everyone' interpret this to refer not only to those who have children currently, but also to those who have had children in the past or will have children in the future. Again, the essential nature of the item is generalised to apply to the whole community, even though its actual relevance is restricted to specific groups at any point in time.

The most common approach used to identify essential items includes only those that a majority identify as essential. This approach has been the advantage that it displays what Gordon (2006) refers to as both face validity (it accords with common sense) and political validity (because as noted earlier, the majority rule is widely endorsed as the basis for decision making in democratic political systems). It is also, however, possible to vary the threshold of support and to examine what difference this makes to the results, as is done later. In this context, it is important that the majority rule is applied to identify essential items after the survey data have been re-weighted to better reflect the structure of the population.

The CUPSE community survey included 61 items about which respondents were asked whether or not they were essential. As implied in the above discussion, essential was defined as 'things that no one in Australia should have to go without today'. The list includes such items as a decent and secure home, a substantial meal at least once a day and access to medical treatment if needed. Other items relate to location (access to a local park or play area for children; streets that are safe to walk in at night), access to services (dental; medical; and financial), items that relate to people's social functioning (a week's holiday away from home; a special meal once a week) and items that affect people's status and identity (being treated with respect by other people; being accepted by others for who you are). Four of the items – damp and mould-free walls and floors; a printer; an answering machine; and a fax machine – were excluded from the client survey in order to minimise its length.

The 61 items were grouped into seven separate domains in the CUPSE questionnaire, the first covering 25 'everyday items' that contribute to overall living conditions, followed by six domains each containing six items. As noted earlier, the focus group discussions helped to identify the scope of each of the domains, which were: accommodation and housing; location and transport; health and healthcare; social and community participation; care and support; and employment, education and skills.

Respondents were asked three questions about each item: Is it essential? Do you have it? And if not, is this because you cannot afford it? In each case, two response options were provided: Yes or No. The third (affordability) question was not asked of those items that cannot be bought by individuals (for example, access to a public telephone, or being treated with respect by other people), where it makes no sense to ask whether or not people can afford the item. Figure 5.1 shows how the responses to the three questions were used to identify the essentials of life, and from there to establish whether or not deprivation exists. The remainder of this chapter focuses on responses to the two questions shown at the top of Figure 5.1, with the responses to the third question analysed in the following chapter.

Figure 5.1: Identifying the essentials of life and deprivation

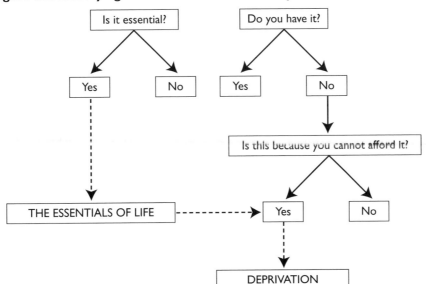

The essentials of life include only those items that received at least 50% support for being essential. Of course, it is possible that different groups have different expectations or attitudes that will affect how they respond when asked whether or not an item is essential. It is often claimed, for example, that because of 'adaptive preferences' and 'bounded realities', people's preferences adapt to their circumstances or reflect existing reference groups, so that whether one regards an item as essential reflects whether or not one has it. Thus:

> People adapt their preferences to fit their actual ability to consume. That is, the fewer economic resources, the fewer consumption items are deemed as desirable. (Halleröd, 2006, p 379)

The possibility alluded to by Halleröd is consistent with evidence showing systematic age differences in the views expressed about which items are essential, as well as evidence relating to whether or not the absence of an item reflects a lack of affordability (McKay, 2004; Van den Bosch, 2004). The first of these possibilities does not in itself create a problem when identifying the essentials of life and estimating deprivation, since it is important that the items identified as essential reflect the individual experiences of community members, even though these are applied to make judgements that are generally applicable. As Van den Bosch argues on the basis of a thorough examination of Belgian data:

> Even though judgments of necessity are colored, if not largely shaped, by personal circumstances and experiences, respondents *do* make the distinction between their own private wishes and a more public point of view ... fairly substantial differences in perceptions of necessity are often found between different social or demographic groups, such as age brackets and household types. These differences do not seem to be the result of divergent views on how stringent or generous the minimum standard of living should be, but, rather, reflect the fact that some items are more important for some kinds of people than for others. (Van den Bosch, 2001, pp 395-6)

Despite this implicit support for the general approach, Van den Bosch goes on to argue that the existence of 'individual uncertainty about judgments of necessity' negates the use of 'such a sharp distinction between necessities and non-necessities' in favour of a weighted approach in which the weight 'can be interpreted as the likelihood that the average person will regard the item in question as a necessity' (Van den Bosch, 2001, p 396).

Even if a weighted approach is rejected in favour of majority rule, the possibility that there are systematic age-related differences in views about which items are essential has important practical consequences if the sample has differential coverage of different age groups, as has been shown to be the case with CUPSE (and many other similar surveys). In this instance, it is important to adjust the raw data by applying weights in order to ensure that the sample responses provide an unbiased estimate of average opinion in the community (not just among sample members) about the identification of which items are essential.

Another concern relates to the possibility that there are systematic differences in the willingness of different groups to acknowledge that they do not have certain items, or to reveal that where this exists, this is because they cannot afford the item. These problems can produce a distorted picture of deprivation that will not be corrected by applying weights that adjust for differential survey response rates. The importance of this issue has been highlighted by McKay (2004), who argues on the basis of data from the British PSE Survey that:

> Put crudely, the young were least likely to believe that particular items are essential but most prepared to say they could not afford them. The old were the most likely to think that some items are essential but most likely to say, when lacking them, that it was a matter of choice rather than an inability to afford them. (McKay, 2004, p 18)

These differences can result in a distorted picture of deprivation that provides a misleading impression of the relative positions of different groups that cannot be adjusted for by applying weights, and this limitation of the results also needs to be borne in mind.

The use of a threshold level of support to identify which items are regarded as essential gives validity to the approach, but its credibility also requires that there is a reasonable degree of consensus on which items are essential. Overall majority support is consistent with systematic differences of views based on factors such as gender (the majority might consist almost entirely of men), age (it might reflect support from specific age groups only) or ethnicity (the majority might mainly consist of those from an Australian/Anglo background). It is therefore also important to establish not only that the items regarded as essential attract majority support, but also that a high degree of consensus exists among different groups in the community about which items to include.

The essentials of life: basic results

Having reviewed a range of issues surrounding the methods used to identify which items are essential, attention now focuses on the key findings produced by the CUPSE community survey. Selected findings from the two client surveys are also presented to provide an insight into differences in the views of different groups and a perspective on the robustness of the results. Figure 5.2 summarises the community sample responses to the 'Is it essential?' question by showing the distribution of the number of items (out of the 61 included in the community survey) regarded as essential by each respondent. The distribution is approximately normal for the range between 20 and 61 items, although the extended left-hand tail contains items regarded as essential by less than 20 respondents.

The mean number of identified essentials is 43.3, the median is 44 and the modal value is 47. In total, only 1.2% of respondents identified less than 20 out of

Figure 5.2: The distribution of the number of items identified as essential by the community sample (*n* = 2,704)

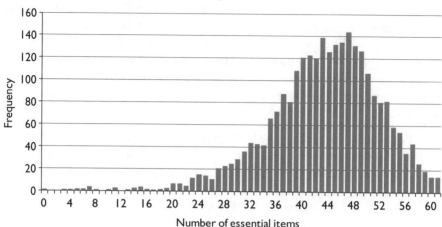

the 61 items as essential, while 19.1% identified more than 50 items as essential. Although this latter figure is high, it is important to remember that the items in the list have been deliberately chosen to relate only to basic needs, so it is no surprise that most are widely regarded as essential. Indeed, this aspect of the results confirms the veracity of the efforts made (through the use of focus groups) to restrict the list of items to those that are necessary to achieve a minimal but acceptable standard of living.

The distribution of responses shown in Figure 5.2 is broadly similar to that produced for Britain from the 1999 Omnibus Survey conducted by the Office for National Statistics (ONS) and analysed by McKay (2004, Figure 2). The British results also indicate that the mean, median and mode of the distribution are close together, although in the British case these summary statistics are a smaller percentage of the total number of items included (54) than is the case for Australia. McKay argues that the degree of variability implied by the distribution of individual responses negates the claim that there is a consensus about the identification of essential items. However, this conclusion has been challenged on the grounds that it is the degree of agreement across broad groups in the community that determines whether or not a consensus exists, not the variability of individual views. Thus, as Gordon (2006) argues:

> Consensus means agreement in the judgment or opinion reached by a group as a whole. It does not mean that there are no individual differences of opinion. (Gordon, 2006, p 113)

Figure 5.3 shows the corresponding distribution of individual responses derived from the 2006 welfare services client sample. As noted earlier, there are four fewer items in this case (57 instead of 61), but this does not affect the broad patterns revealed by the data, which indicate that the distribution is located further to the

Figure 5.3: The distribution of the number of items identified as essential by the 2006 client sample (*n* = 673)

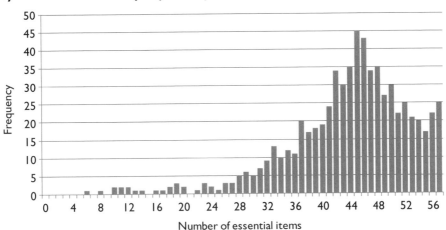

right, and is slightly more concentrated around the mode than the community distribution, but has a longer left-hand tail. Despite the fact that there are four fewer items, both the mean and median are slightly higher in this case, with the mean equal to 43.9 (compared with 43.3) and the median 45 (compared with 44). These differences suggest that the lower standard of living of the client sample does not translate into lower expectations about what is essential. If anything, the reverse is the case, casting doubt on the idea that preferences adapt in the light of experience – at least when it comes to identifying essential items.

Further background information is provided in Figures 5.4 and 5.5, which show the distributions of survey responses to the 'Do you have it?' questions asked in the 2006 community and client surveys, respectively. As expected, the differences

Figure 5.4: The distribution of the ownership of items in the community sample (*n* = 2,670)

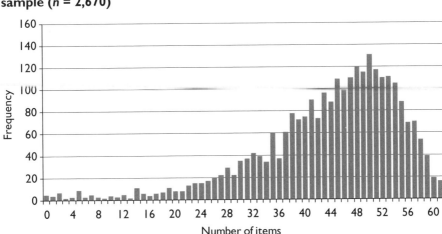

Figure 5.5: The distribution of the ownership of items in the 2006 client sample (*n* = 660)

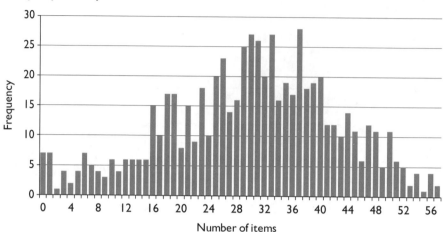

are now more pronounced, with large differences in the positions and the shapes of the two distributions. The mean number of items owned in the community sample (43.7) exceeds that in the client sample (30.1) by almost 50%, the gap providing the first evidence of the degree of material disadvantage faced by those who seek assistance from welfare services.

The pattern of essentials

Having described how the responses are distributed among survey respondents, attention now focuses on which items are identified as essential. The 61 items are listed in Table 5.1, ranked in descending order by the percentage of the community sample that indicated each item was essential. This percentage is shown in raw (unweighted) form in the first column of results, while the estimates in column 2 are adjusted using age-based population weights. Columns 3 and 4 show the (unweighted) percentages based on the welfare client surveys conducted in 2006 and 2008, respectively, while the (unweighted) percentages of each sample who indicated that they have each item are shown in the final three columns.

The main focus of the following discussion is on the results for the community sample, since these will be used to set the benchmark that is applied later to identify and measure deprivation. The results indicate that 48 of the 61 items were regarded as essential by a majority of respondents to the community sample, as were 50 of the 57 items included in both the 2006 and 2008 client samples. Almost half of all items (30) were regarded as essential by more than 90% of the community sample, while more than three quarters of those surveyed indicated that 41 items were essential.

Focusing on the 57 items included in both surveys, all but one of the 47 items (the car) that were regarded as essential by a majority of the community sample

Table 5.1: Identification and possession of the essentials of life in community and client samples, 2006 and 2008 (%)

| | Is it essential? | | | | Do you have it? | | |
| | Community sample 2006 | | Client sample 2006 | Client sample 2008 | Community sample 2006 | Client sample 2006 | Client sample 2008 |
	Unweighted	Weighted					
Medical treatment, if needed	99.9	99.9	99.8	99.4	97.0	88.9	87.3
Warm clothes and bedding if it's cold	99.8	99.8	99.4	99.5	99.6	90.0	89.3
A substantial meal at least once a day	99.6	99.6	98.3	98.8	98.5	84.7	83.0
Able to buy medicines prescribed by a doctor	99.4	99.3	98.9	99.0	95.7	69.0	69.3
Access to a local doctor or hospital[a]	99.3	99.3	98.9	99.1	95.5	91.3	88.6
Disability support services, when needed	98.9	99.0	96.1	96.9	49.8	39.8	44.7
Dental treatment, if needed	98.6	98.5	96.6	96.5	81.3	43.0	45.0
To be treated with respect by other people[a]	98.4	98.5	98.3	97.7	92.6	76.5	76.8
Aged care for frail older people	98.2	98.0	95.7	95.7	49.0	33.5	30.2
To be accepted by others for who you are[a]	98.0	97.9	96.0	96.7	91.9	72.4	74.1
Ability to speak and read English[a]	97.9	97.8	96.8	96.9	98.3	95.3	94.2
Streets that are safe to walk in at night[a]	97.7	97.7	95.0	95.6	71.6	51.7	47.2
Access to mental health services, if needed	97.4	97.2	95.8	95.8	75.1	61.2	68.6
A decent and secure home	97.3	97.3	97.9	98.3	92.1	66.5	65.3
A safe outdoor space for children to play at or near home[a]	96.4	96.1	95.0	95.7	90.2	71.3	68.6
Supportive family relationships[a]	94.9	95.0	95.2	95.2	89.8	65.2	67.5
Children can participate in school activities and outings	94.8	94.7	94.7	94.7	68.9	53.4	49.5
A yearly dental check-up for children	94.7	94.3	95.0	94.0	71.4	41.7	48.2
Someone to look after you if you are sick and need help around the house[a]	93.7	93.2	92.7	91.6	84.4	57.9	54.6

(continued)

Table 5.1 (continued)

	Is it essential?				Do you have it?		
	Community sample 2006		Client sample 2006	Client sample 2008	Community sample 2006	Client sample 2006	Client sample 2008
	Unweighted	Weighted					
Good budgeting skills[a]	93.4	92.4	92.2	92.1	85.1	64.3	60.9
A local park or play area for children[a]	92.9	92.1	94.0	93.5	88.3	79.9	80.6
A hobby or leisure activity for children	92.5	92.5	93.7	91.1	74.1	54.8	49.4
Regular social contact with other people	92.3	92.5	93.7	93.0	87.0	75.8	76.5
A roof and gutters that do not leak	92.3	91.5	92.1	90.9	90.0	77.8	74.0
Good public transport in the area[a]	92.2	92.1	96.9	96.2	60.8	68.6	61.4
Access to a bulk-billing doctor (Medicare)[a]	91.9	91.7	97.1	96.3	73.6	85.7	82.9
Secure locks on doors and windows	91.8	91.6	95.9	96.6	87.5	76.3	71.2
Furniture in reasonable condition	91.2	89.3	92.3	91.9	96.4	80.1	79.5
Access to a bank or building society[a]	91.1	90.2	94.6	94.8	93.0	89.1	89.8
Damp and mould-free walls and floors[a]	90.7	90.7	n/a	n/a	n/a	n/a	n/a
Heating in at least one room of the house	89.0	87.4	88.0	89.1	92.0	75.9	74.8
Up-to-date schoolbooks and new school clothes for school-age children	89.0	88.5	92.1	91.2	66.0	46.9	43.5
Access to a public telephone[a]	88.1	88.5	93.0	92.9	65.9	72.3	72.5
Childcare for working parents	86.0	86.5	93.1	89.7	38.0	31.3	25.7
Someone to give you advice about an important decision in your life[a]	85.0	85.4	87.3	89.3	85.1	71.3	71.1
A separate bed for each child	84.7	84.0	87.5	88.9	85.5	66.4	64.4
A telephone	82.7	81.1	85.1	80.4	96.8	76.4	72.5
Up to $500 in savings for an emergency	82.3	81.1	77.1	76.1	76.1	26.4	25.4
A washing machine	81.8	79.4	86.9	88.7	97.9	80.2	80.8

(continued)

	Is it essential?				Do you have it?		
	Community sample 2006		Client sample 2006	Client sample 2008	Community sample 2006	Client sample 2006	Client sample 2008
	Unweighted	Weighted					
Home contents insurance	77.4	75.1	64.1	70.4	83.8	29.1	32.6
Presents for family or friends at least once a year	73.1	71.6	81.0	78.7	87.5	63.4	58.9
Computer skills	68.5	68.7	67.5	73.2	67.5	56.0	57.4
Attended school until at least Year 12 or equivalent[a]	64.6	63.4	72.3	66.1	66.0	51.2	46.0
Comprehensive motor vehicle insurance	63.4	60.2	53.9	59.9	83.4	29.1	33.6
A week's holiday away from home each year	54.7	52.9	61.0	59.9	56.3	27.4	24.6
A television	54.7	50.9	70.3	71.3	98.8	92.2	91.5
A car	50.4	47.8	50.6	54.4	92.3	47.3	52.1
A separate bedroom for each child aged over 10	50.3	49.1	68.1	71.2	70.4	48.7	47.8
Up to $2,000 in savings for an emergency	46.9	44.4	50.9	46.8	57.9	15.2	14.1
A special meal once a week	36.6	35.9	64.0	58.7	44.8	50.2	43.4
A spare room for guests to stay over	35.7	31.5	36.6	39.5	70.4	35.7	36.3
A night out once a fortnight	35.5	35.6	57.6	53.4	38.7	32.8	29.1
A home computer	25.8	25.9	38.0	42.6	74.8	49.8	51.2
A mobile phone	23.5	23.0	47.7	56.5	81.8	72.7	80.0
A clothes dryer	20.3	18.9	33.2	32.7	61.7	37.4	37.5
Access to the internet at home	19.6	19.7	31.3	37.9	66.7	37.9	37.3
A printer	19.1	18.6	n/a	n/a	n/a	n/a	n/a
A DVD player	19.0	17.2	31.7	39.9	83.1	64.0	74.3
An answering machine	13.6	12.3	n/a	n/a	n/a	n/a	n/a
A dishwasher	8.3	7.6	14.7	13.7	48.6	16.9	16.2
A fax machine	5.7	5.3	n/a	n/a	n/a	n/a	n/a

Notes: [a] Indicates items about which the 'Can you afford it?' question was not asked. n/a = not available.

were also regarded as essential by a majority of the client sample. Service clients also identified three additional items as being essential: up to $2,000 in savings for use in an emergency; a special meal once a week; and a night out once a fortnight. Having some financial security and an occasional break from the daily stresses associated with juggling resources to make ends meet are clearly seen as more important for those who face greatest economic adversity. The only two items where client support for an item being essential falls well below community sample support are home contents insurance and comprehensive motor vehicle insurance, but both items still receive majority support for being essential.

The findings do not vary much when the community sample is weighted to reflect the age structure of the population, or if the weights reflect official estimates of the distribution of income as opposed to the age structure of the general population (although these results are not shown). Nor do they change very much if the 2006 client sample is re-weighted to reflect the age composition of the 2006 community sample. The results for the two client samples show remarkably similar patterns – perhaps not surprising given that they were conducted only two years apart – even though the services and areas covered varied substantially (see Saunders and Wong, 2009, Chapter 4). The fact that the pattern of responses to the 'Is it essential?' question is so stable provides support (albeit guarded) for the robustness of the approach, although this issue is examined in more detail later.

Two of the 48 items that received majority support for being essential on an unweighted basis (a car and a separate bedroom for children aged over 10) failed to do so when the data were re-weighted to reflect the age structure of the population. Further examination of the responses for these two items reveals that support for a car being essential was concentrated among older age groups (those aged 65 and over), while opposition to a separate bedroom for older children being essential was concentrated among those aged under 30 (most of whom were not old enough to have children of their own aged over 10 when the survey was conducted). On the basis of these patterns, the car was removed from the list of identified essentials, but the separate bedroom for older children was retained, reducing the number of essential items from 48 to 47.

The results in Table 5.1 indicate that Australians tend to regard more items as essential than is the case in other countries that have conducted similar surveys, even though this may in part reflect differences in the number of items included in the original list. Thus, the British PSE Millennium Survey, conducted in 1999, found that 35 out of 53 items and activities were regarded as necessary by more than 50% of respondents, and 20 items were regarded as necessary by at least 75% of those surveyed (Pantazis et al, 2006b, Table 4.1). The Japanese Survey on Living Conditions conducted by the National Institute for Population and Social Security Research also found a lower level of support for items being essential, although this could have been because the Japanese Survey allowed for a wider range of response options than the Yes/No choice given in the CUPSE Survey (Abe, 2006; Saunders and Abe, 2010). In South Africa, analysis of data from the South African Social Attitudes Survey finds that 36 out of 50 items received more than

50% support for being necessary in 2006 (Wright, 2008, Table 1), while Barnes (2009, Table 1) found that adults identified only 11 out of 25 child-related items as necessary on this basis in 2007.

The items that appear at the top of the essentials ranking in Australia reflect basic needs relating to food, shelter and heating, and similar items appear at the head of the lists of necessities identified in other countries where similar studies have been conducted. Several items relating to access to medical treatment (including dental treatment and the ability to buy prescribed medications) also feature at the top of the ranking, as does access to services that meet health needs, either generically (doctors and hospitals) or in response to specific contingencies (disability, mental health and aged care). Several of the high-ranking items reflect people's sense of identity (to be accepted by others for who you are), their connections to support networks (supportive family relationships) and perceived levels of safety (streets that are safe to walk in at night).

There is a general tendency for many of the items that appear at the top of the ranking to be associated with providing people with security and protection against unforeseen risks, such as a modest level of emergency savings and different forms of insurance coverage. There is also considerable emphasis on items that increase people's capacity to function in a modern market economy, including budgeting and computer skills, a sound education and English language proficiency. In contrast, consumer items such as a home computer, mobile phone, DVD player and dishwasher, occupy the lower reaches of the essentials ranking and none of these items come close to attracting majority support for being essential.

This aspect of the results suggests that the distinction drawn by the Swedish sociologist Eric Allardt (1992) between 'having', doing' and 'being' is relevant, and that Australians regard items that they can possess ('having') as being less important than items that relate to different forms of participation ('doing') or to people's sense of self-respect and identity ('being'). In overall terms, the ranking of essential items displays few of the hallmarks of consumerism, but is dominated by items that satisfy basic material needs and support people's sense of identity, status and social and economic functioning.

Of the 47 items that were regarded as essential by a majority, 17 were not items that individuals could buy for themselves. In these cases, as noted earlier, the 'Is it because you cannot afford it?' question was not asked. These items were either provided publicly (access to a local doctor or hospital; a safe outdoor place for children to play at or near home; good public transport in the area), or related to people's identity and support networks (to be accepted by others for who you are, supportive family relationships) or to their capacities (ability to speak and read English; good budgeting skills; a Year 12 education).

Deprivation reflects an inability to afford essential items because of a lack of resources, so that those items that cannot be bought by individuals are not relevant when it comes to identifying deprivation. If these items are removed, the number of essential items declines from 47 to 30, and four additional items have also been removed because they reflect specific needs and are thus not relevant to a study of general needs: aged care for frail older people; access to mental health services when needed; childcare for working parents; and disability support services when needed. Their removal reduces the list of essentials further, to 26 items.

Eight of the items shown in Table 5.1 refer specifically to the needs of children and support for all of them being essential exceeds the majority threshold. Five of these items (a safe outdoor space to play at or near home; ability to participate in school activities and outings; an annual dental check-up; a local park or play area; and a hobby or leisure activity) were seen as essential by over 90% of the community sample, and as noted earlier, only one child item (the separate bedroom for older children) ends up close to the majority support cut-off.

Although a case can also be made for removing these items, on the grounds that they too are only relevant to the needs of some groups, it was argued earlier that this is not appropriate for several reasons. Many of those households that do not *currently* have children living with them are older people whose children have grown up and left the parental home. These respondents will have legitimate and informed views about the needs of children and these should be allowed to influence the extent to which the child-related items are seen as essential. In fact, as Figure 5.6 indicates, the level of support for the eight child-focused items being essential is almost identical (the plotted combinations all lie close to the 45° line) for those with and without children living with them at the time they were

Figure 5.6: Differences in support for child-related items being essential by the presence of children in the household

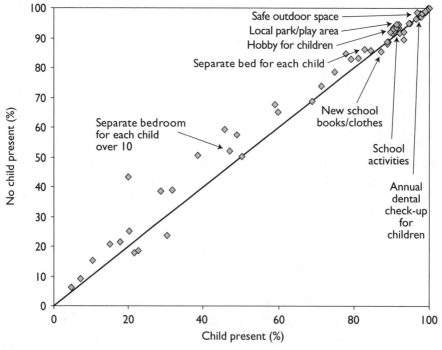

Source: Saunders et al (2007b, Figure 4.D)

surveyed. This highlights the important finding that children's needs are universal and are recognised as such across all sections of society.

Is there a consensus?

Attention has already been drawn to the need to establish that there is a consensus about the items identified as essential that extends across different socioeconomic groups. There is no agreed way of establishing whether or not a consensus exists, since any such decision must rest ultimately on a judgement about whether or not the observed patterns are consistent with the existence of a consensus. In order to inform such a judgement, it is important to document the extent of the differences that exist and this has been done (following Pantazis et al, 2006b) using scatter plots like that shown in Figure 5.6.

These diagrams plot the combinations of support for each item being essential among groups differentiated by such factors as gender, age, income, education and country of birth. The groups can be exhaustive (covering all members of the sample, for example, men and women) or only cover specific sub-groups (for example, those with incomes below a low level and those with incomes above a higher level). The extent to which the views of the two groups coincide is indicated by how close the points on the scatter plot are to the 45⁰ diagonal line that splits the diagram in two, with a consensus existing when all of the points lie close to the diagonal.

Before presenting the scatter plot results, it is worth noting that the above definition of consensus is in fact a good deal more demanding than is required by the approach used to identify which items are essential. Stability of the method requires only that items do not move from one side of the majority support threshold to the other when the views of different groups are compared, not that the two groups have very similar views across all items. A difference in support for an item being essential from 85% to 65%, for example, has no impact on whether or not the item is identified as essential. On this interpretation, all that is required is that most of the points in the scatter plot lie in either the north east or south west quadrants, not that they lie close to the diagonal. There is, however, interest in seeing how the views of different groups compare across the whole spectrum and where this is the case, it provides further evidence that the approach is robust.

The scatter plot results are presented and analysed in detail by Saunders, Naidoo and Griffiths (2007b, Figures 4 and 5), who conclude on the basis of their analysis that:

> ... both the aggregate evidence on the degree of support for items being essential and the detailed breakdowns of support across population sub-groups indicate that there is both a high level of agreement and a high degree of consensus in the community about the identification of which items are essential in Australia today. (Saunders et al, 2007b, p 41)

One area where there are substantial differences in the views expressed by different groups occurs when the sample is differentiated by age. The extent of this difference is illustrated in Figure 5.7, which compares the views of those aged 65 and over with those of people aged under 30 about whether specific items are essential. The differences shown in Figure 5.7 persist if the raw data are re-weighted to reflect the age structure of the population, so they cannot be attributed to any bias in the age structure of the sample.

Almost all of the points plotted in Figure 5.7 lie above the diagonal 45° line, which indicates that the level of support for items being essential is generally higher among older people than among younger people. The specific items where the difference is greatest (identified in Figure 5.7) seem consistent with the view that they reflect the changing priorities of different generations, with older people placing greater emphasis on security and 'home comforts' than their younger counterparts.

Similar age-related patterns have been found in Australian studies of the HES and HILDA financial stress/hardship data (Bray, 2001, Table 8; Siminski and Yerokhin, 2010, Table 1), as well as in studies conducted in New Zealand (Jensen et al, 2006, Figure 3.2), Britain (see McKay, 2004) and in a number of European countries (Van den Bosch, 2004). The reasons for the different age profiles are unclear, although research conducted in Britain by Berthoud, Bryan and Bardarsi

Figure 5.7: Differences in support for items being essential by age

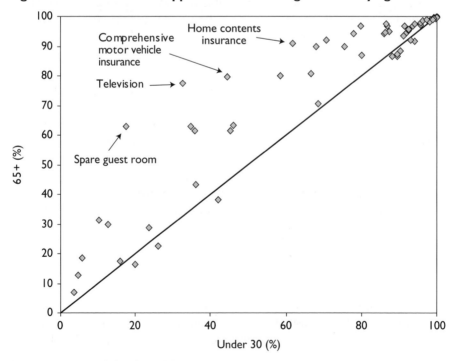

Source: Saunders et al (2007b, Figure 4.C)

(2004) and Berthoud, Blekasaune and Hancock (2006) suggests that they may in part reflect how priorities change as people age over the life course.

The other area where there is a noticeable difference in the level of support for items being essential relates to the tendency for those in the client sample to be more likely to regard items as essential than those in the community sample (see Figure 5.8). The client sample data used to construct Figure 5.8 have been re-weighted using as weights the age structure of the community sample in order to eliminate the impact of the different age structures of the two samples because age has already been shown to be associated with different views about which items are essential.

The results show that which sample one belongs to has an impact on the degree of expressed support for items being essential that is *independent* of any effect associated with age. The fact that a higher percentage of the more disadvantaged members of the client sample regards specific items as essential casts doubt on the 'bounded realities' and 'preference adaption' hypotheses, which both suggest that those with a lower standard of living would have more modest views about how essential items are.

Figure 5.8: Differences in support for items being essential between the 2006 community and client samples

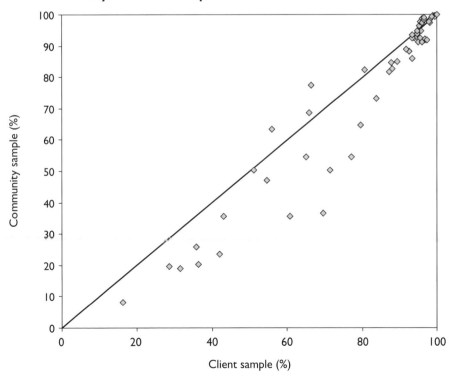

Source: Saunders et al (2007b, Figure 5.B)

The results in Figures 5.7 and 5.8 indicate that there are some systematic differences in the degree of support for items being essential, although the overwhelming picture is one of consensus about the identification of essential items across most dimensions of socioeconomic status. This provides an important rationale for using the items identified as essential to establish the existence and extent of deprivation, as is done in the next chapter.

Is the approach robust?

Attention now turns to the stability of the identification of essential items over time as opposed to between groups at a point in time. This test of stability is important because it affects the ability of the approach to identify community views about the essentials of life in a consistent manner. Particularly over short periods of time, one would not expect views about which items are essential to change very much. If changes are observed, this raises questions about whether the method can capture what it claims to – the strength and nature of community opinion on which items are essential. Of course, the identification of essential items is expected to change over longer periods in response to changes in technology (the emergence of new items and cost reductions for existing items) and in consumer preferences (the more widespread use of items like mobile phones and computers makes it more attractive for others to have them). Results of deprivation studies conducted over longer periods in the UK supports this view, showing that the list of necessities changes to reflect changes in general living standards.

The data are not yet available to test the validity of this proposition in Australia, although the two welfare service client samples provide an initial insight into the robustness of the approach. However, although the two surveys are based on the same questionnaire and were conducted only two years apart, it has already been noted that they cover different services (in relation to both service types and location) and are thus not directly comparable (see Saunders and Wong, 2009 for details). However, it is clear from the client sample data presented in Table 5.1, which is illustrated in Figure 5.9, that despite these differences, the degree of support for specific items being essential is very similar across the two client samples.

The stability in the client sample findings for the two years can be illustrated in a number of ways. In 2006, 32 items (out of a maximum of 57) were regarded as essential by more than 90% of those in the client sample, a further 18 items were regarded as essential by between 50% and 90%, and seven items failed to receive majority support for being essential. The corresponding numbers in 2008 are almost identical – at 31, 19 and 7, respectively. The correlation between the two sets of percentages is 0.9915 while the rank correlation is 0.9907, and both are highly statistically significant ($p = 0.000$).

There are only seven items where the percentage regarding them as essential differs by more than six percentage points between the two years, and in all seven cases, there was an increase between 2006 and 2008. These items are: home

Figure 5.9: Differences in support for items being essential among welfare service clients in 2006 and 2008

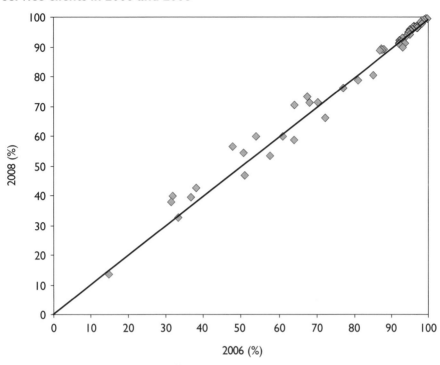

Source: Saunders and Wong (2009, Figure 2)

contents insurance (up by 6.3 percentage points); computer skills (up by 5.8); attended school until at least Year 12 (up by 7.8); comprehensive motor vehicle insurance (up by 6.0); a mobile phone (up by 8.8); access to the internet at home (up by 6.6); and a DVD player (up by 8.2). In at least four of these cases, the increase probably reflects the impact of the price reductions resulting from technological change (reinforced by expanding ownership, which induces others to acquire the item), but the key point is that the evidence is consistent with the view that the method used to identify which items are essential produces stable and sensible findings.

Overall, the evidence thus indicates that although some differences do exist, there is strong support for the claim that a consensus exists among Australians from all walks of life about which items are essential. This is confirmed by evidence from a number of overseas countries, which reveals that there is a broad public consensus about which items constitute the essentials of life 'that cuts across social divisions such as those relating to class, gender, ethnicity and age' (Pantazis et al, 2006b, p 98). This has led some to describe the deprivation approach as 'the consensual method of measuring poverty' (Gordon, 2006, p 43), or as a variant of the 'consensual standard of living approach' (Van den Bosch, 2001). As the authors responsible for refining Townsend's original study over 25 years ago argued at the time:

> The homogeneity of views is striking. People from all walks of life, from across the generations, from widely different family circumstances, and with fundamentally opposed political beliefs, share the same view of the kind of society Britain should be in terms of the minimum standards of living to which all citizens should be entitled. (Mack and Lansley, 1985, p 86)

These remarks and the evidence presented here confirm that it is possible to identify a consensus about which items are essential. This is an important finding, since it represents the first stage in the process of identifying deprivation.

Identifying domains

It was noted earlier that the CUPSE questionnaire was structured so that the items were arranged into a series of living standard domains. Decisions about how these domains were defined and delineated were informed by the feedback provided by the focus groups held with service clients and agency staff about how different spheres of their lives are interconnected. Having identified which items were regarded as essential by a majority of those sampled, factor analysis was used to see whether the responses clustered into distinct groups, and, if so, whether these groups correspond to the domains employed in the CUPSE Survey. Factor analysis has often been used in deprivation and financial stress studies to identify if a small set of items can be identified that capture the essential features of deprivation or financial stress (see Nolan and Whelan, 1996; McKay and Collard, 2003; Bray, 2001; Butterworth and Crosier, 2006).

In applying factor analysis to the essentials of life results, initially no restrictions were imposed on the number of factors and this resulted in 11 factors being identified. However, further examination (of the scree plot) suggested that a smaller number of factors was appropriate and the analysis was repeated after restricting the number of factors to six, but allowing for correlation between each factor (using the Direct Oblimin Rotation technique). The six identified factors and corresponding factor loadings are shown in Table 5.2.

There is a considerable overlap between the factors that emerge from the factor analysis and the domains that that were used to structure the CUPSE survey. The first factor contains items included under the health, housing and accommodation and location and transport domains, factors 2 and 3 contain many of the items included under the 'everyday' domain, factor 4 corresponds closely to the care and support domain, factor 5 is identical to the education and skills domain and factor 6 combines social participation with some relevant everyday items. The mappings are not exact, but close enough to confirm that the information derived from the focus group discussions provided a good representation of the broad structure of community views about what is essential.

Table 5.2: Factor analysis of essentials items in the community survey

	Factor loading		Factor loading
Factor 1: Health and autonomy		*Factor 2: Consumer durables*	
Medical treatment if needed	0.893	Printer	0.846
Access to local doctor/hospital	0.837	Internet access	0.834
Able to buy prescribed medicines	0.819	Home computer	0.830
Dental treatment if needed	0.768	DVD player	0.650
Safe streets at night	0.716	Fax machine	0.630
Access to mental health services	0.660	Dishwasher	0.629
Local park/play area for children	0.557	Mobile phone	0.611
Good public transport	0.535	Answering machine	0.560
Access to bank/building society	0.522	Clothes dryer	0.483
Safe space for children to play	0.514		
Dental check-up for children	0.505	*Factor 3: Accommodation and identity*	
Roof and gutters that do not leak	0.481	Warm clothes and bedding	−0.876
Access to bulk-billing doctor	0.480	Substantial daily meal	−0.856
Public telephone	0.467	Treated with respect by others	−0.753
Secure locks on doors and windows	0.459	Accepted by others	−0.751
Separate bed for each child	0.341	A decent and secure home	−0.734
		Furniture in reasonable condition	−0.607
		Damp and mould free walls and floors	−0.576
		Heating in at least one room	−0.534
		Telephone	−0.395
		At least $500 in emergency savings	−0.394

(continued)

Table 5.2 (continued)

	Factor loading		Factor loading
Factor 4: Services and supports		*Factor 6: Social and family participation*	
Access to disability support services	0.805	Car	−0.506
Access to aged care services	0.800	Spare guest room	−0.501
Someone to look after you when sick	0.723	Home contents insurance	−0.486
Supportive family relationships	0.699	Comprehensive car insurance	−0.477
Someone to give advice on decisions	0.615	Television	−0.460
Regular social contact with others	0.613	Special weekly meal	−0.433
Hobby/leisure activity for children	0.579	Washing machine	−0.427
Childcare for working parents	0.570	Night out every fortnight	−0.419
Annual presents for others	0.399	Week's holiday away	−0.413
		At least $2,000 in emergency saving	−0.348
Factor 5: Basic functioning		Separate bedroom for older children	−0.265
School activities and outings	−0.708		
Ability to speak and read English	−0.705		
New school books and clothes	−0.690		
Good budgeting skills	−0.684		
Computer skills	−0.557		
Education to Year 12	−0.426		

This perception is confirmed by the results in Table 5.3, which compare the reliability statistics based on the CUPSE domain categories and those based on the factors identified in the factor analysis. With two exceptions, all of the Cronbach alpha estimates exceed the acceptable value of 0.7 and the remaining shortfalls are quite small. In general, the scores for the factors identified by the factor analysis exceed those based on the original survey domains, with five of the six factors producing a Cronbach score that exceeds eight (compared with two of the six survey domains). However, the differences are not great and a case can be made for maintaining the original six domains because they emerged from the focus group discussion reported in Chapter Four and are not simply the product of a statistical analysis that takes no account of expressed views or acquired knowledge.

Before completing this examination of the identification of essential items, it is of interest to examine the prevalence or ownership rate for each item. The individual item prevalence rates for the three samples are shown in the final three columns of Table 5.1. It should be noted that these ownership rates are expressed as a percentage of the sample as a whole, even though some items only have relevance to those in specific circumstances (for example, the items that relate to the needs of children). Although it is possible to express ownership rates for the child-related items as a percentage of only those households that contain children, it is not always possible to make similar adjustments for other items. Thus, for example, some of those who say they do not have an item like a roof and gutters that do not leak may live in apartments that do not have a roof, while some who do not have motor vehicle insurance will not own a car. Expressing ownership

Table 5.3: Reliability of the CUPSE domains and identified factors (Cronbach alpha statistics)

	Cronbach scores
CUPSE domains (number of items)	
Everyday items (25)	0.884
Accommodation and housing (6)	0.657
Location and transport (6)	0.760
Health and health care (6)	0.784
Social and community participation (6)	0.720
Care and support (6)	0.811
Employment, education and skills (6)	0.695
Identified factors (number of items)	
Health and autonomy (16)	0.866
Consumer durables (9)	0.859
Accommodation and identity (10)	0.832
Services and supports (9)	0.825
Basic functioning (6)	0.695
Social and family participation (11)	0.808

rates across the whole sample, while imperfect in some instances, provides a useful starting place from which to compare living standards.

The results indicate that most of those in the community sample have all 61 items and in many cases their prevalence is widespread, exceeding 90% for 18 items and above 80% for a further 15 items. As the ownership rate declines, there is a general tendency for the degree of support for the item being essential to also fall, although the extent of the decline in the former is much less pronounced, and several items that appear at the bottom of the essential ranking are widely owned. The large differences between the ownership of some items and whether or not they are seen as essential indicates that people are able to distinguish between what they want (and have) and what they need (and regard as essential). In other cases, however, the gap may be a reflection of the characteristics of respondents: for example, those without children will indicate that they do not have the child-related items, even though they may think that they are essential if children are present in the household.

Another possible reason for some of the low reported prevalence/ownership rates is a lack of relevant information on the part of survey respondents. This may explain the low percentages who say that they do not have access to such items as disability, mental health or aged care services. Many people not faced with these needs may simply not know what services are available if they were to need them, and so answer No when asked if they have them. However, other findings cannot be so readily dismissed. It is striking, for example, that whereas over 97% of the community sample regard streets that are safe to walk in at night as essential, less that 72% say that they actually have this.

The pattern of prevalence rates among the two samples of welfare service clients is similar to that for the community sample, although ownership rates tend to be lower among the client sample, as noted earlier. The largest gaps (in excess of 30 percentage points) in ownership rates reveal what kinds of items those reliant on welfare services for support are missing out on: prescribed medications; dental treatment (for themselves and for their children); emergency savings; a car; comprehensive motor vehicle insurance; a spare room for guests to stay over; access to the internet at home; and a dishwasher. Not all of these items reach the threshold that identifies them as essential, but the fact that they are widely owned in the general community highlights another aspect of the disadvantage facing those in the client sample.

There are also a small number of items that are more widely owned among the two client samples than among the community sample, the most notable being good public transport in the local area, access to a bulk-billing doctor and a public telephone. The fact that all three are provided by the public sector illustrates the important role that public provisions play in supporting the living standards of the most vulnerable groups. The results also suggest that many better-off Australians do not use, and hence may be unaware of, the public services that are available.

Summary

This chapter has focused on the first stage in the deprivation approach, which involves identifying the items regarded as essential by a majority in the community. The methods used to undertake this exercise have been spelt out in detail and the results that emerge when applying them to the CUPSE Survey data described and discussed in depth. Where there is uncertainty about how best to proceed, or about the interpretation of results, alternative approaches have been adopted and the sensitivity of conclusions examined. There are a number of steps in the process where difficult choices have to be made and it is important to recognise the limitations that this can impose on the results that emerge.

Despite the reservations, the results confirm that it is possible to identify which items are regarded as essential by members of the community, and that the results produced appear sensible and robust. They also reveal a high degree of consensus among different groups about which items are essential 'for all Australians' despite considerable variability between individuals in the number of items regarded as essential, as well as in the number of items actually owned. The fact that a broadly based consensus exists means that the deprivation approach is capable of producing results that are consistent with community views about what constitutes the essentials of life.

The results indicate that just under half (26 out of 61) of the items included in the survey that people can buy for themselves were regarded as essential by at least 50% of those in the community sample and by implication, by a majority in the community as a whole. In most of these cases, the degree of support greatly exceeds the 50% threshold, and around half of these items were regarded as essential by more than 90% of those surveyed. Views about which items were essential are similar across the community and client samples at a point in time and appear to be stable over a short period of time. These features of the results confirm that the first stage of the deprivation approach has the capacity to identify the essentials of life and that there is a high degree of agreement about the items so identified.

SIX

Measuring deprivation

Introduction

This chapter uses the 26 items that were identified in the previous chapter as being essential by a majority to provide the first comprehensive, national picture of deprivation in Australia. Results are presented and analysed in detail for the 2006 community sample and a selection of findings from the 2006 and 2008 welfare service client samples are also examined. The basic results are presented on a raw (unweighted) basis and after applying population age weights to adjust for the unrepresentative age profile of the community sample. In general, re-weighting the data in this way has little impact on the results and for this reason, most of the analysis focuses solely on the unweighted data. No attempt has been made to re-weight the two sets of client sample data to make them more directly comparable with each other (or with the community sample), as it is not possible to do this on a consistent basis across the two years.

Several extensions to the basic results are then examined. The first involves varying the filters used to identify deprivation itself. This is followed by an examination of multiple deprivation and by using deprivation index scores to compare the severity of deprivation between different socioeconomic groups. These latter comparisons raise questions about which weighting scheme should be used to derive summary deprivation scores, leading to an examination of the sensitivity of results to the use of alternative weighting schemes.

Tests of statistical reliability and validity are then conducted to see if the number of essential items can be reduced, and factor analysis is used to examine how the deprivation items link together. The relevance and value of the deprivation estimates is then illustrated by using them to compare the adequacy of the incomes received by different groups, including those on low wages or in receipt of different types of social security payment. These results highlight the important role that deprivation studies can play in informing and monitoring income support and related policies.

Identifying deprivation

Deprivation exists when people are prevented from obtaining essential items because they cannot afford them. As Figure 4.1 in Chapter Four indicates, the role of resource constraints is captured by asking people who do not have each item whether or not this reflects a lack of affordability. To be identified as deprived thus requires two conditions to be met: not having an item identified as essential; and missing out on it because of a lack of affordability.

Although it is important to establish that deprivation reflects a lack of resources rather than a choice to go without an item, the method used to establish that those who do not have an essential item cannot afford it is rather rudimentary. What exactly do people mean when they say that they cannot afford an item that they do not have? It is only possible to answer this question if one knows how much the item in question costs, and by making an assumption about how far one's current resources can be stretched or re-allocated in order to acquire it. However, the precise nature of this assumption is likely to vary between people according to their preferences, making it difficult to interpret the responses to the 'Can you afford it?' question.

What one person may perceive as being a consequence of a lack of affordability may be seen by someone else as reflecting the choice to give higher priority to another item. For example, although one's income may make an overseas holiday appear unaffordable, the decision to forego the holiday may also reflect other decisions about what to buy and do and cannot therefore be automatically attributed solely to a lack of income: the holiday probably could be afforded, but current priorities lie elsewhere, so that the decision reflects both constraints and choices. This introduces an element of subjectivity into the deprivation indicators and undermines any claim that they can be regarded as objective measures of living standards (Brewer et al, 2008).

These concerns have been given further impetus by studies like that undertaken by McKay (2004) which have shown that many of those who say they cannot afford essential items do own other, non-essential items. This raises questions about how to interpret responses to the 'Can you afford it?' question and about the identification of essential items, since one would expect them to be acquired first if they are genuinely required to meet basic needs. However, it is important to recall that it is the views of the *community* in general that determine whether or not an item is classified as essential, not the views of specific individuals, and this could explain why some individual consumption patterns appear to be inconsistent with an item being essential or necessary. Furthermore, as Gordon (2006, Figure 2.2) has pointed out, items are acquired at different points in time and people's economic circumstances also vary over time, which can explain the mis-match between resources and ownership of essential items at a point in time.

Despite its limitations, the use of the 'cannot afford' criterion to filter out those who choose to forego particular items places the focus on the constraining influence of a lack of resources (relative to needs) that is the defining feature of poverty. Its use thus serves to strengthen the connection between deprivation studies and those that measure poverty using income. Nevertheless, the uncertainties that arise because of these complexities suggest that it may be wise to explore alternative methods for establishing the role of resource constraints (as is done later in this chapter), and to combine evidence on both deprivation and low income when seeking to identify poverty – an idea that is explored in the following chapter.

Prevalence, deprivation and inferred deprivation

The difficulty in establishing that the lack of essential items is indicative of deprivation reflects the uncertain interpretation that can be placed on responses to the 'Can you afford it?' question. One option explored by Van den Bosch (2004) involves ignoring responses to the affordability question altogether and equating deprivation with not having an item that has been identified as essential. This may over-estimate the extent of deprivation because it will include as deprived those who chose not to obtain the item, even though they had the resources to do so. However, if the numbers in this category are small, the approach will produce reasonably accurate estimates that are simpler to produce and subject to less ambiguity.

The use of information on (lack of) ownership (or the inverse of the prevalence rate) to proxy deprivation will thus over-estimate the extent of the problem, but it is of interest to examine how large this error is, since this indicates the impact on measured deprivation of utilising the responses to the affordability question. It is important to note in this context that the failure to utilise information gathered in response to the 'Can you afford it?' question does not imply rejection of the *principle* that resource constraints (or enforcement) are an important feature of deprivation. Rather, it reflects the *practical* limitations of the method used to establish empirically that enforcement is the underlying cause.

There is an alternative way of inferring that deprivation is enforced that does not rely solely on lack of ownership, or depend on responses to the 'Can you afford it?' question. The rationale for this approach is as follows: it is known from the responses to the 'Is it essential?' question whether or not each individual regards each item as essential. If an individual does not have an item that has been identified as essential by the majority, and that individual also regards the item as essential, then it can be inferred that the lack of ownership of the item must reflect an inability of that individual to afford it, implying that deprivation exists in this case. If, on the other hand, the individual does not regard the item as essential (even though a majority did), then it can be inferred that they chose not to acquire the item and should not therefore be regarded as deprived of it.

This inferential approach rejects the information contained in responses to the 'Can you afford it?' question, relying instead on the expressed views on whether the item is regarded as essential to infer whether a lack of ownership can be equated with deprivation. The approach has its limitations, particularly in relation to the treatment of items that may not be relevant to individuals in specific circumstances – for example, the views expressed by people who do not have children living with them about whether or not child-related items are essential. Despite these limitations, it is useful to examine how the results produced by the inferential approach differ from those produced by the standard approach as a check on the robustness of the methods used to identify deprivation.

Reflecting this discussion, Table 6.1 uses the unweighted community sample data to compare the inverse of the ownership rate for each of the 26 items identified by a majority as essential, with the deprivation rate derived by applying the affordability filter as indicated in Figure 5.1 (Chapter Five), and with the inferred deprivation rates derived from the *individual* views on whether each essential of life item is essential, as explained above.

Table 6.1: Ownership, deprivation and inferred deprivation rates

Essential items	Inverse ownership rate – does not have (%)	Deprivation rate – does not have and cannot afford (%)	Inferred deprivation – does not have but regards as essential (%)
A decent and secure home	7.87	6.65	7.43
A substantial meal at least once a day	1.54	1.07	1.27
Warm clothes and bedding, if it's cold	0.36	0.24	0.28
Heating in at least one room of the house	7.96	1.78	2.68
Furniture in reasonable condition	3.62	2.58	2.61
Comprehensive motor vehicle insurance	16.62	8.59	6.68
A telephone	3.2	1.46	1.92
A washing machine	2.13	0.83	0.99
A television	1.18	0.16	0.28
Up to $500 in savings for an emergency	23.9	17.61	16.81
Secure locks on doors and windows	12.54	5.11	8.87
Home contents insurance	16.2	9.49	8.44
A roof and gutters that do not leak	9.95	4.64	7.64
A separate bed for each child	14.48	1.59	10.28
A separate bedroom for each child aged over 10	29.56	6.11	11.66
Medical treatment if needed	2.97	1.99	2.98
Able to buy medicines prescribed by a doctor	4.28	3.89	4.17
Dental treatment if needed	18.66	13.86	18.03
A yearly dental check-up for children	28.65	9.09	25.35
Regular social contact with other people	12.99	4.73	10.47
A week's holiday away from home each year	43.72	22.42	19.13
Presents for family or friends at least once a year	12.46	6.61	5.36
A hobby or leisure activity for children	25.86	5.66	21.09
Computer skills	32.48	5.20	20.74
Up-to-date school books and new school clothes for school-age children	33.96	3.79	28.52
Children can participate in school activities and outings	31.11	3.52	28.86

By definition, the deprivation estimates in columns 2 and 3 of Table 6.1 are smaller than the (lack of) ownership rates in the first column, because each applies an additional filter designed to better identify deprivation. However, interest focuses on the difference between the estimates in columns 2 and 3, since this reveals what difference it makes when identifying deprivation on the basis of individual responses to the 'Can you afford it?' and 'Is it essential?' questions. In the majority of cases, the difference is small – less than two percentage points for 14 of the 26 items included. The differences are most marked for the six child-related items, and in these cases the inferred deprivation rates are (except for the separate bedroom for older children) closer to the lack of ownership rates than to the deprivation rates. This presumably reflects the problems that those without children have in deciding whether or not the child-related items are essential where, as suggested earlier, the inferred deprivation approach breaks down because the items are not relevant to current circumstances.

Aside from these cases, however, the results in Table 6.1 suggest that *for items that meet general needs*, one could dispense with the affordability question and infer deprivation from responses to the question asking whether or not items are essential. This is an important conclusion because it suggests that the much-criticised question that asks about the affordability of items that are not owned may not be a crucial component of the deprivation approach. Importantly, the inferential approach relies on majority opinion to identify essentials and thus maintains the credibility attached to this aspect of the approach. It does, however, rely on drawing inferences from the responses that may not be warranted, whereas the standard approach draws more directly on the responses. For this reason the standard approach is used now to examine the deprivation profile.

The deprivation profile

The conventional (don't have and cannot afford) deprivation rates for each of the 26 essentials of life items are shown for the community and two client samples in Table 6.2 and illustrated in Figures 6.1 and 6.2. In this instance, the client sample estimates in Figure 6.1 have been re-weighted so that the age structures of both samples are the same, although this makes relatively little difference to the general picture. It does not, for example, make any difference to the marked differences in the item-specific deprivation rates between the two samples.

As explained earlier, the incidence rates in Table 6.2 have been expressed as a percentage of the total sample in each case, not just of those in each sample whose circumstances are relevant to each form of deprivation. Thus, for example, the numbers who cannot afford those items that relate to children are expressed as a percentage of all survey respondents, not just those who have children. If the latter approach was adopted, the incidence rates of the children's items would be considerably higher than those shown. The logic underlying the approach adopted (see Figure 5.1 in Chapter Five) assumes that those respondents who do not have items that are not relevant to their current circumstances will indicate that their

Table 6.2: The incidence of deprivation in community and client samples

	Community sample		Client sample (unweighted)	
	Unweighted	Weighted[a]	2006	2008
A decent and secure home	6.6	7.1	28.2	29.6
A substantial meal at least once a day	1.1	1.2	12.6	14.7
Warm clothes and bedding, if it's cold	0.2	0.3	8.1	9.5
Heating in at least one room of the house	1.8	2.1	15.6	17.6
Furniture in reasonable condition	2.6	2.8	18.2	17.2
Comprehensive motor vehicle insurance	8.6	9.8	43.3	41.9
A telephone	1.5	1.9	15.4	17.7
A washing machine	0.8	1.1	13.4	13.2
A television	0.2	0.2	5.2	4.6
Up to $500 in savings for an emergency	17.6	19.6	57.7	59.8
Secure locks on doors and windows	5.1	5.0	17.5	18.2
Home contents insurance	9.5	11.1	46.3	46.0
A roof and gutters that do not leak	4.6	4.8	12.5	14.6
A separate bed for each child	1.6	1.7	12.4	11.4
A separate bedroom for each child aged over 10	6.1	6.7	20.7	18.8
Medical treatment if needed	2.0	2.1	9.3	10.3
Able to buy medicines prescribed by a doctor	3.9	4.5	25.3	26.4
Dental treatment if needed	13.9	14.5	46.0	45.7
A yearly dental check-up for children	9.1	9.8	34.7	26.0
Regular social contact with other people	4.7	4.7	15.0	15.0
A week's holiday away from home each year	22.4	23.6	53.1	54.8
Presents for family or friends at least once a year	6.6	6.8	29.7	31.6
A hobby or leisure activity for children	5.7	5.7	23.8	24.7
Computer skills	5.2	4.6	17.5	14.9
Up-to-date school books and new school clothes for school-age children	3.8	4.0	18.5	19.4
Children can participate in school activities and outings	3.5	3.6	16.2	17.9
Mean incidence rate	**5.8**	**6.1**	**23.7**	**23.9**

Note: [a] Weighted by ABS population weights.

absence does *not* reflect a lack of affordability so that they will *not* be identified as deprived of these items.

It is, however, important to note that the fact that the items that relate to children are only relevant to those households containing children introduces an element of non-comparability into the estimates. This follows because, if the logic described above is correct, the maximum deprivation score for households without children will be lower than the maximum score for households with children. Although this does not affect the comparisons of deprivation across individual items, it does

Figure 6.1: The incidence of deprivation in the community and client samples in 2006

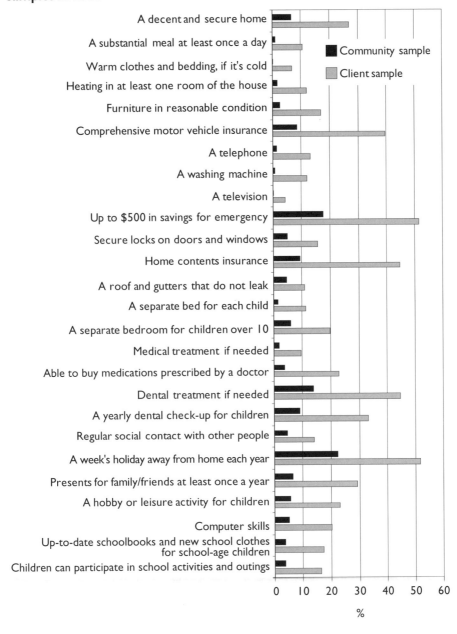

make it more difficult to compare the extent of deprivation in households with and without children, and this needs to be borne in mind when interpreting some of the results presented later.

The deprivation estimates for the community sample are presented in Table 6.2 in both raw (unweighted) form and after weighting to reflect the age composition

Figure 6.2: The incidence of deprivation in the client sample in 2006 and 2008

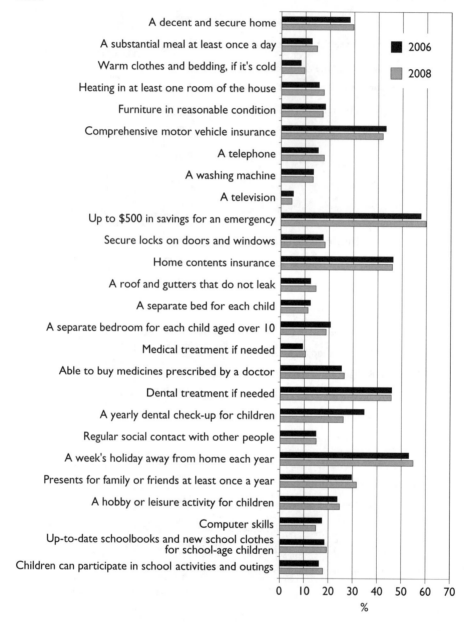

of the population. As noted earlier, re-weighting the data in this way makes little difference to the results and for this reason, only the unweighted estimates are discussed from now on. The client sample estimates for the two years vary by more than the difference between the unweighted and weighted community sample estimates, but the difference is statistically significant ($p = 0.01$) in only one instance – an annual dental check-up for children. For this reason, discussion focuses on the client sample estimates for the earlier year, when comparisons with the community survey can be made.

Table 6.2 and Figure 6.1 indicate that less than one per cent of those in the community sample are deprived of such items as a substantial daily meal, warm clothes and bedding, a washing machine or a television. In contrast, deprivation rates exceed 10% in the case of three items and approach 10% for three others. The items where deprivation is most severe are: a week's holiday away from home each year (22.4%), $500 in savings for use in an emergency (17.6%), dental treatment when needed (13.9%), home contents insurance (9.5%), an annual dental check-up for children (9.1%) and comprehensive motor vehicle insurance (8.6%). It is interesting to note that the deprivation rates in Table 6.1 are similar to the hardship rates shown in Table 3.5 (Chapter Three) for those items that are the same or similar, adding credence to the results presented here.

The mean incidence rate across all 26 essential items is around 6% – a figure that is well below the estimated poverty rate of 11.1% in 2005-06 presented in Chapter Two. In conjunction with the low incidence of specific forms of deprivation in the community sample, the results in Table 6.2 indicate that relatively few Australians are unable to afford most essential items. However, there are pockets of deprivation that give rise to concern, particularly when viewed against a backdrop of the high level of material prosperity that most Australians were enjoying at the time.

This overview of the deprivation profile suggests that the items can be separated into three roughly equal-sized groups according to the level of deprivation experienced: first are the eight items that satisfy the most important basic needs such as food, clothing, heating and health, where the incidence of deprivation is generally less than 2%; next comes nine items related to accommodation, basic skills and some of the children's items where deprivation lies between 2% and 6%; finally, there are a further nine items that include access to dental treatment, and different forms of social participation, where the deprivation rate exceeds 6%.

All but one of the items where deprivation is most pronounced reflect actions that people need to take to protect their longer-term security against unpredictable risks: an adequate level of *savings* for use in an emergency; appropriate *insurance coverage*; and access to dental care *when needed*. The absence of these items among large sections of the community highlights the fact that many Australians are only a minor mishap (a faulty refrigerator, a scrape in the car or a toothache) away from becoming deprived.

In terms of the ordering of individual item deprivation rates, with the exception of a decent and secure home, deprivation is less prevalent among those items that relate to material possessions (furniture in reasonable condition; a telephone; a washing machine) than among those items that reflect different forms of participation (regular social contact with others; a week's holiday away; a hobby or leisure activity for children; children can participate in school outings and activities) or access to basic support services (medical treatment when needed; prescribed medications; dental care). This reinforces the idea, captured by the essentials of life themselves, that Australians have a broad understanding of the diverse range of items required to meet their many needs. It also highlights the crucial role that public provision of key services plays, not only in meeting community needs, but also in combating deprivation among individuals.

The findings on the incidence of deprivation among the client sample paint a bleaker picture than those revealed by the community sample. This is hardly surprising since the client sample was deliberately chosen to include those who are among the most vulnerable and disadvantaged members of society. However, the important point is not so much that deprivation is *higher* among the client sample than among the community sample (which is not unexpected), but rather that the *absolute level* of deprivation faced by those in the client sample (in both years) is so high.

Thus in 2006, close to half of those in the client sample were deprived of four essential items: $500 in savings for use in an emergency (57.7%); a week's holiday away (53.1%); home contents insurance (46.3%); and dental treatment if needed (46.0%). The client deprivation rate exceeds one quarter for more than one third (9) of the 26 essential items, whereas it never reaches this level in the community sample. In overall terms, the (unweighted) average incidence of deprivation across all 26 essential items among the client sample (23.7%) is more than four times that for the community sample (5.8%). The severity of deprivation among the client sample is further highlighted by the fact that around one in eight are not able to afford some of the most basic items, including a substantial meal at least once a day, to heat at least one room in the house, to own a washing machine, a separate bed for each child, to have regular social contact with other people, or can afford to pay for their children's participation in school outings and activities.

These results also suggest that many Australian children are being raised in circumstances that are likely to have adverse effects not only on their current level of well-being, but also on their longer-run life chances. Among the client sample in particular, between one in eight and one in five are deprived of an adequate number of bedrooms for their children, up-to-date school books and new school clothes, and participation in school activities and outings. Around one quarter cannot afford a hobby or leisure activity for their children, and over one third are not able to afford an annual dental check-up for their children. Even among the community sample, close to 10% have children who are deprived of an annual dental check-up, while around 6% are denied the opportunity for their children to participate in hobby or leisure activities or are deprived of a separate bedroom for older children.

In overall terms (as measured by the average deprivation rate) there was little change in deprivation among the clients of welfare services between 2006 and 2008, although there were some marked changes for specific items. The deprivation rate increased by two percentage points or more for five items: a substantial daily meal; heating in at least one room; a telephone; up to $500 in emergency savings; and a roof and gutters that do not leak. These increases occurred at a time of rising real incomes and falling unemployment and raise serious questions about the relevance of the 'trickle down' theory that is often used (by those with access to power and resources) as a justification for giving priority to economic growth over redistributing resources to those in greatest need.

However, there is also some good news implicit in the client sample figures, since deprivation did not increase across the board. In fact, the deprivation rate declined for 10 of the 26 essential items and was constant in one instance, and although some of these changes were small, declines of two percentage points or more were experienced for two items – a yearly dental check-up for children; and computer skills – with the former decline being statistically significant. The improved access to preventative dental care for children by 2008 is indicative of some progress being made in an area that was shown to be highly problematic in 2006.

Such conclusions must be treated with a degree of caution because differences in the services that participated in the client survey in each year make it difficult (and dangerous) to compare the results without acknowledging this. It is also likely that some of those who were least disadvantaged in 2006 will have benefited from the improved economic conditions and found employment by 2008, leaving those who were still relying on welfare services for assistance somewhat more disadvantaged on average than they were two years earlier.

If the changes in the services that participated in the two client surveys are controlled for by focusing only on changes among the clients of those services that participated in both surveys, the increase in average deprivation is actually *greater* than that shown in Table 6.2, and there are more instances of increased deprivation (Saunders and Wong, 2009, Table 10). On the basis of this restricted but more comparable sample, the mean deprivation rate rose from 26.0% to 32.3% between 2006 and 2008, while deprivation increased for all but one item (a television), with the increase being statistically significant ($p = 0.05$) in the case of five items: a decent and secure home; warm clothes and bedding; furniture in reasonable condition; an annual dental check-up for children; and children can participate in school activities and outings. In overall terms, the evidence thus suggests that while deprivation among welfare service clients remained broadly constant over the period, there is evidence that it increased in some instances.

Multiple deprivation

The results presented so far treat each form of deprivation as an isolated event, but it is also important to know the extent to which deprivation clusters together in the same individuals or households. This involves examining the incidence of multiple deprivation, and how it is distributed among members of the community. When people are forced to go without several essential items at the same time, the evidence that needs are not being met becomes more compelling. Previous studies have shown that many of those who experience deprivation in one dimension also face it in others, compounding the problems faced and adding to the complexity (and urgency) of finding solutions.

The incidence of multiple deprivation in the community and two client samples is shown in Table 6.3. The final row shows the mean deprivation scores for each sample, which have been derived by summing the number of deprivations and averaging the resulting scores across each sample. The multiple deprivation incidence rate takes no account of the depth or severity of deprivation, because it treats, for example, someone who is deprived of 10 essential items the same as someone who is deprived of six items. And although the mean deprivation score implicitly takes account of individual differences in the severity of deprivation, these are concealed in the overall group averages. It is possible to develop more sophisticated measures that take account of the severity of deprivation (see Borooah, 2007, for an example), but this has not been attempted here.

The results indicate that almost two fifths (38.5%) of those in the community sample experience at least one form of deprivation and more than one quarter (26.4%) experience two or more forms of deprivation. One in nine (11.1%) were missing out on at least five essential items simultaneously – a similar proportion to those with incomes below half of the median (Table 2.2 in Chapter Two). The percentage deprived of three or more essential items (18.8%) is similar to the percentage with incomes below 60% of the median. These similarities are exploited in the overlap analysis described in the following chapter.

Whichever year is considered, the extent of multiple deprivation in the client sample is indicative of a severe level of deprivation among this group. Focusing on the results for the earlier year, more than two thirds (68.0%) experienced two or more forms of deprivation, while close to half (48.2%) were missing out on five or more essential items. Approaching one third (29.5%) of those in the client sample were deprived of at least eight items, and were thus missing out on around one in three of the items identified as essential by a majority.

Table 6.3: The incidence of multiple deprivation in community and client samples (unweighted percentages)

Number of essential items lacking because they cannot be afforded	Community sample	Client sample 2006	2008
0	61.5	21.9	21.3
1 or more	38.5	78.1	78.7
2 or more	26.4	68.0	70.4
3 or more	18.8	61.9	63.6
4 or more	14.2	55.2	56.2
5 or more	11.1	48.2	48.5
6 or more	8.1	41.4	42.1
7 or more	6.0	34.3	35.9
8 or more	4.4	29.5	30.8
9 or more	3.3	24.0	26.1
10 or more	2.2	19.1	22.0
Mean deprivation score	**1.38**	**5.40**	**5.64**

The extent of the difference in multiple deprivation between the community and client samples is illustrated by the fact that the percentage of the community sample that are deprived of two or more items (just over one quarter) is similar to the percentage of the client sample that are deprived of eight items – four times as many. This sharp difference is reinforced by the fact that the mean deprivation score in the client sample (5.40) is almost four times higher than that for the community sample (1.38). This difference cannot be assumed to imply that those in the client sample are experiencing four times as much deprivation as those in the community sample, since the relationship between the number of items lacking and the extent of deprivation may not be linear. Even so, the results indicate that multiple deprivation was widely experienced among the welfare service client sample, and point to the inadequacy of the support that many in this group were receiving from government and non-government sources.

Patterns of deprivation

The incidence of deprivation in different sub-groups defined on the basis of their socioeconomic characteristics provides important information on the nature and impact of deprivation, allows the circumstances of different groups to be compared and can help to identify where existing policies are absent or ineffective. The indicator used to capture differences in the extent of deprivation experienced is the mean deprivation score, derived by summing the number of deprivations experienced by those in each group and averaging the resulting scores across the group. No attempt has been made to weight the data to adjust for differences in sample composition, nor to assign a different weight to each item. It is important, however, to recall the point made earlier about the non-comparability of those scores that depend on household circumstances (such as those with and without children, or those with and without a disability).

The relationship between age and deprivation in the community and client samples is shown in Figure 6.3. The results for the community sample indicate that there is a clear negative age gradient to deprivation, with those in the youngest age range (under 25) experiencing the highest level of deprivation (index score of 2.13). The deprivation index then declines to between 1.7 and 2.0 for those aged between 25 and 44, falls further for those aged 45 and over, reaching a minimum of below 0.9 (less than half the value of the index for those aged under 25) for those in their late 50s and remaining low for those aged 65 and over. A similar pattern is apparent among those in the client sample, although in this case there is less variation among those aged up to 54 (with the maximum index value reached for those aged between 50 and 54), and more variation among those aged 65 and over. The number of older participants in the client sample is, however, very small, and the estimates for those aged 40 and over should be treated with caution.

For both samples, there is a clear life cycle pattern to the profile of deprivation. Although the numbers are small, particularly in the lower age ranges (under 25) for the community sample and upper age ranges (over 50) for the client sample,

Figure 6.3: The age profile of mean deprivation scores in the community and client samples

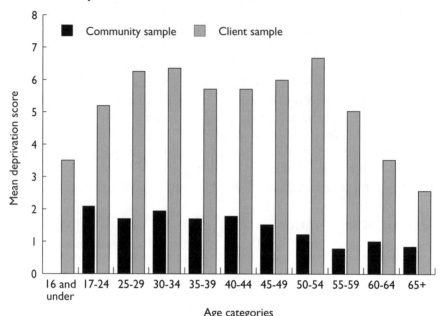

the pattern is one of rising deprivation until about age 30, after which it plateaus out until declining markedly after age 50. Although deprivation remains high in the client sample for those aged 50 and over, the numbers are very small, but the decline in deprivation among older age groups is clear (although more modest) in the community sample, which contains a large number of respondents in this age range.

The contrast between the degree of deprivation in the two samples is again evident in the fact that the minimum value of the age-specific deprivation score among the client sample (2.60 for those aged 65 and over) is higher than the maximum value of the score among the community sample (2.13 for those aged under 25). In overall terms, however, Figure 6.3 shows that the age-related pattern of deprivation that is clearly apparent in the community sample is muted by the greater level of disadvantage (possibly reinforced by the distorted age composition) that exists in the client sample.

The age-related variations in deprivation scores shown in Figure 6.3 seem somewhat at odds with the conventional view that average living standards are lower for those in older age groups. This view is based primarily on income-based comparisons over the life cycle, which show that mean incomes tend to decline at older ages, and that this translates into higher poverty rates (see Table 2.3, Chapter Two). However, income comparisons can only be used to draw implications about living standards after an equivalence adjustment has been applied to allow for differences in household needs. Once the equivalence adjustment has been applied, income becomes a better indicator of the standard of living, and can be more readily compared with mean deprivation scores, since both now capture the ability of available resources to meet needs.

Figure 6.4 compares the age profiles of mean deprivation scores and mean equivalised incomes for those in the community sample. It shows that the two indicators suggest quite different implications about the relative living standards achieved at different stages of the life course. For example, mean incomes reach a maximum between the ages of 25 and 29 and the mean adjusted income of those aged 65 and over is only just over 60% of this maximum figure. In contrast, deprivation (which is an inverse indicator of the standard of living) reaches its minimum value between the ages of 55 and 59, and remains close to this level at older ages, despite the sharp drop in mean equivalised income.

The different age profiles shown in Figure 6.4 suggest that the two indicators cannot both be capturing the same thing – or at least not doing so with equal accuracy. Several factors might explain the differences, particularly as they apply to those in the older age groups. First, the equivalence adjustment may not adequately capture the variations in needs that occur over the life cycle. If needs decline as adults age (or if a larger proportion of their needs are met from services provided and paid for by the public sector rather than by goods that consumers have to pay for themselves), then the equivalence adjustment may understate the relative living standards of older people. Another possible explanation is that deprivation may be understated among older people because the essential items are identified by majority opinion and fail to identify items that meet the specific

Figure 6.4: Age profiles of equivalised mean income and mean deprivation scores in the community sample

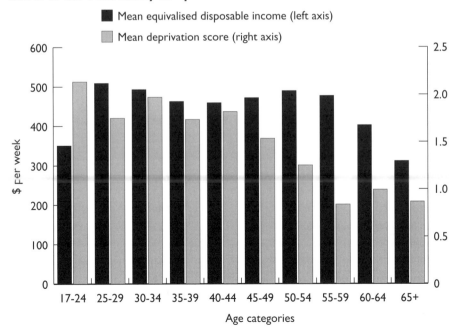

needs of older people. Another possibility is that the items themselves may be relevant, but older people are less willing to admit that they cannot afford items that they do not have.

The evidence from overseas studies tends to be consistent with both of these latter propositions, as studies by Berthoud et al (2004), McKay (2004) and Van den Bosch (2001, 2004) have demonstrated. However, this evidence is largely drawn from static (cross-sectional) studies, and longitudinal surveys that track the circumstances of the same people through time suggest a somewhat different relationship exists between deprivation and the ageing process (Berthoud et al, 2006; see also Siminski and Yerokhin, 2010).

Turning to how deprivation varies with socioeconomic circumstances more generally, Table 6.4 compares mean deprivation scores for households classified by a range of characteristics. Whether deprivation within each specified sub-group is above or below the average for the entire sample can be seen by comparing the deprivation score for the group with that for all households shown (in bold) in the final row of Table 6.4. The variations in deprivation across family types in both community and client samples are consistent with the declining age gradient just described. These disaggregated results also indicate that deprivation is higher among single working-age and older people than among couples, is higher among couples with children than among childless couples, and is considerably higher among lone-parent families than among couples with children. Deprivation among mixed family households is also high – about the same as among single working-age people living alone.

Deprivation tends, on average, to be lower in the less populous states (aside from Tasmania), particularly in Western Australia and the Australian Capital Territory (ACT) than in the more densely populated states along the eastern seaboard.

Table 6.4: Mean deprivation scores by selected socioeconomic characteristics in 2006[a]

Characteristic	Community sample	Client sample
Family type[b]		
Single, working age	2.14	5.41
Single, older person	1.33	3.13
Working-age couple, no children	0.84	4.71
Older couple	0.55	2.67
Working-age couple, with children	1.29	4.28
Lone parent	3.48	7.44
Other (mixed family households)	2.29	6.18
State/territory		
NSW	1.41	6.00
Victoria	1.46	4.23
Queensland	1.51	5.42

(continued)

Table 6.4 (continued)

Characteristic	Community sample	Client sample
State/territory (continued)		
South Australia	1.30	5.82
Western Australia	0.95	7.46
Tasmania	1.52	2.91
ACT	0.78	–
Main activity[c]		
Employed	1.15	2.92
Unemployed	3.66	5.85
Retired	0.81	2.85
Studying	1.53	6.26
Caring for children or adults	2.66	8.45
Principal source of income		
Wages, salaries or interest	1.06	2.59
Social security payment	2.28	6.41
Education		
Degree/higher degree	0.80	4.15
High school or less	1.70	5.62
Housing tenure		
Owner/purchaser	0.81	2.58
Private renter	3.49	6.14
Public renter	3.91	5.79
Country of birth		
Australia	1.43	5.62
Another English-speaking country	0.86	4.42
Another non-English-speaking country	1.61	5.48
Indigenous (ATSI)[d]		
No	1.33	5.28
Yes	5.60	7.17
Has an ongoing disability		
No	1.24	4.78
Yes	1.96	6.64
All households	**1.38**	**5.40**

Notes: [a] Not all of the categories shown are exhaustive, but the excluded categories contain a diverse range of groups and often contain very small numbers of cases. It should also be noted that the numbers in some of the client categories are quite small.

[b] Single working-age people are aged between 18 and 64; older people are aged 65 or over; older couples are those where the respondent is aged 65 or over; children include only dependent children, aged under 18; mixed family households include all other households with three or more adults (for example, those with unrelated adults living together as a group household, or adult children living with their parents).

[c] Main activity refers to the respondent only and excludes those who provided multiple responses.

[d] ATSI = Aboriginal or Torres Strait Islander.

Western Australia was in the midst of a mining boom in 2006, while the ACT is dominated by Canberra, home of the federal government, and its low mean deprivation reflects the high incomes of many of its inhabitants. Overall, the ranking of states/territories by their deprivation score in Table 6.4 is very similar to the corresponding poverty ranking shown in Table 2.3 in Chapter Two.

Being unemployed is associated with a substantially higher deprivation score (relative to those in employment), while those caring for a child or an adult with a disability also face high levels of deprivation – particularly carers in the client sample. Deprivation is more than twice as high among households that are mainly reliant on a social security payment than among those whose income is mainly derived from earnings or interest. This raises questions about the adequacy of social security benefits and this issue is examined in more depth later.

High levels of deprivation are also associated with having a low level of education and being a renter (in either the private or public sectors). Differences in deprivation scores by country of birth show that those born in Australia fall between the two immigrant groups, with those born in other English-speaking countries faring best, and those who have migrated from non-English-speaking countries experiencing the highest level of deprivation on average. This latter finding does not automatically imply that language proficiency explains the observed differences in deprivation, since cultural and other factors will also affect the opportunities and experiences of different groups of immigrants.

The level of deprivation experienced by Indigenous Australians is very high – the highest in any single category identified in this analysis – and among the community sample it exceeds that of the non-Indigenous population by a factor of more than four to one. Finally, those with a disability or ongoing restrictive medical condition also experience above-average deprivation, and although it is not possible to establish what is contributing to this difference, the additional costs associated with disability is one possible factor (see Saunders, 2007).

Deprivation scores for sub-groups within the client sample exhibit a broadly similar pattern to those among the community sample, but are consistently higher across all groups. It is interesting to note, however, that many of the within-category deprivation relativities in the community sample are larger than those in the client sample. Although this in part reflects the numerical limits on the index scores, the comparisons based on educational attainment, housing tenure, country of birth and disability status all show less variation in the client sample than in the community sample. As was the case for the age variations discussed earlier, it seems that the experience of extreme disadvantage tends to dampen the impact of specific socioeconomic characteristics.

It is striking that large differences in deprivation between the community and client samples remain even when comparing the deprivation scores *within* sub-categories. Thus, the mean deprivation score among those in the client sample who are unemployed (5.85) is considerably higher than that for unemployed people in the community sample (3.66). Even more interesting is the fact that those in the client sample who are employed experience only slightly less deprivation than those in the community sample who are unemployed (an index score of 2.92 compared with 3.66).

These differences highlight the fact that the factors identified in Table 6.4 (the differences in respondent characteristics, and between membership of the community and client samples) exert an important but differential impact on the level of deprivation experienced. Thus, for example, the deprivation 'penalty' associated with having a low level of education (an increase in the mean deprivation score of between 0.9 and 1.5) is much less (in either sample) than that associated with being a member of the client sample for those with a given level of education (an increase in the mean deprivation score of between 3.4 and 3.9 points). In contrast, the mean deprivation score of Indigenous Australians in the community sample is similar to that of non-Indigenous members of the client sample.

These comparisons suggest that the deprivation outcomes in Table 6.4 reflect a complex range of influences that have their origins in a broad range of factors. While some of these are directly amenable to policy (for example, labour force status, level of education or reliance on community sector agencies for assistance), others are intrinsic and cannot be altered. This does not mean that reducing the deprivation gaps is an impossible task, but it highlights the fact that action will need to be substantial and sustained in order to have an impact.

Sensitivity analysis: the weighting issue

The mean deprivation scores used to describe the deprivation profile assign an equal weight to each item that satisfies a threshold level of support for being essential. This approach has been criticised because no account is taken of differences in the degree of support for each item being essential, or of differences in item ownership or participation rates. Reflecting these concerns, it has been argued that a weighted approach is more appropriate and can be applied in a way that avoids the need to set a threshold that distinguishes between essential and non-essential items.

The two alternative weighting schemes that have been proposed in the literature are prevalence weighting and preference weighting (Willitts, 2006). The former approach applies weights that reflect the ownership of each item, while the latter applies weights that reflect the degree of support for each item being essential. The results presented earlier (in Table 5.1 in Chapter Five) suggest that the choice of weighting scheme can have an important bearing on measured deprivation. For example, while almost everyone (99.6% of those surveyed) think that a substantial daily meal is essential, only 75.1% think that home contents insurance is essential. Furthermore, a greater proportion of those surveyed have the former item (98.5%) than have the latter item (83.8%). These differences suggest that not being able to afford a substantial meal implies a greater degree of deprivation than not being able to afford home contents insurance – because more people think that the daily meal is essential, and because more people actually have it.

Although there is merit in the arguments used to support a weighted approach, it is unclear which approach should be used. Those who have applied a weighted approach have tended to favour prevalence weighting on the grounds that patterns of ownership capture prevailing norms, so that to miss out on an item that most people have is a visible maker of deprivation. The use of prevalence weighting thus better captures an important feature of deprivation – being unable to take part in widely enjoyed forms of consumption or participation. Another advantage of using prevalence weights is that they avoid the need to ask whether those who lack an item cannot afford it – a question that has been shown to be subject to interpretational problems. In contrast, the use of preference weighting replaces a readily comprehensible and easily disseminated method for identifying necessities (do a majority agree that the item is essential?) by a more complex method that is harder to describe (and possibly also, more difficult to justify). The discomfort associated with going hungry or having inadequate heating, for example, is no greater if 90% think that the items are essential than if only 60% think so.

One advantage of adopting a weighted approach is that if it is applied to all items on the list, not just those that exceed the threshold that identifies them as essential, it avoids the need to set a threshold in the first place. If applied in this way, the whole process of identifying deprivation becomes much simpler. Against this, the abandonment of reliance on community views to identify essential items reduces the credibility of the approach to some degree – possibly to a substantial degree. In addition, the original selection of which items to include in the list now becomes more critical since all are retained.

One study that has ignored views about which items are essential altogether and based the measurement of deprivation on ownership rates alone has been undertaken by Van den Bosch (2004). Using EU–SILC data the study shows that if deprivation is based solely on the *lack* of essential items (as opposed to the dual criteria of lack of ownership *and* lack of affordability), the situation of single older people appears much worse. This change occurs because the reluctance of older people to admit that they do not want an item that they do not have no longer affects whether or not they are identified as deprived.

It can also be argued that any weighting scheme should also reflect differences in the cost of acquiring each item. This idea is consistent with the role of resource constraints in determining deprivation, but is difficult to apply in practice because no single price adequately captures the cost of items that vary greatly in terms of the frequency with which they are purchased (compare a decent home with a substantial daily meal) and are also (deliberately) specified rather imprecisely in the survey questions. Even the cost of a hobby or leisure activity for children or home contents insurance varies greatly according to the quality of the product and where and how it is purchased.

Studies that have examined the impact of applying different weighting schemes have found that it makes relatively little difference to who is identified as deprived (Halleröd et al, 1997), although there is evidence that the deprivation ranking of some groups is sensitive to the use of different weighting schemes (Van den Bosch,

2001, 2004). This suggests that there is value in examining the sensitivity of the deprivation results presented earlier to the use of alternative weighting schemes. In order to expand the scope of the analysis, the impact of applying different weights is accompanied by also examining the sensitivity of the results to changes in the level of support used to define which items are essential.

Table 6.5 shows the impact of applying four alternative indices of deprivation:

1. An unweighted deprivation index, derived by summing those items that receive at least *50%* support for being essential (DEP50)
2. An unweighted deprivation index, derived by summing those items that receive at least *90%* support for being essential (DEP90)
3. A preference weighting approach, under which the weights reflect the degree of *support* for each item being essential (PREFWT)
4. A prevalence approach under which the weights reflect the *ownership rate* of each item (PREVWT)

The earlier results in Table 5.1 (Chapter Five) indicate that while the basic deprivation index (DEP50) is based on the 26 items identified as attracting majority support for being essential, only 12 of these items exceed the 90% support threshold that is relevant when constructing the DEP90 index. These 12 items are: medical treatment if needed; warm clothes and bedding if it's cold; a substantial meal at least once a day; ability to buy prescribed medications; dental treatment if needed; a decent and secure home; children can participate in school activities and outings; an annual dental check-up for children; a hobby or leisure activity for children; regular social contact with other people; a roof and gutters that do not leak; and secure locks on doors and windows.

Because the two weighting schemes do not require a threshold that distinguishes between essential and non-essential items, they have been applied to all 44 of the items that can be purchased by individuals (those items not indicated by the superscript [a] in Table 5.1). These differences in the number of items used to construct the different indices means that their absolute values are not comparable, and attention thus focuses on the relative values of the mean deprivation score for different groups.

The values of the four alternative indices are shown in Table 6.5 for households differentiated by age, family type and Indigenous and disability status. (The patterns are broadly similar for the other breakdowns presented earlier.) The patterns of deprivation relativities between different households exhibited by the different indexes are similar. This can be most readily seen by comparing the index values for younger (under 30) and older (65 and over) age groups, which vary between 1.31 and 1.43, and between 0.63 and 0.75, respectively. Although the relative deprivation status of older people improves when the two weighting approaches are employed (a finding that is consistent with other studies), the differences do not affect the main conclusion about the relative deprivation status of older and

Table 6.5: Comparing alternative deprivation indices by household characteristics (mean index scores)

	Deprivation index[a]							
	DEP50		DEP90		PREFWT		PREVWT	
Household characteristic	Abs	Rel	Abs	Rel	Abs	Rel	Abs	Rel
Age								
Under 30	1.97	1.43	0.73	1.31	2.39	1.36	2.64	1.37
30-64	1.43	1.04	0.58	1.04	1.81	1.03	1.96	1.02
65 and over	0.87	0.63	0.35	0.63	1.23	0.70	1.45	0.75
Family type								
Single, working age	2.14	1.55	0.84	1.50	2.59	1.47	2.97	1.54
Older person	1.33	0.96	0.60	1.07	1.90	1.08	2.18	1.13
Working-age couple, no children	0.84	0.61	0.33	0.59	1.10	0.63	1.18	0.61
Older couple	0.55	0.40	0.19	0.34	0.81	0.46	0.96	0.50
Working-age couple, with children	1.29	0.93	0.51	0.91	1.67	0.95	1.78	0.92
Lone-parent family	3.48	2.52	1.54	2.75	4.34	2.47	4.73	2.45
Indigenous/ATSI								
Yes	5.60	4.06	2.00	3.57	7.06	4.01	7.66	3.97
No	1.33	0.96	0.54	0.96	1.71	0.97	1.87	0.97
Has an ongoing disability								
Yes	1.96	1.42	0.81	1.45	2.49	1.41	2.74	1.42
No	1.24	0.90	0.49	0.88	1.59	0.90	1.74	0.90
All households	**1.38**	**1.00**	**0.56**	**1.00**	**1.76**	**1.00**	**1.93**	**1.00**

Note: [a] Abs = absolute value of the index; Rel = relative value of the index (relative to the value for all households, which is set equal to 1.00).

younger age groups. Older people appear less deprived than those aged under 65, whichever index of deprivation is used.

The comparisons in Table 6.5 also reveal that the value of the relative deprivation index for couples with children remains virtually unchanged, at around 0.93 across all of the four deprivation indices, whereas the corresponding values for lone-parent families vary between 2.45 (PREVWT) and 2.75 (DEP90). In all four instances, however, lone parents are seen to experience far greater deprivation than couples with children. The use of any of the four indices also has no impact on the finding that Indigenous Australians and people with a disability both experience above-average levels of deprivation.

In overall terms, the rankings of relative deprivation scores are also stable across the four indices: Indigenous Australians always appear as most deprived, followed by lone-parent families, while working-age couples without children and older couples always appear as the two least deprived groups. The deprivation rankings within age groups and family types are also the same across all four indices. The similarity in the four indices is confirmed by the very high correlation coefficients (in excess of 0.99) between the different indexes shown in Table 6.6.

Table 6.6: Correlation matrix for alternative deprivation indices

	Deprivation index:			
	DEP50	**DEP90**	**PREFWT**	**PREVWT**
DEP50	1.000	0.915**	0.972**	0.954**
DEP90	–	1.000	0.891**	0.850**
PREFWT	–	–	1.000	0.986**
PREVWT	–	–	–	1.000

Note: ** = statistically significant (p = 0.01).

The sensitivity analysis thus indicates that it makes little difference to the deprivation relativities of different groups whether a threshold is used to identify which items are essential, the level at which that threshold is set or whether or not all items above and below the threshold are weighted when constructing the index of deprivation. In light of these findings, there is a strong case for applying the unweighted, majority rule deprivation index (DEP50) because of its transparency and political validity.

Identifying core deprivation items

When evidence on deprivation is used to help identify poverty, it is important to establish that the individual components of deprivation are associated with independent indicators of poverty and social disadvantage. The DEP50 deprivation index considered above is based on 26 items and raises the question of whether the information it contains can be captured using a simpler index based on a smaller number of items. One way of reducing the number of essential items is to raise the threshold used to identify essential items above 50%, although the use of a threshold set at 90% support has already been shown to have little impact on the patterns revealed by the results.

Two other ways to reduce the number of items used to identify deprivation involve applying more detailed statistical analysis of the list of deprivation items. The first, associated with the work of Gordon (2000, 2006) applies tests of reliability and validity as a way of checking whether the different items are capturing the same underlying idea – the existence of a standard of living that is linked to poverty. The second approach has been developed by researchers at the Economic and Social Research Institute (ESRI) in Ireland (Callan and Nolan, 1993; Nolan and Whelan, 1996) and by McKay and Collard (2003), who apply the approach to British data. It involves conducting exploratory factor analysis to see if it is possible to identify a smaller group of items that still captures most of the information contained in the full list.

The rationale for adopting the latter approach is explained by Nolan and Whelan as follows:

> ... not all of the ... items may be considered appropriate as indicators
> of deprivation [while] simply aggregating them in a single index
> ignores the fact that different items may reflect different dimensions of
> deprivation and adding them together may lose valuable information.
> (Nolan and Whelan, 1996, p 86)

They go on to note that Townsend himself identified different dimensions of deprivation, which implies that the construction of an index should reflect this – or should at least investigate whether such dimensions can be identified in the data. Nolan and Whelan's study was based on 24 deprivation items that were shown using factor analysis to group into three broad dimensions: basic lifestyle deprivation (which contained eight items); secondary lifestyle deprivation (nine items); and housing deprivation (seven items).

The eight items included in the first dimension were: not going without heating; not going without a substantial meal; absence of arrears or debt; new not second-hand clothes; a meal with meat, chicken or fish every second day; a warm waterproof overcoat; at least two pairs of strong shoes; and a roast meat joint or its equivalent at least once a week. These items include several that are included among the essentials of life identified for Australia in Table 5.1, but also reflect the specific customs (and climate!) of Ireland. Only the eight basic lifestyle deprivation items were later incorporated into the poverty targets adopted by the Irish government (Nolan, 2000), although that list was subsequently amended (and re-labelled 'economic strain') by removing two items (going without a substantial meal due to lack of money, and going into debt to meet ordinary living expenses) and adding in five new ones (keep the home adequately warm; buy presents for family or friends at least once a year; replace any worn-out furniture; have family or friends for a drink or meal once a month; and have a morning, afternoon or evening out in the last fortnight, for entertainment) (Whelan et al, 2006, Table 3).

Tests of reliability and validity

Following Gordon (2006), the reliability of the 26-item deprivation index was assessed by calculating the Cronbach alpha statistic, which reflects how well a set of items (or variables) capture a single underlying latent construct. A low value (a value of 0.7 or higher is normally considered satisfactory) implies either that the items do not measure the same construct, or that a multi-dimensional structure exists. One way of testing for the reliability of a set of items involves calculating the Cronbach alpha score for all the items together, and then re-calculating it after each item in turn is omitted. A marked decline in the statistic will imply that the omitted item captures the underlying structure well, while if the omission results in an unchanged or higher Cronbach statistic, this suggests that the item plays little role in capturing the latent structure.

The first column of Table 6.7 shows that the Cronbach alpha reliability statistic for the 26 deprivation items that satisfy the 50% majority rule for being essential is equal to 0.8542. Removal of each item in turn results in a decline in the statistic in all except three cases: a washing machine; computer skills; and a television set. In the first two cases, the increase in the Cronbach alpha when the items is removed is very small, and only the removal of the television set results in a noticeable increase (from 0.8542 to 0.8558) – although even here the decline is not large.

The validity of the 26 items was assessed, again following Gordon (2006), by calculating the odds ratios derived from a series of log-linear regressions that included each item separately in a model that has each of the following five indicators of poverty or disadvantage as dependent variable:

i.   Subjective health status is 'poor' (the lowest of four response categories)
ii. Current standard of living is 'very low' (the lowest of five response categories)
iii. Does not have enough income to get by on (the first of four response categories)
iv. Very dissatisfied with overall financial situation (an assessed score of 1, 2 or 3 on a 10-point scale)
v.   Self-describes oneself/one's family as poor (yes/no choice)

All five variables are likely to be highly correlated with poverty, either because they indicate that resources are inadequate (indicators iii and v), or because they imply a standard of living that is symptomatic of poverty (indicators ii and iv), or because they represent an outcome that is often associated with poverty (indicator i). Since it is the *strength* of these relationships that is important, attention focuses on whether or not the estimated odds ratios are statistically significant, rather than on the size of the estimated effects.

As can be seen from columns 2 to 6 of Table 6.7, most of the estimated odds ratios are statistically significant ($p = 0.05$), with only two items (warm clothes and bedding, if it's cold; and a television) recording more than one insignificant estimate. Of these two, only the television set also performed poorly on the reliability test, which suggests that the television is the only item that can be removed from the list of essential items. It should be noted that the removal of the television set is unlikely to have a marked bearing on the results, since Table 5.1 indicates that the television ownership rate is close to 99% for the community sample and over 92% in the client sample. However, it is also of interest to note that despite its widespread ownership, the level of support for a television being essential was less than 55% on an unweighted basis and only 50.9% on a weighted basis, so that its original inclusion among the list of essentials was marginal.

Factor analysis of deprivation

Exploratory factor analysis has been widely used in deprivation studies to produce a more manageable list of items that receive majority support for being essential. If a set of core items can be identified, fewer questions would need to be included in deprivation surveys, lowering the cost and possibly also increasing the response

Table 6.7: Reliability and validity test results

Deprivation indicator	Cronbach alpha scores	Poverty correlates:					
		Poor health	Low standard of living	Not enough to get by	Financially dissatisfied	Subjectively poor
All items	**0.8542**	–	–	–	–	–
Medical treatment if needed	0.8501	*	*	*	*	*
Warm clothes and bedding	0.8541	n/s	*	*	n/s	n/s
A substantial meal at least once a day	0.8479	*	*	*	*	*
Able to buy prescribed medicines	0.8482	*	*	*	*	*
Dental treatment if needed	0.8391	*	*	*	*	*
Decent and secure home	0.8479	*	*	*	*	*
Children can participate in school activities/outings	0.8483	*	*	*	*	*
Yearly dental check-up for children	0.8424	*	*	*	*	*
A hobby or leisure activity for children	0.8458	*	*	*	*	*
Regular social contact with other people	0.8478	*	*	*	*	*
Secure locks on doors and windows	0.8486	*	*	*	*	*
A roof and gutters that do not leak	0.8502	*	*	*	*	*
Furniture in reasonable condition	0.8503	*	*	*	*	*
Up-to-date schoolbooks/clothes for school-age children	0.8483	*	*	*	*	*
Heating in at least one room	0.8519	*	*	*	*	*

(continued)

Table 6.7 (continued)

Deprivation indicator	Cronbach alpha scores	Poverty correlates:				
		Poor health	Low standard of living	Not enough to get by	Financially dissatisfied	Subjectively poor
A separate bed for each child	0.8525	*	*	*	*	*
A telephone	0.8524	n/s	*	*	*	*
Up to $500 in emergency savings	0.8459	*	*	*	*	*
A washing machine	0.8543					*
Home contents insurance	0.8432	*	*	*	*	*
Presents for family or friends at least once a year	0.8454	*	*	*	*	*
Computer skills	0.8545	*	*	*	*	*
Comprehensive motor vehicle insurance	0.8492	*	*	*	*	*
A week's holiday away from home each year	0.8440	*	*	*	*	*
A television	0.8558	n/s	n/s	n/s	n/s	n/s
Separate bedroom for each child aged over 10	0.8514	*	*	*	*	*

Note: n/s = not statistically significant (*p* = 0.05).

141

rate. The concept also then becomes more manageable to construct, and easier to describe, disseminate and debate.

It has already been noted that factor analysis was used to develop the deprivation index that was adopted by the Irish government to monitor poverty trends (Nolan, 2000). It has also been used to assist the development of the poverty measures used by the British government to assess its efforts to reduce child poverty (Calandrino, 2003; McKay and Collard, 2003). The technique has also been used in New Zealand by Jensen et al (2002) in their development of the ELSI scale.

In Australia, factor analysis was used by Bray (2001) to assess whether it was possible to reduce the 13 financial stress questions that were introduced into the 1998-99 HES to a smaller set of uncorrelated components that could capture distinct components of stress. This resulted in the identification of three distinct components of financial stress: 'missing out' (six items); 'cash flow problems' (three items); and 'hardship' (four items) (Bray, 2001, Appendix D). Breunig et al (2005) have also applied factor analysis on the set of financial stress questions included in HILDA since 2001 (see also Headey and Warren, 2007, pp 54-6; and Butterworth and Crosier, 2006).

Although exploratory factor analysis has been widely used to develop deprivation and related living standards indicators, the technique has been subject to criticism. For example, McKay and Collard (2003) note that:

> There are no hard and fast rules about what variables should be used to explain the underlying structure of the data ... [and because factor analysis is] ... entirely data driven ... different solutions are likely to be obtained from different samples or from the same sample over time. (McKay and Collard, 2003, p 45)

In a similar vein, Tomlinson, Walker and Williams (2008) have emphasised the limitations of factor analysis, arguing that not only are the results subject to measurement errors in the original variables, the factors that emerge from the analysis cannot always be compared over time. They also note that:

> ... factor analysis is essentially an *exploratory* technique. No strong theoretical justification is required in deciding which variables to include or exclude from the analysis, and the researcher has little control over how the variables form the resulting factors. (Tomlinson et al, 2008, p 601; emphasis added)

Reinforcing these observations, McKay and Collard (2003, p 48) note that even though 'interpretable factors can indeed be derived from the datasets' using factor analysis, the factors that emerge are not always consistent over time.

Reflecting these uncertainties, Nolan and Whelan (1996) used factor analysis to identify how different variables cluster together, but argued that judgement should be used before reaching any definitive conclusions, and applied such judgements to derive their final list of core deprivation items. They classified two items (presents for family/friends each year and having a hobby or leisure activity) into the secondary lifestyle deprivation category, even though the factor analysis results suggested that they formed part of basic lifestyle deprivation. The use of judgements to refine the results that emerge from factor analysis suggests a pragmatic and flexible approach that is informed by theoretical reflection on how different items are related before deciding how the different components of deprivation cluster together.

Exploratory factor analysis has been used in this way to examine the underlying structure of the 25 deprivation items that remained after the reliability and validity tests had been applied. Initially, an unconstrained principal components analysis was applied, resulting in the identification of eight factors, although it was clear that most of the variance was explained by a small number of these. After experimenting with a variety of constrained analyses, a three-factor solution was identified as the superior model. It made little difference whether or not orthogonality was imposed and a rotated solution was chosen because of its greater flexibility.

The results (derived using the Oblimin method with Kaiser normalisation) are presented in Table 6.8, which shows the factor loadings for each of the 25 items. The identified groupings contain items that meet related needs in three broad areas: basic needs and risk protection; accommodation and household deprivation; and children's needs. These three factors explain about 36% of the variance in all 25 items, with around two thirds of that due to the first factor alone. (The overall explanatory power is little changed if the number of factors is increased to four or five, and these additional factors contain very few items.) The need to apply judgements to the factor analysis results is highlighted in Table 6.8 by the substantial daily meal, which has factor loadings that are virtually identical in factors 2 and 3. However, it makes more conceptual sense to include this item in factor 3 because of its similarity with the other items in that group.

On the basis of these results, a case can be made for reducing the 25 essentials of life items to the 11 basic needs and risk protection items shown in Table 6.8. This shorter list covers access to basic health-related services, items that serve an important social functioning role (an annual holiday away; presents for family and friends; regular social contact with other people; and computer skills) and two items that contribute to a sense of security at home (secure locks; and absence of leaks). These latter two items could equally be located among the second grouping, which contains seven items, all but one of which relates to the quality of the dwelling and its contents. The third grouping relates to items that either meet the specific needs of children, or items such as a substantial meal and warm clothes that are particularly important for children.

It is interesting to note that there is a high degree of overlap between the 11 basic needs and risk protection items identified in Table 6.8 using factor analysis and the 12 items that receive at least 90% support for being essential (on a weighted basis) shown in Table 5.1. Seven items are common to both lists: dental treatment if needed; an annual dental check-up for children; able to buy prescribed medicines; regular social contact with other people; medical treatment if needed; secure locks on doors and windows; and a roof and gutters that do not leak. All

Table 6.8: Deprivation item factor loadings

	Component		
	Factor 1: Basic needs and risk protection	Factor 2: Accommodation and household deprivation	Factor 3: Children's needs
Basic needs and risk protection			
Dental treatment if needed	0.749	0.255	0.145
Annual dental check-up (children)	0.691	0.142	0.150
A week's holiday away each year	0.663	0.192	0.225
Up to $500 in emergency savings	0.622	0.263	0.070
Presents for family or friends yearly	0.562	0.243	0.262
Able to buy prescribed medicines	0.561	0.322	0.183
Regular social contact with others	0.473	0.128	0.382
Medical treatment if needed	0.473	−0.027	0.273
Secure locks on doors and windows	0.470	0.102	0.294
Computer skills	0.438	0.045	0.120
A roof and gutters that do not leak	0.429	0.136	0.095
Accommodation and household deprivation			
A telephone	0.144	0.607	0.133
A washing machine	0.000	0.587	0.179
Home contents insurance	0.564	0.578	0.063
Comprehensive motor vehicle insurance	0.437	0.536	−0.062
Furniture in reasonable condition	0.343	0.470	0.126
A decent and secure home	0.427	0.451	0.131
Heating in at least one room	0.260	0.438	0.111
Children's needs			
A substantial meal at least once a day	0.159	0.431	0.430
A separate bed for each child	0.159	0.146	0.672
Warm clothes and bedding if it's cold	0.041	0.433	0.570
Children participate in school activities and outings	0.447	0.066	0.533
Up-to-date school books and new school clothes	0.427	0.096	0.533
A hobby or leisure activity for children	0.496	0.118	0.506
A separate bedroom for children over 10	0.295	0.136	0.448

but one of these items (regular social contact with other people) also appears in the first factor ('health and autonomy') identified in the earlier analysis of the original 26 essential items (see Table 5.2, Chapter Five).

Given this overlap in the results derived from the different methods, a case can be made for prioritising the seven items identified above into an even shorter list. However, this would omit many items that meet important needs (particularly those relating to the needs of children) and would thus provide a restricted perspective on deprivation, and how it affects different Australians.

Thus, while the factor analysis results provide an interesting perspective that confirms some of the earlier findings, they do not add a great deal of new information or insight, or allow the existing information to be presented more economically. The case for rejecting the list of 25 essential items in favour of a sub-set of indicators on the basis of the factor analysis or threshold sensitivity analysis is not compelling and is therefore not pursued further.

An application: deprivation and pension adequacy

Research on the adequacy of income support payments has been of great interest to social security analysts and those who advocate on behalf of the recipients of social security benefits. It has generated intense debate between those who favour higher payments to protect and promote the interests of vulnerable Australians and those who express concern about the budgetary cost of such measures and their impact on incentives to work. Much of this debate has been informed by comparisons between levels of income support payments and poverty lines, but the resulting inferences depend crucially on the confidence attached to poverty lines, which has been shown to be weak.

The Melbourne Institute still publishes quarterly updates of the poverty line developed by the Commission of inquiry into Poverty (1975) – the Henderson poverty line – and compares them with other possible benchmarks, and with levels of social security payments (for example, Melbourne Institute of Applied Economic and Social Research, 2009). As noted earlier, these and other comparisons (for example, those based on percentages of median income) are used by bodies like ACOSS to advocate on behalf of the poor and argue for increased payments, or to even out the variations that favour one group over another (ACOSS, 2003).

As poverty lines have come under increased scrutiny, their use to assess the adequacy of social security payments has also become increasingly problematic. Even when they are used to draw conclusions about the *relative* adequacy of different payments (for example, to single and partnered beneficiaries, or to families with differing numbers of children), the comparisons reflect the balance between the existing payment relativities and the equivalence scale embedded in the poverty lines. Use of a different scale can change the comparisons to favour one group over another, yet the choice of scale is often as arbitrary as the level at which the poverty line itself is set.

The limitations of using poverty lines to establish the adequacy of income support payments were highlighted in the 2009 *Pension review report*, which adopted a broad perspective on the adequacy issue, noting in its report that 'the question of adequacy can be conceived in both absolute and relative terms' and arguing that 'ultimately it needs to be answered in the context of contemporary society, and the living standards of others' (Harmer, 2009, p xiii). Comparisons were drawn between pension rates and various poverty lines (Harmer, 2009,

Charts 5 and 6), although the poverty measures were described as limited because they 'deal poorly with some resources available to households, including the high level of housing assets of older Australians and access to subsidised rents in public housing' (Harmer, 2009, p 35).

In reaching its final determinations on pension adequacy, the report drew on a range of indicators including income benchmarks, budget standards and well-being outcomes. Evidence on deprivation was not given serious attention, even though the living standards and outcome focus that is a feature of deprivation studies have much in common with the overall approach taken by the report.

The insights generated by adopting a deprivation perspective on the adequacy of income support payments can be illustrated by comparing deprivation rates among recipients of different social security payments and other low-income groups, identified on the basis of their main source of income. Table 6.9 lists the income sources identified in the CUPSE community survey and provides a breakdown of the responses in each category. Most of the categories are self-explanatory, although two require further discussion. (It should be noted that the word 'pension' has a generic meaning in the Australian social security system and does not refer only to the age pension paid to retirees, as it does in many other countries. (The Australian Age Pension is paid to those over the eligibility age who also satisfy the income and assets tests.)

Low-wage workers include working-age households containing at least one full-time worker with gross family incomes between $500 and $799 a week. (This range was set to approximate the total income of workers receiving the federal minimum wage, which was equal to $484.50 a week at the time; see Australian Fair Pay Commission, 2006.) The self-funded retirees group includes those aged 65 and over whose main source of income was interest, dividend or superannuation who have been prevented from receiving an Age Pension by the income and assets tests. These two categories were included in the comparisons to provide a broader perspective on the results for those in receipt of a social security benefit.

One specific focus of the *Pension review report* was on the appropriateness of the relativity between payments for single and couple pensioners. This in part

Table 6.9: Income source categories and sample sizes

Main source of income	Sample breakdown	
	Numbers	%
Earnings (low-wage workers)	205	24.9
Interest (self-funded retirees)	98	11.9
Age Pension	320	38.8
Service Pension (paid to war veterans)	48	5.8
Disability Support Pension	76	9.2
Parenting Payment Single (lone parents)	38	4.6
Newstart Allowance	39	4.7
Total sample	**824**	**100.0**

reflected the political controversy about the (in)adequacy of the single rate of pension that had led to the establishment of the Review that produced the report (see Saunders and Wong, 2008, 2011: forthcoming). Attention was also directed to the payments to pensioners in different circumstances and to illustrate these issues, the age pensioner groups identified in Table 6.9 were further disaggregated into the sub-groups shown in Table 6.10. Sample size is small for some of the disaggregated groupings, particularly since not every sample member provided all of the information required to conduct the comparisons. However, the data can be used to illustrate how the deprivation approach can assist in assessing income adequacy without using a poverty line or having to select an equivalence scale.

The number of essential items used to compare deprivation among the groups identified in Tables 6.9 and 6.10 was reduced to 19 by excluding, in addition to the television set, the six items that relate specifically to the needs of children. The child items were removed because they are not relevant to Age Pension recipients and, as noted earlier, because the inclusion of items relating to the needs of children creates difficulties when comparing deprivation scores between those with and without children.

The resulting mean deprivation scores and multiple deprivation incidence rates are compared in Table 6.11 across the income source categories identified in Table 6.9, while the comparisons within the age pensioner categories defined in Table 6.10 are shown in Table 6.12. The estimates are illustrated in Figures 6.5 and 6.6 respectively, where the incidence of multiple deprivation is defined as missing out on four or more items.

The results in Table 6.11 indicate that, on average, the self-funded retiree group experiences very little deprivation (mean deprivation score = 0.09), whereas those receiving either an Age Pension or a Service Pension are deprived of about one essential item on average, and low-wage workers are deprived of around two items

Table 6.10: Sub-categories within the age pensioner group

	Sample breakdown	
Sub-category	**Numbers**	**%**
Gender		
Male	145	45.3
Female	175	54.7
Age		
Up to 74 years	200	62.5
75 and over	120	37.5
Living arrangement		
Single, lives alone	102	37.8
Married, lives as couple	168	62.2
Housing tenure		
Owner/purchaser	241	83.4
Renter (public or private)	48	16.6

Table 6.11: Deprivation mean scores and multiple incidence rates, by income source

	Income category:						
Indicator	Earnings (low-wage workers)	Interest (self-funded retirees)	Age Pension	Service Pension	Disability Support Pension	Parenting Payment Single	Newstart Allowance
Mean deprivation index score							
	2.14	0.09	1.0	0.87	3.01	5.00	4.18
Incidence of multiple deprivation (number of items lacking and unaffordable)							
0	43.1	93.9	61.3	71.7	24.3	7.9	12.8
At least 1	56.9	6.1	38.7	28.3	75.7	92.1	87.2
At least 2	44.5	2.0	21.2	28.3	59.5	76.3	74.4
At least 3	31.7	1.0	14.7	15.2	48.6	73.7	66.7
At least 4	23.8	0.0	9.8	8.7	32.4	63.2	59.0

Note: Percentages are expressed after omitting missing values.

Table 6.12: Deprivation mean scores and multiple incidence rates among age pensioners

	Gender:		Age:		Living arrangement:		Housing tenure:	
	Male	Female	Under 75	75 and over	Lives alone	Lives as a couple	Owner/ purchaser	Renter
Mean deprivation index score								
	0.87	1.10	1.21	0.61*	1.34	0.72**	0.68	2.56**
Incidence of multiple deprivation (number of items lacking and unaffordable)								
0	64.7	58.3	56.4	69.6	54.1	65.8	68.7	20.9
At least 1	35.2	41.7	43.6	30.4	45.9	34.1	31.3	79.1
At least 2	19.4	22.6	26.7	11.6	29.6	14.6	14.6	53.5
At least 3	12.9	16.1	17.9	8.9	21.4	9.8	9.9	39.5
At least 4	8.6	10.7	12.3	5.4*	14.3	6.7*	5.6	27.9**

Note: The asterisks (*/**) indicate that the deprivation differences between the two categories are statistically significant ($p = 0.05/0.01$).

on average. Disability pensioners are deprived of about three items on average, while those receiving Parenting Payment Single (restricted here to cover lone parents only) and Newstart Allowance (paid to the unemployed) are deprived of more than four items on average.

In terms of their inability to buy items that a majority of the community regard as essential for everyone, these results thus suggest that on average, age pensioners are more deprived than self-funded retirees (as is to be expected given the means-tested nature of the Australian pension system). Age pensioners face a similar degree of deprivation to those receiving a Service Pension, but are considerably

Figure 6.5: Comparing deprivation between income source categories

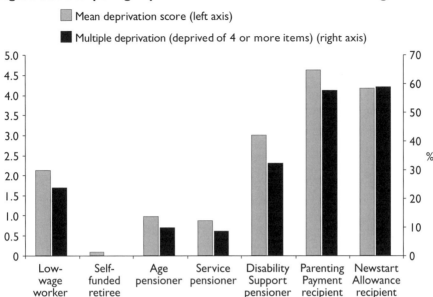

Figure 6.6: Comparing deprivation between age pensioner categories

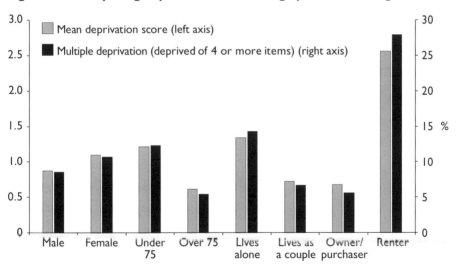

better off than low-wage workers and those receiving a social security benefit on account of disability, lone parenthood or unemployment.

The ranking of groups by the incidence of multiple deprivation is similar to that based on the mean index scores and this result is unaffected if multiple deprivation is based on missing out on two instead of four items. When the indicator is based on the harsher definition, the incidence of deprivation in the community sample as a whole is 14.2% – around one in seven (see Table 6.3). Table 6.11 indicates that none of the self-funded retiree group faces this degree of multiple deprivation, whereas around 10% of those receiving the Age Pension and Service Pension, close to one quarter of low-wage workers, almost one third of disability pensioners and well over one half of those receiving Parenting Payment Single and Newstart Allowance are deprived of at least four essential items.

Those in these last two categories face a level of multiple deprivation that is above the average experienced by the welfare client samples in either 2006 or 2008 (see Table 6.3). In terms of income adequacy, the results in Table 6.11 thus suggest that while some receiving Age Pension are facing severe deprivation, this problem is much more common among other groups of social security recipients.

Table 6.12 presents the mean deprivation scores and incidence of multiple deprivation across the age pensioner sub-categories differentiated on the basis of gender, age, living arrangements and housing tenure. As noted earlier, some of these differentiations result in small samples and the statistical significance of the observed differences has been indicated.

The differences in mean deprivation scores are statistically significant when the groups are differentiated by age, living arrangement and housing tenure, but not when they are differentiated by gender. Although the difference is not statistically significant, female pensioners have a deprivation score that is more than one quarter (26.4%) above that for males, despite the fact that female pensioners are on average older than males and that deprivation tends to decline with age, being only half as high for those aged 75 and over than for those aged under 75.

The difference in mean deprivation scores between pensioners living alone and those living with their partner is large and statistically significant. However, by far the largest difference relates to housing tenure: those receiving Age Pension who are renting their homes have a mean deprivation score that is almost four times higher than those who either own their home outright or are paying off a mortgage (the vast majority of whom are outright owners). The level of deprivation among this group is two-and-a-half times higher than the average for all age pensioners and approaching the level experienced by those receiving a disability pension.

Tests of the statistical significance of the estimates have only been applied to one of the indicators of multiple deprivation – the incidence of four or more items – since the patterns are again similar across the different indicators. The patterns displayed by these results is again similar to those for the mean deprivation scores, and the differences are again statistically significant between groups differentiated by age, living arrangements and housing tenure, but not for those differentiated by gender.

These results illustrate how the deprivation approach is capable of providing valuable information that can be used to assess and compare the adequacy of the incomes received by different groups. This information is a vital ingredient into decisions about the setting of income support payments (including the payment relativities for different groups). The results provide clear guidance to where increases in benefit rates should be targeted if the goal is to reduce existing levels of deprivation among recipients. They can also assist in the determination of the level of minimum wages and the design of the income test that affects benefits received when there is other income. Unlike poverty lines, deprivation indicators tap more directly into the living standards actually attained by different groups without the need to set a poverty line threshold or to choose an equivalence scale. Although they are not perfect – no such indicator ever will be – the results illustrate how a deprivation approach can inform assessments of living standards and income adequacy in ways that poverty lines cannot.

Summary

This chapter presents the first Australian estimates of deprivation in Australia and examines variations in the level of deprivation using mean scores, and differences in the incidence of multiple deprivation. The estimates provide a new perspective on the material dimension of social disadvantage and how it varies between groups differentiated by socioeconomic characteristics such as age, location, educational attainment, housing tenure, disability and Indigenous status. The variations in deprivation between these groups highlight a dimension of inequality that is closely related to living standards differentials.

Statistical examination of the original 26 deprivation items suggests that only one item (a television set) can be dropped without affecting the cohesiveness of the list of items, and that it is possible to identify sub-sets of items that group together in ways that correspond to the domains that emerged from the focus groups discussions described in Chapter Four. Factor analysis has been used in other countries to identify a set of core items that can capture the central features of deprivation. Previous Australian studies have used such analysis to identify broad areas of financial stress and when that approach is used to restrict the list of deprivation items, it produces results that are similar to those produced by setting a higher threshold of support to identify essential items.

Estimates of deprivation can shed important light on the adequacy of different forms of income, including social security payments. The results in the previous section show that deprivation among those above pension age who are not eligible to receive a pension because of the income or assets tests (self-funded retirees) is far lower than that among age pensioners, confirming that the means tests are successful in preventing those with resources of their own from accessing the public pension system.

However, the results also show that, among social security recipients, age pensioners face a lower level of deprivation on average than those who are receiving support because of disability, lone parenthood or unemployment. They also reveal large differences in deprivation among those receiving an Age Pension, with those aged under 75, living alone and in rental accommodation being most deprived. These latter results suggest that the political attention that was directed in 2008 and 2009 at highlighting, and then addressing the inadequacy of the single rate of Age Pension would have been better directed at improving the adequacy of other payments in the social security system, and improving the targeting of the Age Pension itself.

Overall, the results in this chapter show that the deprivation approach can be implemented in practice to produce sensible and stable results. These results can be used to shed important new light on patterns of social disadvantage and provide an evidence base for reform designed to improve the adequacy of social benefits and to reduce living standard inequalities.

SEVEN

A new poverty measure

Introduction

The previous two chapters have applied the deprivation approach using Australian survey data, identified the essentials of life, examined the deprivation profile, assessed the sensitivity of the findings to changes in the methods used to derive them and illustrated their relevance with an example. This chapter extends earlier work by Saunders and Naidoo (2009) to compare the deprivation estimates with poverty rates estimated from the same data, focusing on how they differ and where they overlap. It then combines information on deprivation and poverty to produce a new poverty measure to complement the existing income-based measures (poverty lines) that were shown earlier to contain important weaknesses.

The analysis begins by comparing differences in the profiles of deprivation and poverty and then examines the incidence of specific forms of deprivation among those who are identified as being deprived or poor. The results indicate that deprivation and poverty capture different aspects of social disadvantage, but this alone does not indicate which is the better indicator. In order to address this issue, the relationship between each of them and a series of indicators of subjective well-being is investigated. This analysis is predicated on the view that a good indicator of social disadvantage should be able to predict poor well-being outcomes among those it identifies as disadvantaged.

These results suggest that deprivation provides a sounder basis for identifying disadvantage than comparing incomes with a poverty line. This does not mean that poverty studies should be abandoned and replaced by deprivation studies, since it has already been argued (in Chapter Two) that poverty line studies have much to contribute to an understanding of the risk of experiencing social disadvantage. Such studies are best viewed as part of a broader attempt to identify how different dimensions of disadvantage translate into standards of living that fail to meet community standards of acceptability.

An examination of the overlap between poverty and deprivation provides the point of departure for the development of an approach that combines evidence on low income and poor outcomes in terms of living standards. The resulting notion of consistent poverty is then applied to produce new estimates of the extent and nature of poverty in contemporary Australia.

The profiles of deprivation and poverty

In order to compare deprivation and poverty, it is necessary to develop specific empirical definitions of both concepts. Although these definitions are inevitably somewhat arbitrary, the impact of applying alternative definitions can be assessed using sensitivity analysis. In practice, this involves measuring poverty using poverty lines set at different percentages of median (equivalised) income, as was done in earlier chapters. Alternative definitions of deprivation are derived by varying the level of support used to identify essential items, and by varying the number of essential items that individuals are forced to go without when identifying deprivation.

The threshold level of support used to identify essential items is set (as before) at either 50% or 90%, while the number of items foregone that define deprivation is varied between two and four. For some purposes, it is convenient to adopt definitions that result in similar poverty and deprivation rates, because this allows the extent of overlap and difference to be established more consistently. The precise definitions used are described at each stage of the analysis, along with the justification for the option selected.

The analysis commences by showing, in the first two columns of Table 7.1, the mean deprivation scores of different groups based on the number of items regarded as essential by 50% (DEP50) and 90% (DEP90) of the community sample. The next two columns show the incidence of multiple deprivation, defined as being deprived of at least four of the 25 DEP50 items, or at least two of the 12 DEP90 items, respectively. These combinations of definitions of essential items and multiple deprivation have been chosen to produce overall rates (shown in the final row of Table 7.1) that are close to the estimated income poverty rate of 14.4% shown in the lower right-hand side corner cell.

This poverty rate is higher than that presented in Chapter Two because it has been derived from the information on income reported in the CUPSE Survey that is less accurate than the ABS income data that were used to generate the poverty estimates presented in Chapters Two and Three. The main role of the poverty estimates in this chapter is to provide a basis for *comparing* the estimates produced using different indicators for different groups, and the CUPSE income data, while imperfect, are robust enough to serve this purpose.

Information on gross (before tax) income was collected in the CUPSE Survey in ranges in order to minimise non-response because individuals are known to be reluctant to provide details of their incomes in surveys. In order to derive a precise estimate, income was set at the mid-point of the designated range and an imputed estimate of income tax payments was deducted in order to derive disposable (after tax) income. Each step in this process is likely to induce errors and as a consequence the poverty estimates will be somewhat imprecise, although this should not affect the broad conclusions derived from the analysis.

Because the mean deprivation scores in Table 7.1 have been presented and discussed earlier (see Table 6.4 in Chapter Six), the following discussion focuses

Table 7.1: The socioeconomic profiles of deprivation and poverty

Household characteristic	Mean deprivation score (unweighted)		Incidence of multiple deprivation (%)		Poverty rate (<50% median income)
	DEP50	DEP90	DEP50 ≥4	DEP90 ≥2	
Age					
Under 30	2.00	0.75	21.4	18.5	21.2
30-64	1.45	0.59	15.2	14.8	11.8
65 and over	0.87	0.35	8.5	8.0	18.8
Family type					
Single, working age	1.40	0.86	25.0	20.3	9.2
Older person	1.32	0.59	13.0	12.3	7.8
Working-age couple, no children	0.86	0.33	7.9	9.1	3.4
Older couple	0.56	0.19	5.6	4.9	14.1
Working-age couple, with children	1.30	0.52	13.6	13.5	15.4
Lone-parent family	3.55	1.58	40.4	39.7	28.9
Principal source of income					
Wages or interest	1.06	0.43	10.8	10.8	6.6
Social security payment	2.42	0.96	27.0	22.9	33.3
Educational attainment					
High school or below	1.75	0.70	18.7	17.6	18.4
Trade certificate	1.28	0.56	13.3	13.6	12.0
University	0.80	0.30	7.5	6.8	12.0
Housing tenure					
Owner/purchaser	0.82	0.33	7.8	8.4	9.9
Private renter	3.46	1.40	39.4	34.6	20.9
Public renter	4.07	1.60	47.4	38.5	37.5
Indigenous/ATSI					
Yes	5.60	2.00	60.0	50.0	38.1
No	1.36	0.54	14.1	13.5	14.1
Has an ongoing disability					
Yes	2.06	0.85	22.9	21.4	25.1
No	1.25	0.50	12.8	12.2	11.9
All households:	**1.40**	**0.56**	**14.6**	**13.9**	**14.4**

mainly on the results for multiple deprivation (which forms the basis of later analysis). The general patterns displayed by both multiple deprivation indicators (based on DEP50≥4 and DEP90≥2) are similar, although the gap between them is widest for those groups that are most susceptible to severe deprivation, including single working-age people, those reliant on a social security payment, public and private renters and Indigenous Australians. Multiple deprivation is more severe among all of these groups when the DEP50≥4 indicator is used.

The final column of Table 7.1 shows the poverty rates, derived by comparing equivalised disposable income with a poverty line set at 50% of median equivalised income (derived using the modified OECD scale). There are some important differences between these group-specific poverty rates and the incidence of multiple deprivation, even though the specifications were deliberately chosen to produce similar *overall* incidence rates. In general, the gap between the multiple deprivation and poverty rates is largest for those groups that have the highest poverty rates. Thus, the incidence of multiple deprivation is considerably higher than the poverty rate among single working-age people, lone-parent families, renters (public and private) and Indigenous Australians.

In contrast, the incidence of multiple deprivation is below the poverty rate for older people, particularly older couples, those with a university degree and (to a lesser extent) those mainly reliant on a social security payment. The latter finding reflects the large number of age pensioners in the CUPSE sample, and the bunching together of social security recipients just below the poverty line. The latter confirms the earlier observation that this bunching can lead to estimates of the degree of social disadvantage among social security recipients that are highly sensitive to where the poverty line is set. These differences provide the first clear evidence that the identification of which groups are most disadvantaged is sensitive to whether unmet need is assessed by comparing income with a poverty line, or is based on the reported inability to afford items regarded as essential by a majority of the community.

Tables 7.2 and 7.3 compare the deprivation incidence rates of each of the 25 essential items for households classified by their deprivation and poverty status, respectively. Multiple deprivation is now defined as experiencing an enforced lack of at least two items for both DEP50 and DEP90 indicators, while poverty is defined as having an income below poverty lines set at 50% and 60% of median income. These definitions have been selected to produce similar estimates of deprivation and poverty (shown in the top rows of each table), because the focus is now on comparing patterns among similar numbers of households identified as disadvantaged using different indicators. This also explains why the estimates based on the higher poverty line are presented first in Table 7.3.

This approach allows the estimates derived from alternative approaches to be compared, while assessing the sensitivity of the comparisons and examining how well the classifications discriminate between households based on their deprivation and poverty status. It is specifically designed to identify the sub-set of items that best predicts overall deprivation status, and draws on studies undertaken by McKay and Collard (2003) and Whelan, Nolan and Maître (2008) that apply a similar approach using British and EU-SILC data, respectively.

The individual items are listed in Tables 7.2 and 7.3 in increasing order of the strength of community support for them being essential. The results highlight the importance of distinguishing between items on the basis of the *degree of support* for

Table 7.2: The incidence of deprivation items by deprivation status

	DEP50		DEP90	
		Not		Not
	Deprived	deprived	Deprived	deprived
Item	DEP50≥2	DEP50<2	DEP90≥2	DEP90<2
Overall incidence rate:	**27.0**	**73.0**	**14.0**	**86.0**
Medical treatment, if needed	7.2	0.1	13.3	0.2
Warm clothes and bedding if it's cold	0.8	0.0	1.5	0.0
A substantial meal at least once a day	4.0	0.0	7.4	0.0
Able to buy medicines prescribed by a doctor	14.7	0.1	26.9	0.3
Dental treatment, if needed	49.2	1.0	76.7	3.6
A decent and secure home	22.8	0.9	33.2	2.4
Children can participate in school activities and outings	12.3	0.2	20.3	0.6
A yearly dental check-up for children	33.2	0.4	56.0	1.2
A hobby or leisure activity for children	20.0	0.3	31.8	1.0
Regular social contact with other people	17.7	0.1	29.4	0.8
Secure locks on doors and windows	18.2	0.3	28.4	1.3
A roof and gutters that do not leak	15.9	0.6	24.1	1.5
Furniture in reasonable condition	9.3	0.2	13.9	0.8
Up-to-date school books/clothes for children	12.7	0.3	18.8	1.1
Heating in at least one room of the house	6.5	0.1	8.6	0.7
A separate bed for each child	5.5	0.1	6.2	0.7
A telephone	5.5	0.1	6.5	0.7
Up to $500 in savings for an emergency	56.2	3.5	59.2	11.0
A washing machine	2.9	0.1	4.1	0.3
Home contents insurance	33.4	0.9	41.8	4.5
Presents for family or friends at least once a year	24.6	0.1	33.3	2.4
Computer skills	18.0	0.4	22.3	2.4
Comprehensive motor vehicle insurance	28.7	1.6	30.8	5.3
A week's holiday away from home each year	70.4	4.7	72.4	14.5
A separate bedroom for each child over 10	18.7	1.6	22.3	3.5

them being essential, and on the basis of their *rates of deprivation*. With one exception (access to dental treatment if needed) the six items where deprivation is highest (shown in shading) are not the same as those regarded as most essential (the first six entries in the list of items). In fact, using the more restrictive deprivation measure DEP90, the average individual item incidence rate is *higher* for the 13 items not included as essential on this definition (those below the dotted line in the first column), than for the 12 items that are essential (shown above the dotted line).

It is also clear that the deprivation classifications in Table 7.2 provide a clearer demarcation between the individual item deprivation rates then the poverty classifications based on income in Table 7.3. This is the case for those items where deprivation is high overall (for example, dental treatment, if needed), as well as for those items where deprivation is much lower (for example, a substantial daily meal). This suggests that the deprivation approach provides a better basis for

Table 7.3: The incidence of deprivation items by poverty status

Item	Poverty line set at 60% of median income		Poverty line set at 50% of median income	
	Poor	Not poor	Poor	Not poor
Overall incidence rate:	**23.8**	**76.2**	**14.4**	**85.6**
Medical treatment, if needed	4.3	1.3	4.3	1.6
Warm clothes and bedding if it's cold	0.6	0.1	0.6	0.1
A substantial meal at least once a day	3.4	0.4	4.2	0.6
Able to buy medicines prescribed by a doctor	9.4	2.5	10.8	2.9
Dental treatment, if needed	29.2	9.6	30.8	11.3
A decent and secure home	15.3	4.1	17.2	5.0
Children can participate in school activities and outings	9.6	1.7	10.5	2.3
A yearly dental check-up for children	18.6	6.5	20.1	7.3
A hobby or leisure activity for children	15.1	2.9	17.4	3.7
Regular social contact with other people	10.8	3.0	12.6	3.5
Secure locks on doors and windows	10.6	3.6	12.5	4.0
A roof and gutters that do not leak	9.7	3.3	11.8	3.6
Furniture in reasonable condition	5.9	1.7	6.2	2.1
Up-to-date school books/clothes for children	10.1	1.9	11.9	2.4
Heating in at least one room of the house	3.4	1.3	3.9	1.4
A separate bed for each child	4.5	0.7	5.2	1.0
A telephone	3.6	0.9	4.3	1.1
Up to $500 in savings for an emergency	31.6	13.9	32.5	15.5
A washing machine	1.7	0.6	2.2	0.6
Home contents insurance	21.2	6.3	22.3	7.7
Presents for family or friends at least once a year	17.1	3.7	19.3	4.7
Computer skills	14.4	2.6	15.3	3.6
Comprehensive motor vehicle insurance	21.9	5.1	25.9	6.2
A week's holiday away from home each year	43.6	16.7	45.0	19.2
A separate bedroom for each child over 10	12.7	4.6	13.1	5.3

identifying who is actually experiencing a poverty-level standard of living than an approach based on comparing income with a poverty line. This conclusion is even stronger for the results based on the broader deprivation indicator (DEP50) than for those based on the DEP90 measure, because the latter measure excludes many people who face high rates of deprivation in specific instances.

Table 7.3 shows that many of those with incomes above the poverty line are more likely to be deprived of specific items than those identified as not deprived in Table 7.2. The extent of this problem is not reduced when the poverty line is lowered from 60% to 50% of median income; if anything, it gets worse. It is difficult to condone a poverty measure that fails to identify as poor those who cannot afford items that are widely regarded as things that no one should have to go without.

Poverty, deprivation and well-being

One property that all indicators of disadvantage should possess is the ability to track differences in well-being. At the individual level, one would expect to find lower levels of well-being among those identified as poor or deprived than among those not so identified. However, two factors may compound this relationship: first, individuals differ in the way that the objective conditions they experience affect their subjective assessment of their well-being (and possibly also their willingness to acknowledge this when asked in surveys); second, there is no definitive way of distinguishing between those who are poor (or deprived) and those who are not, leading to some incorrect classifications that will affect the mean well-being scores of those identified as being in different disadvantaged states.

Even so, the better the indicator is able to separate those who are disadvantaged from those who are not, the clearer the well-being differential should be between those who fall on either side of the dividing line. This suggests that it is possible to gain an insight into the ranking of alternative disadvantage indicators by comparing how well they segregate people according to their expressed level of subjective well-being. Table 7.4 explores this idea by comparing the values of a range of indicators of subjective well-being (defined in the notes to Table 7.4) for people classified by whether they are identified as deprived or poor by the indicators used in Tables 7.2 and 7.3.

The results provide an interesting insight into the relationship between whether or not people are identified as disadvantaged using alternative objective measures and differences in several dimensions of their subjective well-being. Thus, for example, while around 37% of those who are deprived of two or more essential items indicate that their standard of living is fairly or very low, this is true of only around 5% of those who are not identified as deprived on this measure. And while just under one third of those with incomes below the 50% of median income poverty line regard themselves as poor, this is also true for just over 9% of those with incomes above that poverty line.

The estimates shown on the right-hand side of Table 7.4, based on the more restrictive measures of deprivation and poverty, display lower average levels of well-being among both the disadvantaged and not disadvantaged groups than those on the left-hand side of the table. This is because some of those who were least disadvantaged among the group identified as disadvantaged using the less restrictive measures are shifted into the not disadvantaged group when the definition is tightened. This reduces the average level of well-being of those who remain disadvantaged, while also pulling down the average level of well-being of the larger pool of people who are now identified as not disadvantaged.

Thus, for example, when the poverty line is shifted downwards from 60% to 50% of median income, households with incomes between 50% and 60% of the

Table 7.4: Indicators of subjective well-being by deprivation and poverty status

Well-being domain/ indicator	DEP50			DEP90		
	Deprived DEP50≥2	Not deprived DEP50<2	Ratio	Deprived DEP90≥2	Not deprived DEP90<2	Ratio
Life satisfaction						
Standard of living is low	36.7	4.7	7.81	46.3	8.0	5.79
Dissatisfied with standard of living	34.7	5.4	6.43	43.5	8.4	5.18
Financial well-being						
Dissatisfied with financial situation	41.8	5.4	7.74	52.6	9.1	5.78
Regards self/family as poor	36.2	4.2	8.62	48.0	7.1	6.76
Does not have enough to get by on	16.7	2.6	6.42	24.2	3.5	6.91
	60% median			50% median		
	Poor	Not poor	Ratio	Poor	Not poor	Ratio
Life satisfaction						
Standard of living is low	29.9	8.2	3.65	32.5	10.1	3.22
Dissatisfied with standard of living	24.8	9.7	2.56	25.9	11.1	2.33
Financial well-being						
Dissatisfied with financial situation	31.3	10.4	3.01	33.4	12.3	2.72
Regards self/family as poor	30.8	7.3	4.22	32.9	9.4	3.50
Does not have enough to get by on	14.4	3.9	3.69	16.0	4.8	3.33

Notes: The first and second well-being indicators are based on questions that provide five possible responses, ranging from very high/very satisfied to very low/very dissatisfied and show the percentages in the lowest two categories (fairly or very low, or dissatisfied). The third indicator is based on responses to a 10-point scale ranging from very dissatisfied (= 1) to very satisfied (= 10), and shows the percentages with a score of three or less. The fifth indicator is based on Yes/No responses to the question 'Would you describe you/your family as poor?', while the fifth indicator is based on responses to a four-option income managing question.

median are shifted out of the disadvantaged group and into the not disadvantaged group. Since the average level of well-being among this group is likely to be above those with incomes below 50% of the median but below that of those with incomes above 60% of the median, the shift results in an increase in average well-being among both disadvantaged and not disadvantaged groups.

What is most interesting about the results in Table 7.4 is not how sensitive well-being is to where the benchmark for identifying poverty or deprivation is set, but how well the alternative indicators used to identify disadvantage are able to capture differences in subjective well-being. This issue is explored, following Saunders and Zhu (2009), by comparing the average well-being ratios for those identified as disadvantaged on the basis of their incomes (poverty) and on the basis of their living standards (deprivation).

When the well-being ratios in columns 3 and 6 of Table 7.4 are compared, it is clear that identifying disadvantage on the basis of deprivation status is better able to capture differences in well-being than identifying disadvantage on the basis of poverty status. For example, those identified as deprived are between 6.8 and 8.6 times more likely to think that they are poor than those not deprived, whereas those with income below a poverty line are only between 3.5 and 4.2 times more likely to think that they are poor than those with incomes above the line.

The deprivation-based well-being ratios in Table 7.4 are consistently higher than those based on poverty, and the generally low values of the latter cast further doubt on the use of income alone to establish whether or not disadvantage exists. It is also of interest to note that the ratios are lower in both cases when the more restrictive definitions are used to identify disadvantage. This suggests that these measures are probably too restrictive, because they classify as not poor or deprived many people whose low level of well-being suggests that they are experiencing disadvantage and doing it tough. A similar decline is evident when the more restrictive poverty line is used, although the impact in this case is much smaller.

The clear message that emerges from this analysis is that identifying disadvantage using a deprivation approach is better able to capture what Bradshaw and Finch (2003) argue is a desirable feature of any poverty measure – that it is able to identify those who perceive themselves to have a low level of well-being and are struggling financially.

Predicting the risk of poverty and deprivation

It is common to present results on the profiles of disadvantage in the form shown in Table 7.1, that is, by comparing poverty and/or deprivation rates experienced by different sub-groups in the population. Such presentations provide a useful summary of the risks facing different groups and the resulting comparisons can help to highlight where problems are most pressing and where policy intervention is most urgently needed. However, the estimates are based on a series of independent classifications of individuals based on each characteristic, whereas in reality individuals have characteristics that place them into several groups simultaneously – a younger, unemployed, Indigenous private renter, for example. In order to calculate the marginal risks of being disadvantaged associated with each specific characteristic (that is, being unemployed, or an Indigenous Australian), it is necessary to isolate the impact of each effect using multivariate analysis.

The method normally adopted for this purpose is regression analysis, since this allows the impact of each identified characteristic to be quantified holding constant the impact arising from all other characteristics. The regression approach has been applied in this context by Wilkins (2008) to identify the determinants of poverty in Australia, and by Nolan and Whelan (1996) and Halleröd et al (2006) to explain differences in deprivation scores within and between countries.

Although the most common form of regression analysis is ordinary least squares (OLS), this approach is not appropriate when the dependent variable is dichotomous (that is, whether or not someone is poor or deprived), or has a restricted range (that is, mean deprivation scores), because these variables do not conform with the assumptions that underlie the standard OLS model. An alternative estimation method that is appropriate when the dependent variable is dichotomous is probit analysis, and the specifications described below were estimated using both OLS and probit methods to assess how much of an impact the choice of estimation technique has on the results produced. In broad terms, the answer to this question is 'not much' – at least in relation to the statistical significance of different variables and the ability of the models to explain the variation in different indicators of disadvantage. Because of their greater theoretical appropriateness, only the estimates derived from the probit regressions are presented and discussed.

The aim of the regression analysis is not to develop a rigorous structural model that is capable of identifying the causal determinants of poverty and deprivation, but to compare how well the alternative indicators of disadvantage are correlated with variables that are known from previous research to increase the likelihood of experiencing disadvantage, or are a likely outcome of that experience. The focus is thus primarily on *comparing* the poverty and deprivation indicators in terms of their ability to be statistically related to variables known to be associated with disadvantage. While not definitive, the regression findings will add to the mounting array of evidence being used to discriminate between the two indicators that will help to establish which approach is superior.

In light of these considerations, the regression modelling was applied with the aim of identifying a common set of variables that are strongly associated with variations in poverty and deprivation. Initial experimentation included a large number of variables that capture differences in the individual (and household) characteristics thought to be associated with disadvantage, with variables being dropped if they did not show up as statistically significant across a range of specifications. The variables included in the final regression results that formed the basis of the comparisons are defined in Table 7.5, which also shows the (community) sample mean values of each variable.

Where the variables are defined dichotomously, the sample means in Table 7.5 indicate the percentage of the sample that has each characteristic. Thus, the mean value of 0.272 for the variable ASSETS indicates that 27.2% of the sample did not have assets of at least $50,000, while the mean value of 0.129 for SUBPOV indicates that 12.9% of the sample identified themselves or their family as being poor. The sample means of other variables have to be interpreted differently so that, for example, the mean of 0.737 for GONEWO indicates that on average, respondents missed out on less than one of the 10 items specified in the question, while the mean of 5.879 for FINSAT shows where the average respondent placed themselves on the 10-point financial satisfaction scale.

One variable that is not shown in Table 7.5, but was included in the initial modelling, was whether or not the respondent was a lone parent. Despite the fact that the descriptive results in Table 7.1 (and in earlier tables) show that lone parents face a high risk of exposure to both poverty and deprivation, the estimated parameter on this variable, while significant initially, became insignificant when other variables were included in the model. This probably reflects the collinearity

Table 7.5: Specification of variables employed in the regression analysis

Variable name	Specification and definition	Mean value
Dependent variables		
DEPST	Deprivation status = 1 if deprived of four or more items (based on DEP50), = 0 otherwise	0.142
POVST	Poverty status = 1 if income below the poverty line (50% of median income), = 0 otherwise	0.144
Independent variables		
ASSETS	Ownership of assets = 1 if assets less than $50,000, = 0 otherwise	0.272
NOSAVING	Ability to raise $2,000 in a week in an emergency = 1 if cannot, = 0 otherwise	0.142
GONEWO	Number of adverse events (out of 10) experienced in the last year due to a shortage of money. Events are: gone without food when hungry; got behind with rent or mortgage; moved house because rent/mortgage was too high; couldn't keep up with utility bills; had to pawn or sell something or borrow money from a money lender; had to ask a welfare agency for assistance; wore bad-fitting or worn-out clothes; couldn't go out with friends and pay one's way; unable to attend a wedding or funeral; couldn't get to an important event because of lack of transport	0.737
NOHLTH	Number of health-related items (out of three) that could not be afforded in the last year. Items are: see a doctor when self or family member was sick; see a dentist when self or family member needed to; unable to afford medicines prescribed by a doctor	0.212
NOTREAT	Special treat = 1 if had not spent $100 or more on a special treat for self in the last year, = 0 otherwise	0.301
INCMAN	Ability to manage on current income = 1 if does not have enough to get by, = 0 otherwise	0.422
FINSAT	Financial satisfaction: score on a 10-point scale measuring satisfaction with financial situation where 1-3 = very dissatisfied and 9-10 = very satisfied	5.879
SUBPOV	Subjective poverty status = 1 if assesses self as poor, = 0 otherwise	0.129
UNEMP	Unemployment status =1 if unemployed, = 0 otherwise	0.039
OLDERAGE	Age, in years = 1 if age 65 or over, = 0 otherwise	0.217
NESC	Country of birth = 1 if born in a non-English-speaking country, = 0 otherwise	0.108
ATSI	Indigenous status = 1 if indigenous, = 0 otherwise	0.008
PRIVREN	Renter status =1 if renting privately, = 0 otherwise	0.136

between lone parenthood and some of the other variables, although it may also be a consequence of other unidentified factors.

Another variable that was omitted after initial experimentation was the level of (equivalised) income. This variable was highly significant in the initial specification, but was rejected by more complex specifications of the model because it is so highly correlated with the poverty rate. Income also appeared as statistically significant in the initial specifications of the deprivation model (an issue that is examined further below), but again became insignificant once other variables were included in the model.

In order to provide an overview of the results, the output generated by four specifications is presented in Table 7.6. The first specification includes a small number of variables that capture the level of economic resources available to the household, including its assets and access to savings. The initial specification was extended in the second specification to include four variables that reflect limited access to resources and a lack of discretionary spending power – three relating to going without important items, the fourth reflecting reported difficulty making ends meet. The third specification adds variables that measure the adverse impact of disadvantage on two aspects of subjective well-being – satisfaction with one's financial status, and whether or not one regards oneself as poor. The final specification also includes some of the demographic variables shown to be closely associated with poverty and deprivation in the earlier analysis (Table 7.1).

These last two extensions initially included more variables than are shown in the reported results in Table 7.6. Inspection of the preliminary results revealed a consistent pattern of performance across the alternative specifications (and between the probit and OLS estimations) and the variables that did not perform well were therefore dropped from all four specifications in order to strengthen the basis for the comparisons.

As before, the dependent variables were specified so that they each resulted in a similar estimate of the overall extent of disadvantage. Using a poverty line set at 50% of median income, the poverty rate was estimated to be 14.4% (see Table 7.1), so the number of items used to identify deprivation was chosen to produce a deprivation rate that is as close as possible to this estimate. This resulted in deprivation being defined as missing out on four or more items, a definition that produced a deprivation rate of 14.2% – slightly below the figure shown in Table 7.1 because the sample is now restricted to those for whom it is possible to identify both their poverty and deprivation status.

Virtually all of the estimated parameters shown in Table 7.6 are statistically significant, although this is partly a reflection of the selection process used. Even so, the results indicate that it is possible to explain a considerable amount of the variation in different indicators of disadvantage using a relatively small number of variables. Interest focuses on comparing the statistical significance of the variables in the alternative models, and their overall explanatory power.

A summary indication of explanatory power is provided by the likelihood ratio (LR) Chi-squared test statistic and the pseudo R^2 shown in the penultimate

Table 7.6: Probit estimates of deprivation and poverty status models

Independent variable	Dependent variable: DEPST				Dependent variable: POVST			
Intercept	−1.76** (34.10)	−2.50** (26.42)	−1.49** (7.43)	−1.60** (7.60)	−1.38** (32.27)	−1.60** (28.87)	−1.21** (7.64)	−1.34** (8.17)
ASSETS	1.01** (14.06)	0.65** (7.38)	0.56** (6.14)	0.48** (4.85)	0.47** (6.56)	0.31** (4.03)	0.28** (3.44)	0.26** (3.08)
NOSAVING	1.23** (15.07)	0.54** (5.40)	0.46** (4.49)	0.44** (4.10)	0.74** (8.92)	0.52** (5.43)	0.48** (4.90)	0.46** (4.53)
GONEWO		0.27** (8.50)	0.22** (6.58)	0.19** (5.27)		0.51 (1.80)	0.02 (0.55)	0.05 (1.49)
NOHLTH		0.52** (7.45)	0.46** (6.40)	0.45** (6.09)		−0.09 (1.37)	−0.13 (1.86)	−0.12 (1.71)
NOTREAT		0.26** (2.91)	0.14 (1.49)	0.19* (1.89)		0.15 (1.91)	0.09 (1.11)	0.05 (0.61)
INCMAN		0.62** (5.82)	0.37** (3.16)	0.41** (3.36)		0.45** (5.59)	0.36** (4.06)	0.32** (3.57)
FINSAT			−0.15** (5.34)	−0.15** (4.93)			−0.05** (2.55)	−0.05* (2.22)
SUBPOV			0.37** (3.34)	0.36** (3.13)			0.26* (2.45)	0.15 (1.36)
UNEMP				0.07 (0.40)				0.65** (4.39)
OLDERAGE				−0.18 (1.42)				0.28** (3.10)
NESC				0.33* (2.47)				0.23* (2.19)
ATSI				0.93* (2.46)				−0.03 (0.08)
PRIVREN				0.48** (4.35)				−0.00 (0.04)
n	2,608	2,506	2,485	2,352	2,449	2,365	2,345	2,290
LR Chi²	603.3	1,012.3	1,055.1	1,026.8	178.2	230.3	247.5	261.1
Pseudo R²	0.280	0.487	0.512	0.524	0.088	0.119	0.129	0.141

Notes: z scores are shown in brackets; statistical significance indicated by */** (p = 0.05/0.01); LR = likelihood ratio..

two rows of Table 7.6. Although the latter cannot be interpreted as measuring the percentage of the variance of the response variable that is explained by the model, it does allow the performance of the alternative specifications to be compared. The parameter estimates shown in the body of the table also need to be interpreted with caution, because the size of the impact on the dependent variable of a one-unit increase in each predictor variable depends on the values of the other predictors in the model, and on the starting value of the predictor itself. It is possible to estimate the implied marginal effects that would operate if each predictor is set equal to its mean value (following Wilkins, 2008), but this has not been attempted because the focus is on comparing the *strength* of the effects associated with each independent variable (predictor) as opposed to their size.

The estimates in Table 7.6 suggest that the first specification performs better in explaining variations in deprivation than in poverty, as can be seen by comparing the strength of individual impacts as well as the overall explanatory power of the model. This feature of the results remains present and is unaffected when the other specifications are considered. The variables that are expected to be correlated with disadvantage all show up strongly when the deprivation indicator is used, but their associations with the poverty indicator are weaker – at times far weaker. Thus, while there is a strong relationship (across all four specifications) between being deprived and the number of items that people missed out on because of a shortage of money (GONEWO), there is no such relationship between going without and poverty status. The one variable that does perform better at explaining poverty status is not having enough money to get by on, and this makes sense in terms of the difference between being deprived and being poor. When the two well-being indicators (FINSAT and SUBPOV) are included, they appear as significant in both models, but are again more strongly determined in the deprivation model than in the poverty model.

The household characteristic variables included in the fourth specification tend to perform rather poorly in both models, but this does not influence the relative superiority of the deprivation approach. These estimates provide some weak confirmation of the earlier finding that deprivation is lower among older people (although the estimated effect is not statistically significant), but the contrast with the poverty approach (which shows clearly that poverty is higher among older people) is striking. Deprivation is also shown to be higher among immigrants from non-English-speaking countries, Indigenous Australians and private renters, yet none of these demographic effects are found to be significantly associated with poverty once the other effects are included in the model.

The superiority of the deprivation approach is reinforced by the fact that all four specifications explain a far greater proportion of the variation in the dependent variable than is the case for poverty. In relation to the most comprehensive (final) specification, this difference is substantial: 51% in the case of deprivation, compared with only 14% in the case of poverty. This difference, along with the better statistical performance of individual variables (that have been deliberately chosen because they are important signposts of disadvantage) leads to the conclusion that the case for choosing deprivation over poverty is compelling. However, the choice between the two indicators is a false one, in the sense that both embody important information and a better approach may involve combining them in a composite measure.

Is there a deprivation threshold?

Before considering such a composite measure, it is of interest to examine the relationship between income and deprivation in more detail. One aim of this is to establish whether or not an income threshold exists below which deprivation rises sharply. If so, it might be possible to use this threshold as the basis for a new deprivation-based income poverty line, as Townsend tried to do in his original study. However, it is important to acknowledge that the usefulness of a deprivation threshold depends crucially on its robustness, since a threshold that is sensitive to how it is derived will be subject to all of the ambiguities that surround existing poverty lines.

Figure 7.1 shows the relationship between estimated equivalised disposable income (re-grouped into the income categories specified in the survey) and two indicators of deprivation: the mean deprivation score (upper panel) and the incidence of those missing out on two or more essential items (lower panel). In both cases, deprivation is based on the revised 25 items (DEP50) index, although very similar results are produced if the more restrictive (DEP90) index is used in its place.

Visual inspection of both diagrams suggests that an income threshold may exist in the range bounded between $200 and $300 a week of (equivalised) disposable income. There is a noticeable plateau to deprivation over the range $300 to $500 a week, but when income falls below $300 a week, deprivation begins to rise sharply. The incomes that define the limits of the threshold correspond to 52.9% and 79.4% of the survey-based estimate of median equivalised disposable income of $378 a week, respectively, while the mid-point of the income range ($250) corresponds to 66.2% of median income.

Although it is not possible to locate the threshold more precisely (or even to establish convincingly that a threshold exists), it is interesting to note that the identified income range is not only close to existing median income-based poverty lines, but is also similar to the threshold range identified for Ireland by Nolan and Whelan (1996). They concluded from their examination of the relationship between poverty and deprivation that:

> ... it may be possible to apply sensible upper and lower limits to the range to be considered. In broad terms, such a range may be bounded by the 50 per cent and 70 per cent [of mean equivalised disposable income] relative lines. (Nolan nd Whelan, 1996, p 123)

Given the inaccuracies associated with the CUPSE Survey income variable, there is little point in trying to locate more precisely where a deprivation-based income

Figure 7.1: Relationship between alternative deprivation measures and equivalised disposable income

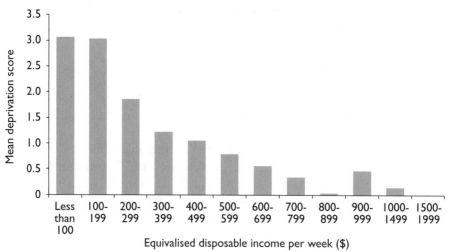

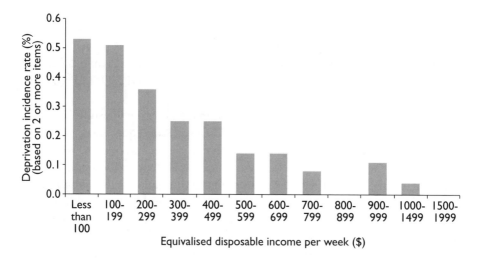

threshold fits in the income distribution, although the range identified here is used later to guide the development of a composite indicator.

Overlap analysis

Previous studies have examined the degree of overlap between deprivation and poverty as a way of illustrating that they capture different dimensions of unmet need (Bradshaw and Finch, 2003), or reflect different aspects of living standards (Perry, 2002). Most of these studies find that the overlap between poverty and deprivation is low in individual countries, and this finding has been confirmed across a range of countries by analysis showing that:

> ... the extent of material deprivation and financial hardship across the
> EU is reflected only to a limited extent by the income-based indicator
> [set at 60% of median income] conventionally used to measure the
> risk of poverty. (Ward, 2009, p 130)

The lack of overlap between poverty and deprivation suggests that the two
indicators are capturing different aspects of disadvantage and this in turn suggests
that they can be combined into a composite measure.

The degree of overlap between those with incomes below the poverty line
and those identified as deprived is illustrated for the community and 2006 client
samples in Figures 7.2 and 7.3, respectively. These overlaps are based on a poverty
line set at 50% of median income, and define deprivation as being deprived of at
least four of the 25 essential items that appear in the variable DEP50.

It has already been shown (see Table 7.1) that these definitions produce similar
estimates of poverty and deprivation for the community sample, and the same
definitions were applied to the client sample (so that the disadvantage indicators
applied to the welfare service client sample are, as before, derived using community
benchmarks). It should be noted that the client sample overlaps are based on
poverty rates estimated using gross income because income tax was not imputed
(mainly because the client sample income variable was even less precise than the
community sample income variable). This simplification is unlikely to induce a
marked distortion into the client sample overlap estimates, although they should
be seen as illustrative.

Figure 7.2 indicates that there is a low degree of overlap between the poverty
and deprivation estimates for the community sample: only around 36% ($5.1/14.2
= 0.359$) of those with incomes below the poverty line are deprived of four or
more essential items, while only 35% ($5.1/14.6 = 0.349$) of those identified as
deprived on this basis have incomes below the poverty line. Figure 7.3 shows not
only that the absolute levels of both poverty and deprivation are much higher for
those in the client sample, but also that the overlap is much greater in this case.

Thus, whereas only 36% of those identified as poor in the community sample
are also deprived, the corresponding overlap is almost 60% ($36.7/61.5 = 0.597$)
for the client sample. This is an important finding, since it indicates that poverty
and deprivation tend to produce converging estimates when they are applied to
more disadvantaged groups. This in turn suggests that the different components
of disadvantage tend to cluster together more strongly as the level of disadvantage
increases.

A number of factors can explain why the overlap estimates shown in Figures
7.2 and 7.3 are so low (particularly among the community sample). They include
the broader concept of resources implicit in the lack of affordability criterion
used to identify deprivation, the possibility that needs are not captured well by
the equivalence scale implicit in the poverty line (which, for example, makes no
allowance for special needs associated with disability or the age of adults), or that
income is not shared equally within the household as is assumed in the poverty

Figure 7.2: Estimated overlap between poverty and deprivation in the community sample

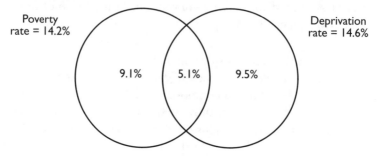

Poverty
rate = 14.2%

Deprivation
rate = 14.6%

9.1%   5.1%   9.5%

Figure 7.3: Estimated overlap between poverty and deprivation in the client sample

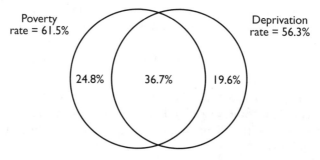

Poverty
rate = 61.5%

Deprivation
rate = 56.3%

24.8%   36.7%   19.6%

line methodology. One conclusion that could be drawn from the overlap results is that different indicators should be used to identify disadvantage among different groups in the community. However, if the aim is to develop indicators that have *general applicability* that allow the circumstances of different groups to be quantified and compared, then a common approach is needed.

Because of the limitations of the client survey income variable, only the community sample data have been used to examine the overlap issues more thoroughly. Table 7.7 shows how the size of the overlap changes when alternative definitions of poverty and deprivation are used. For each poverty line, the number of items used to identify deprivation has been chosen, as before, to minimise the gap between the estimated deprivation and poverty rates. This becomes difficult to achieve when the higher poverty lines are used because the number of items used to define deprivation cannot fall below one, and this produces deprivation rates that are below the corresponding poverty rates. In these cases, the overlap measure becomes sensitive to whether it is expressed relative to the poverty rate (that is, the percentage of the poor who are also deprived), or relative to the deprivation rate (that is, the percentage of the deprived who are also poor). The estimates in the final column of Table 7.7 follow the above discussion of Figures 7.2 and 7.3 in using the poverty rate as the base for estimating the overlap.

In general, Table 7.7 indicates that the size of the overlap increases as the poverty line is raised, and is slightly bigger when the broader deprivation index (DEP50) is used. However, at all poverty lines between 50% and 80% of median income, only between one third and just over one half of those identified as poor are also deprived. These are the income limits which were shown in Figure 7.1 to define the boundary around a possible deprivation threshold. These low overlaps confirm that how social disadvantage is measured makes a great deal of difference to who is identified as experiencing it. They also suggest that it would not be wise to rely on any single measure to estimate the extent of the problem, or as the basis for evaluating the impact of policy.

Consistent poverty

A composite indicator may be preferable. This insight has led to the development of the concept of consistent poverty, which identifies those with incomes below the poverty line who also experience a specified degree of deprivation (Nolan and Whelan, 1996; Maître, Nolan and Whelan, 2006; Whelan and Maître, 2007). Strong support for the concept of consistent poverty was expressed during the public consultations organised by the Department for Work and Pensions in the UK to develop measures of child poverty that could be used to monitor the British government's commitment to abolish child poverty (DWP, 2003a, 2003b). A measure that combines both low income and deprivation received most support from those consulted because:

> ... it resonates well with the perception that poverty should encompass some idea of the practical effects of low income ... [and is] ...

Table 7.7: Overlaps between different indicators of poverty and deprivation

	Poverty rate (P)	Deprivation rate (D)	Poor and deprived (P & D)	Neither poor nor deprived	Overlap (P & D)/P
50% median income					
DEP50≥4	14.2	14.6	5.1	76.3	35.9
DEP90≥2	14.2	13.9	4.7	76.6	33.1
60% median income					
DEP50≥2	23.3	26.8	11.7	61.6	50.2
DEP90≥1	23.3	24.2	10.6	63.2	45.5
70% median income					
DEP50≥2	32.0	26.8	14.6	55.7	45.6
DEP90≥1	32.0	24.2	12.9	56.7	40.3
80% median income					
DEP50≥1	39.8	38.8	22.7	44.1	57.0
DEP90≥1	39.8	24.2	15.1	51.1	37.9

concerned with outcomes rather than processes and in this sense it was believed to reflect the public perceptions of poverty and the feelings of distress felt by those in poverty ... a measure that chimes better with the public understanding of poverty would be able to gain public and political credibility. (DWP, 2003a, pp 20-1)

The term 'consistent poverty' carries the implication that other estimates (for example, those based on income alone) are in some sense inconsistent and the term 'validated poverty' might be preferable since it captures the idea (already examined in Chapter Three) that the existence of deprivation is used to confirm (or validate) that those whose incomes place them at risk of poverty are actually experiencing poverty (Saunders, 2003b). However, the term consistent poverty is used here to conform to other studies and avoid unnecessary confusion.

Tables 7.8 and 7.9 compare the composition and incidence of conventional and consistent poverty, respectively. Results are presented for poverty lines set at 60% and 70% of median income. The choice of these income benchmarks reflects the earlier threshold results, as well as the overlap results in Table 7.7, which show that a lower poverty line produces a low overlap, while a higher poverty line identifies many people as poor who are not experiencing deprivation. These income thresholds also correspond to the poverty lines used in the EU Laeken indicators and in countries like Ireland and Britain that have developed indicators that combine poverty and deprivation as a basis for monitoring change and assessing the impact of policy.

Table 7.8 shows how the structure of poverty changes when alternative measures are used to identify it. The patterns are similar whether the poverty line is set at either 60% or 70% of the median, so only the former results are discussed. When the measurement of poverty is changed from being based on income alone to the combination of income and deprivation (based on DEP50≥2), the composition of those identified as poor changes markedly. In particular, the proportion of the poor who are aged 65 or older declines from around one third of all poor households to around one fifth. This decline is most marked among older couples, and reinforces the evidence presented in the previous chapter showing that older couples receiving the Age Pension are better off than single age pensioners.

The shift from poverty to consistent poverty also leads to increases in the proportions of the poor who are working-age single people and lone-parent families. When the consistent poverty indicator is used, there is a sharp decline in the proportion of the poor who are owner/purchasers and an equally sharp increase in the proportion who are renters, particularly those in the private rental sector. The proportion of the poor who are Indigenous Australians also rises, but remains low because the group itself is a small proportion of the population (and an even smaller proportion of the community sample). The same patterns are apparent when the harsher deprivation measure (based on DEP90) is used, although the changes are less dramatic.

Table 7.9 examines how the change from poverty to consistent poverty affects the poverty rates facing different groups. Again, the discussion focuses

Table 7.8: The structure of poverty and consistent poverty by household type

Household characteristic	60% of median income:	Consistent poverty		70% of median income:	Consistent poverty	
	Poverty	DEP50≥2	DEP90≥2	Poverty	DEP50≥2	DEP90≥2
Age						
Under 30	15.3	18.5	16.2	14.2	17.6	15.8
30-64	52.6	60.6	66.5	51.4	61.6	68.3
65 and over	32.1	20.9	17.4	34.4	20.7	15.8
Family type						
Single, working age	9.3	12.2	11.4	6.8	9.8	9.4
Older person	10.9	8.7	6.6	8.0	7.0	5.4
Working-age couple, no children	7.3	3.5	3.6	9.7	7.3	5.4
Older couple	11.9	5.6	4.8	19.2	8.4	5.4
Working-age couple, with children	39.0	42.5	46.1	36.2	39.8	44.1
Lone-parent family	9.0	11.5	15.6	9.7	14.3	20.3
Principal source of income						
Wages or interest	33.5	34.3	33.1	36.6	35.6	35.3
Social security payment	63.2	62.4	62.0	60.8	61.6	60.6
Educational attainment						
High school or below	70.5	73.1	77.1	68.9	72.2	35.6
Trade certificate	19.4	16.4	14.5	20.8	16.8	14.9
University	10.1	10.5	8.4	10.3	11.0	8.5
Housing tenure						
Owner/purchaser	55.2	40.1	37.7	60.3	42.9	39.6
Private renter	19.5	28.9	32.3	17.7	29.1	33.7
Public renter	10.5	15.7	15.6	8.8	13.4	13.9
Indigenous/ATSI						
Yes	1.5	2.5	3.7	1.4	2.5	3.5
No	98.5	97.5	96.3	98.6	97.5	96.5
Has an ongoing disability						
Yes	32.7	32.9	37.3	32.2	33.4	36.8
No	67.3	67.1	62.7	67.8	66.6	63.2
All households:	**100.0**	**100.0**	**100.0**	**100.0**	**100.0**	**100.0**

on comparing the estimates shown in the first two columns, although the other estimates produce similar patterns. In overall terms, the poverty rate falls by half, from 24% to 12%, when the consistent poverty measure replaces the conventional poverty measure. This decline is not spread equally across all demographic groups, but is concentrated among older people (where the poverty rate declines by more than two thirds, from 37% to 12%), those mainly dependent on wages or

Table 7.9: Poverty and consistent poverty rates, by household type

Household characteristic	60% of median income: Poverty rate	Consistent poverty rate DEP50≥2	Consistent poverty rate DEP90≥2	70% of median income: Poverty rate	Consistent poverty rate DEP50≥2	Consistent poverty rate DEP90≥2
Age						
Under 30	28.5	16.9	8.6	36.1	20.1	10.2
30-64	18.6	10.6	6.8	24.9	13.4	8.4
65 and over	37.4	12.3	5.9	54.7	15.1	6.5
Family type						
Single, working age	28.1	18.2	9.9	28.2	18.2	9.9
Older person	50.0	20.5	9.0	50.0	20.5	9.0
Working-age couple, no children	8.6	2.0	1.2	15.6	5.2	2.2
Older couple	24.1	5.6	2.8	52.9	10.6	3.9
Working-age couple, with children	21.6	11.6	7.3	27.3	13.5	8.4
Lone-parent family	33.3	21.2	16.7	49.1	32.7	26.3
Principal source of income						
Wages or interest	23.7	5.1	2.9	15.3	6.5	3.7
Social security payment	10.2	29.8	17.4	79.5	36.2	20.4
Educational attainment						
High school or below	31.2	16.2	9.9	41.7	19.9	11.9
Trade certificate	20.6	8.7	4.4	30.2	11.1	5.5
University	9.7	4.9	2.3	13.5	6.4	2.8
Housing tenure						
Owner/purchaser	17.6	6.3	3.4	26.2	8.3	4.4
Private renter	33.4	24.5	15.9	41.6	30.7	20.1
Public renter	64.6	49.5	28.6	74.0	52.8	30.8
Indigenous/ATSI						
Yes	42.9	35.0	30.0	52.4	45.0	35.0
No	23.5	11.4	6.5	32.1	14.2	7.9
Has an ongoing disability						
Yes	41.6	21.1	13.9	55.8	26.7	16.6
No	19.6	9.6	5.2	26.9	11.8	6.3
All households	**23.8**	**11.7**	**6.8**	**32.4**	**14.6**	**8.3**

interest incomes and those who either own their own home or are in the process of purchasing it.

In stark contrast to these declines, the incidence of consistent poverty *increases* by a factor of three among those mainly dependent on a social security payment, even though the overall poverty rate declines by more than half. Other groups where the (proportionate) decline in the poverty rate is greater than the overall decline are single working-age people, lone parents, public renters and Indigenous Australians. Similar patterns are apparent when the stricter definition of deprivation is used and when the poverty line is raised from 60% to 70% of median income. Thus, relative to the income poverty measure, the consistent poverty measure (however it is defined) reveals a poverty landscape in which those groups that are most vulnerable to income poverty appear even more disadvantaged relative to other groups.

It remains unclear, however, which of the two indicators of consistent poverty shown in Tables 7.8 and 7.9 provides the better basis for examining the quantitative dimensions of social disadvantage. In addressing this issue, the regression approach adopted earlier is again employed, this time with a focus on comparing the relative performance of the two main consistent poverty indicators used in the above analysis. The approach adopted is the same as that described earlier, and results derived from the same four model specifications are compared. (The general comments made earlier about the performance of variables not included in the reported results apply equally to the results now discussed.)

Table 7.10 presents the regression results based on the two variants of consistent poverty identified in columns two and five of Tables 7.8 and 7.9 using the same format used to generate the earlier results in Table 7.6. The variable CONPOV60 includes those with incomes below 60% of the median who are also deprived of at least two essentials items (based on DEP50), while CONPOV70 includes those with incomes below 70% of the median who are also deprived of at least two of the same list of essentials items.

As before, the first three sets of independent variables included in the modelling all show up as being significantly related to both specifications of consistent poverty. The pseudo R^2 for the two economic resource variables alone is around 20%, and this increases to around 30% when the four outcome variables are included. Both subjective well-being indicators (FINSAT and SUBPOV) are statistically significant and their inclusion leads to a further rise in explanatory power. When the final set of five demographic variables are included, there is a further modest increase in explanatory power although only the first three of these variables are statistically significant ($p = 0.05$).

In overall terms, the results suggest that the second formulation (CONPOV70) outperforms the first specification, although the difference is not great and a case could be made for preferring either approach. Because the most commonly used poverty measure in Australia sets the poverty line at 50% of median income, the first consistent poverty approach represents less of a departure from current practice and, on these grounds, could be regarded as preferable. Use of a poverty line set at 60% of median income is also consistent with the approach used in the compendium of social inclusion indicators for Australia (see ASIB, 2009a and the following chapter).

Importantly, whichever version of consistent poverty is adopted, it is clear from comparing the results in Table 7.10 with those in Table 7.6 that the consistent poverty framework is far superior to that based on income alone, in the sense that

Table 7.10: Probit estimates of alternative consistent poverty models

Independent variable	Dependent variable: CONPOV60				Dependent variable: CONPOV70			
Intercept	−1.73**	−2.25**	−1.38**	−1.47**	−1.62**	−2.15**	−1.31**	−1.40**
	(32.80)	(26.53)	(7.25)	(7.57)	(32.97)	(27.90)	(7.25)	(7.60)
ASSETS	0.78**	0.47**	0.41**	0.37**	0.85**	0.52**	0.45**	0.41**
	(10.14)	(5.48)	(4.57)	(3.96)	(11.57)	(6.38)	(5.22)	(4.54)
NOSAVING	0.97**	0.47**	0.42**	0.42**	1.06**	0.53**	0.45**	0.45**
	(11.31)	(4.74)	(4.12)	(3.99)	(12.71)	(5.43)	(4.57)	(4.38)
GONEWO		0.15**	0.09**	0.11**		0.16**	0.10**	0.12**
		(5.03)	(2.96)	(3.34)		(5.46)	(3.33)	(3.70)
NOHLTH		0.07	0.01	0.02		0.11*	0.04	0.05
		(1.10)	(0.10)	(0.25)		(1.74)	(0.59)	(0.79)
NOTREAT		0.18*	0.09	0.06		0.29**	0.19*	0.17
		(2.07)	(0.95)	(0.66)		(3.38)	(2.21)	(1.90)
INCMAN		0.75**	0.54**	0.51**		0.68**	0.47**	0.44**
		(7.26)	(4.86)	(4.47)		(7.19)	(4.57)	(4.11)
FINSAT			−0.13**	−0.13**			−0.12**	−0.12**
			(4.92)	(4.87)			(4.87)	(4.81)
SUBPOV			0.29**	0.24*			0.39**	0.36**
			(2.62)	(2.13)			(3.74)	(3.29)
UNEMP				0.41*				0.42*
				(2.52)				(2.50)
OLDERAGE				0.26*				0.26*
				(2.30)				(2.47)
NESC				0.27*				0.27*
				(2.17)				(2.20)
ATSI				−0.05				0.07
				(0.13)				(0.21)
PRIVREN				0.11				0.14
				(1.04)				(1.36)
n	2,419	2,336	2,318	2,266	2,419	2,336	2,318	2,266
LR Chi²	334.8	489.5	524.4	534.0	424.5	614.5	656.5	670.6
Pseudo R²	0.192	0.291	0.316	0.327	0.212	0.319	0.344	0.357

Notes: z scores are shown in brackets; statistical significance indicated by */** ($p = 0.05/0.01$); LR = likelihood ratio.

it identifies as disadvantaged those households that other information confirms have few economic resources and are unable to meet their basic needs. However, it is also the case that an approach based on deprivation alone (using DEP50≥4, as shown in Table 7.6) produces results that are, in some regards, superior on statistical grounds to those produced by either version of consistent poverty. The explanatory power of the deprivation model is greater than that of the consistent poverty models and there are noticeable differences in the relative performance of some of the independent variables included in the models. The only demographic variable that is statistically significant across all three specifications is ethnicity (as captured in the country of birth variable, NESC), with the remaining variables performing differently in the different specifications.

These differences make it difficult to choose between the deprivation approach (based on DEP50≥4) and the two versions of consistent poverty. What is clear is that deprivation adds an important new dimension to our understanding of the causes and consequences of social disadvantage that is missing if the focus is on income alone. Both versions of the consistent poverty approach maintain a role for low income as a factor that contributes to disadvantage, and thus represent less of a radical departure from current practice than the deprivation approach which dispenses with a direct role for income altogether.

Income has always played an important role in Australian debates about poverty and social disadvantage and is the focus of most government redistributive programmes, particularly those that operate through the tax, transfer and wage determination systems. These arguments suggest that income poverty should be maintained as an important dimension of social disadvantage. The consistent poverty approach that combines evidence on low income with that on deprivation provides a sharper focus on outcomes and is consistent with community understanding of the meaning of poverty. These features make the concept of consistent poverty a better basis on which to generate the evidence needed to convince policy makers that poverty exists, and that action is needed to address it.

Summary

Australian poverty studies have lacked conviction because of the arbitrary tools used to identify and measure poverty, because they do not capture the impact of resources other than money income and because the existence of poverty is presumed, not established. These limitations have made it difficult to defend the estimates and have resulted in their failure to influence policy. Poverty rates may make good media headlines, but they are not seen as reliable enough to convince those who can bring about change. More effort is needed to identify those who are actually missing out in order to provide the impetus for action and to guide what form of action is needed. This is all the more pressing in a country like Australia, which has a long tradition of targeting its public welfare resources on those in greatest need.

Estimates of deprivation differ in many ways from those based solely on reported income, and these differences remain when alternative measurement techniques are used to identify both poverty and deprivation. The results presented in this chapter indicate that many of those identified as income poor are not deprived, while many of those who face deprivation have incomes above the poverty line. They also reveal that some of the groups shown to be most susceptible to poverty are not equally susceptible to deprivation, although those who face the highest poverty rates appear even more disadvantaged in terms of their deprivation. These findings present a challenge to the income poverty approach and raise questions about the effectiveness of existing income support policies.

The consistent poverty approach that combines poverty in the sense of low income with deprivation has been adopted in other countries with similar welfare policy settings and institutional structures, and there is much to be gained from adopting it in Australia. It is over three decades since the Poverty Commission gave its stamp of authority to the use of a poverty line tied to the basic wage. The conceptual framework and research instruments developed by the Commission helped to stimulate and guide a generation of Australian poverty studies, but those instruments and the ideas and constructs that underpinned them are no longer applicable in today's economic and social circumstances. A new approach is needed to take Australian poverty research forward and the concept of consistent poverty extends the earlier approach in ways that make it more relevant to current and future conditions.

EIGHT

Defining social exclusion and the social inclusion agenda

Introduction

Social exclusion has emerged over the last three decades as a major research topic and a new organising theme for social policy. It has influenced how social issues are conceived, debated, researched and addressed, particularly in Europe. Its modern usage began in France in the 1970s to capture the idea that certain marginalised groups face multiple barriers (not just economic) that effectively exclude them from the French social protection system (Peace, 2001; Whiteford, 2001). The fight against exclusion has been at the centre of the EU's social agenda since the Maastricht Treaty was first signed in 1992 and its significance has grown in line with the expansion of the EU itself. Following increased interest in the topic in Britain, social exclusion was identified as one of the thematic priorities of its ESRC (1997) and exerted a powerful influence on the formulation of British social policy under the Labour governments of Tony Blair and Gordon Brown.

Government commitment to an inclusion agenda in Australia has lagged behind developments in Europe but is fast catching up. The social policy agenda of the Howard government in the period 1996-2007 was built around a concept of mutual obligation that had a weak philosophical basis (Goodin, 2001), and did little to offer real opportunities to those with limited capacities who were unable to compete in the labour market (Saunders, 2001). The Reference Group on Welfare Reform, established to develop a new blueprint for the social support system, was motivated by a vision that 'the nation's social support system must be judged by its capacity to help people participate economically and socially' (Reference Group on Welfare Reform, 2000, p 3) although this had relatively little impact on the recommendations developed, and even less on those that were implemented.

The focus in Australia over much of this period (and more recently in New Zealand; see Welfare Working Group, 2010) has been on joblessness and exclusion from the labour market and the need for reform of the social security ('welfare') system to make work more attractive (and welfare less attractive) to working-age benefit recipients. Despite this narrow focus, the underlying idea of social inclusion has persisted as a feature of Australian social policy and debate over its scope, meaning and implications has gradually broadened (in both academic and policy circles). This trend has brought the Australian inclusion agenda closer to that adopted in Europe – particularly in Britain – and it is therefore appropriate that the following discussion begins by outlining key features of European development.

Inclusion as a policy priority

Along with other EU member states the social inclusion strategy adopted by the UK government involved agreeing to a set of common objectives informed by a range of indicators. Beginning in 1999, its *Opportunity for all* reports provided an annual overview of government action to tackle poverty and social exclusion. It produced three-year National Action Plans that identified indicators, reported trends and compared performance with other EU countries (DWP, 2008). The goal of combating social exclusion played a central role in these developments, which reflected a commitment to:

> ... building an inclusive cohesive and prosperous society with fairness and social justice at its core, in which child poverty has been eradicated, everyone who can work is expected to contribute to national prosperity and share in it, and those who can't work are supported.... The commitment is to build a society in which social exclusion is reduced by improving employment prospects for people facing the greatest disadvantage, such as ex-offenders, the homeless and drug users, providing equality for ethnic minorities, disabled people and older people and eradicating child poverty. (DWP, 2008, pp v–vi)

As noted, the EU has played a major role in placing social inclusion at the centre of the European social policy agenda (Atkinson, 2007). The development of indicators, building on work conducted by Atkinson et al (2002), has re-invigorated the use of indicators to monitor social progress more generally (Stiglitz et al, 2009; OECD, 2010).

The UK's suite of *Opportunity for all* indicators provide a regular overview of progress achieved in tackling poverty and the many dimensions of social exclusion. Indicators are presented separately for children and young people, people of working age, people in later life and for communities, with trends since the baseline (1997) and recent changes identified for each indicator across each socioeconomic group (DWP, 2007). Ireland's National Anti-Poverty Strategy was first introduced in 1997, and has subsequently been modified in the light of experience, research and the availability of better data as part of a broader effort to promote inclusion (Nolan, 2000; Layte, Nolan and Whelan, 2000; Office for Social Inclusion, 2004). Through these developments, broad political acceptance of social exclusion as a key policy goal brought many European countries closer to the point where 'real progress in the social domain can only be achieved if social objectives are on the agenda at the highest level of policy making' (Atkinson, 2007, p 26).

Underlying the European embrace of social inclusion as a key policy goal is an intellectual framework in which:

> Society is seen by intellectual and political elites as a status hierarchy or as a number of collectivities, bound by sets of mutual rights and obligations that are rooted in some broader moral order. Social

exclusion is the process of becoming detached from this moral order. (Room, 1995, p 6)

This insight provides an important link between the literature on social exclusion and that on welfare state regimes (Esping-Andersen, 1990, 1999), and illustrates how the values and institutional structures that underpin welfare states influence how the problems it addresses are conceptualised, analysed and addressed.

This explains why the re-negotiation of rights and responsibilities under welfare to work programmes in countries like Australia, New Zealand and the US have not been informed by a broader desire to promote social inclusion, but by the narrower goal of maximising employment participation. These developments highlight the impediments to adopting a social exclusion perspective in a country like Australia that has never fully embraced the use of an extensive state apparatus to promote egalitarian citizenship in the broad sense originally identified by Marshall (1981) and reinforced more recently by writers such as Giddens (1998).

Possibly reflecting this narrow conception of the meaning and significance of inclusion as a policy goal, many Australian researchers have expressed ambivalence about its academic benefits and warned against the dangers of using social exclusion simply to re-label poverty using more 'acceptable' language (Arthurson and Jacobs, 2004; see also Catholic Social Services Australia, 2010). Thus, it has been argued that:

> ... although the term social exclusion has political utility, as an academic concept it provides little advantage compared to other widely used concepts, such as poverty, other than to emphasise relational factors that shape material and cultural deprivation.... Social exclusion's potential appears to be at the level of policy implementation. In stressing the interconnected aspects of deprivation [it] can be used to endorse policies that seek to adopt a multi-agency or "joined-up" government approach, for instance on housing estates. (Arthurson and Jacobs, 2004, p 37)

Following the election of the ALP government in 2007, Deputy Prime Minister Julia Gillard was assigned responsibility for social inclusion and announced in 2008 that the new government was developing 'a new framework for national policy based on the powerful idea of social inclusion' (Gillard, 2008a, p 4). A Social Inclusion Unit was established within the Department of Prime Minister and Cabinet to support the work of a new Australian Social Inclusion Board comprised of experts, practitioners and community leaders in advising the government about how to examine, monitor and address specific forms of exclusion.

The importance of these initiatives was reinforced by delegates to the 2020 Summit, who identified social inclusion as a 'first order issue' and proposed the development of a national action plan for social inclusion that would use 'evidence-based goals and measurable targets' along with a national poverty strategy to tackle Australian disadvantage (Department of Prime Minister and Cabinet,

2008a). Since then, the government has articulated the principles underlying its inclusion agenda and set out its policy priorities (Australian Government, 2008, 2009). The Social Inclusion Board has overseen the release of a series of reports on different aspects of social inclusion (see, for example, Vinson, 2009a, 2009b) and the development of a compendium of social inclusion indicators designed to 'reflect on both the social achievements of the recent past and those aspects which, on a comparative basis, might warrant greater attention' (ASIB, 2009a, p ix). A companion volume provides a detailed profile of social exclusion in Australia using the indicator framework developed in the compendium (ASIB, 2009b). In addition, a special module on social inclusion has been included in the 2010 General Social Survey, which will provide the first large-scale nationally representative picture of the extent of social exclusion in Australia.

In developing its policy agenda and collecting the evidence required to support it, the Australian government has drawn on the experience of several state governments that acted earlier to give priority to tackling social inclusion. This has been most notable in South Australia, where a social inclusion initiative was introduced in 2002 (Cappo, 2002; Rann, 2002; Government of South Australia, 2004). A central feature of the initiative was the creation of a South Australian Social Inclusion Board to provide advice to the Premier on an agenda that 'is evidence-based and seeks innovative mobilisation of government and non-government resources' (Hayes et al, 2008, p 5). The *Fairer Victoria* strategy is also underpinned by a desire to build 'stronger and more inclusive communities' (Brumby, 2008), while the Tasmanian Premier announced in 2008 that: 'A social inclusion strategy for Tasmania is a key component of my Government's commitment to building a clever, kind and connected Tasmania' (Bartlett, 2008; see also Tasmania Social Inclusion Unit, 2008).

These developments in part reflect the role that state governments play in Australia in providing many of the services that play an important role in promoting social inclusion through better integrated policies. With the sharing of responsibilities under Australia's federal system of government, such integration must involve closer cooperation and collaboration between federal and state governments. If this can be achieved, these initiatives have the potential to bring about a sea change in Australian social policy, particularly if an effective partnership can be forged to address the underlying issues in a coordinated and sustained way. However, the lack of an effective partnership between federal and state governments has often in the past been a formidable obstacle to the development of the kind of integrated approach that is a key feature of the social inclusion policy response.

Without a genuinely cooperative approach to federalism, the prospects for addressing exclusion effectively will be severely compromised, and this makes the Australian inclusion agenda to some degree hostage to the vagaries of the political cycle. Progress is being made in this area through the work of the Council of Australian Governments but much remains to be done before the political and administrative structures are in place to translate terms such as 'whole of government' and 'joined-up government' from political rhetoric into policy reality. This challenge is likely to become more difficult following the election of a conservative governments in Victoria and Western Australia (with several other states likely to follow) and the much reduced majority of the ALP government following the 2010 federal election.

Over the longer term, however, a number of other factors have created a climate that has become more conducive to the adoption of a social inclusion agenda in Australia. Between 1993 and 2008, strong and sustained economic growth resulted in declining unemployment and focused the attention of policy makers on extending the benefits to those who had missed out. This approach began to unwind in the wake of the global financial crisis, which exposed the inherent weaknesses of *laissez faire* economics. The government responded to the crisis by introducing a series of successful stimulus measures that played a major role in supporting domestic demand in the face of declining world trade and cut-backs in investment in the face of growing global uncertainty. In this context of an increased role for government, the idea of social inclusion has resonated more with post-crisis public opinion, and the 'powerful idea of social inclusion' began to exert its influence on the social policy agenda, even though the evidence needed to support such a change was largely lacking.

This discussion has highlighted the central role that issues of social exclusion and inclusion now occupy on the social policy agenda in an increasing number of countries. Very rarely can an idea have been so quickly embraced by government and had such a dramatic impact on the entire policy apparatus. It has influenced policy objectives, the collection of data, the mechanisms used to translate evidence into policy, the relations between the different tiers of government and how government interacts with the research community and the non-government sector. At the same time, insufficient attention has been paid to identifying the key features of exclusion and the factors that drive it, and the emphasis given to reforming the welfare system in English-speaking countries to encourage (or coerce) beneficiaries into employment continues to produce an unbalanced policy response.

These developments highlight the important role that politicians have played in the emergence of the social inclusion agenda in Australia, as in Europe. Such support has obvious advantages, but the dominant influence of political actors in setting the inclusion agenda also has its weaknesses. In many instances, for example, policy priorities determined politically have influenced what evidence is collected ('policy-based evidence') rather than the normal scientific sequence in which conceptual examination is used to identify what evidence is needed, and data are then collected to produce this evidence and allow the policy implications to be drawn ('evidence-based policy') (Levitas, 2006). Focusing attention on the *concept* of social exclusion is not popular among those driving the policy agenda, but is necessary to ensure that the right kind of evidence is collected, its interpretation scrutinised and the implications debated.

Definition, discourse and metaphor

There has always been a degree of tension between the lack of conceptual clarity about the meaning of social exclusion and the pressure within government to generate the evidence to support its policy imperatives. Concern has been expressed that its embrace of an inclusion agenda has allowed government to avoid addressing other aspects of disadvantage, such as poverty (Bradshaw, 2004), although these fears have been allayed as poverty and (to a much more limited extent) inequality have been incorporated into the inclusion agenda.

Even so, there is still a concern that the focus on inclusion has diverted attention away from issues of inequality that have traditionally occupied a central place on the social policy agenda. Leading Third Way proponent Anthony Giddens (1998, p 102; emphasis in the original) has sought to deflect such criticism by arguing that 'the new politics defines equality as *inclusion* and inequality as *exclusion*', pointing out that: 'Exclusion is not about gradations on inequality, but about mechanisms that act to detach groups of people from the social mainstream' (Giddens, 1998, p 104). Others remain unconvinced by such claims, with Béland (2007) providing a forceful critique of this interpretation, arguing that:

> ... the current political focus on social exclusion has helped to shift policy attention away from other forms of inequality, including income inequality between the wealthy and the rest of the population ... as mobilised in centre-left and Third Way political discourse, the idea of social exclusion can become a powerful ideological tool that legitimises modest policy reforms entirely compatible with moderate understandings of economic liberalism and, ultimately, [is] unable to fight the social evils this idea refers to. (Béland, 2007, p 124)

These disputes are a direct consequence of the close relationship between scholars and policy makers that has characterised the emergence and evolution of the social inclusion agenda, making it difficult to disentangle conceptual issues from the underlying political and ideological motivations.

It is important that policy is guided by a concept that lacks ambiguity, not least in this case because some of the most crucial aspects of exclusion cannot be easily captured in the indicators used to shape policy. With the focus on a 'can do, pragmatic and flexible' approach, academic debate over conceptual issues is seen as sterile and an unnecessary obstacle in the way of progress. A central feature of the policy response to exclusion is the need for a coordinated approach that seeks integrated solutions to the many factors that produce exclusion. This makes it all the more important that policy is guided by a definition of exclusion that is conceptually robust but capable of providing the flexibility required of both the issue itself and of the political context that provides legitimacy to the policy response.

The use of indicators as signposts of exclusion and inclusion reflects the difficulty of producing a concrete definition. By its nature, exclusion is a multi-faceted concept whose manifestation is constantly evolving, making it impossible to produce precise measures that have ongoing relevance. Flexibility is needed and an indicator approach provides this, although it is important to recognise that even the most extensive list of indicators is no substitute for a rigorous definition. Such a definition is needed to guide the identification of indicators and to raise questions about the extent to which movements in the indicators signify progress.

Much has been made in the literature about the existence of competing definitions of social exclusion. At one level, the lack of agreement over definitional issues can be seen as reflecting a deep-seated deficiency in the concept itself. Some academic analysts have expressed concern that the lack of conceptual clarity creates ambiguity, leaving policy makers with the freedom to define an inclusion agenda that suits their own interests. Others (generally those closer to policy making) have welcomed the flexibility it provides to acknowledge new dimensions of exclusion as they emerge, while avoiding the definitional and measurement controversies that are seen as a diversion.

There are a number of definitions of social exclusion, each of which draws attention to different aspects of what Vinson (2009a) has described as 'an underlying metaphor' that seeks to represent certain aspects of the social world. A similar point has been made by Saraceno (2002), who emphasises the close links with political discourse to argue that:

> … social exclusion is a politically flexible concept. Indeed, there are good grounds for claiming that social exclusion has been more developed as a discourse than as a concept: that is, the idea has been most used and articulated in the service of the language of politics. Hence it constitutes a relatively loose set of ideas that represent particular settings, rather than a concept with theoretical substance and coherence that transcends national and political contexts. (Saraceno, 2002, p 49)

On this view, the lack of an agreed definition allows the political forces needed to address social exclusion to be mobilised in the light of changing priorities, contexts and opportunities.

One problem with this interpretation is that it gives those in positions of political power the authority to set and adjust priorities and the ability to promote definitions that suit their own purposes. This risk has been identified by Ringen (2007) in relation to the setting of 'official' poverty lines and poverty reduction targets, although he notes that the same risks also apply to the exclusion agenda:

> The meaning of social exclusion is determined in the political apparatus of the European Union and exclusion thus defined is then explored scientifically with appropriate social indicators.… The advantage of this way of doing it is that normative questions that cannot easily be answered scientifically are taken to be answered democratically and that politicians can be held to account by standards they have themselves

committed to. But there are also serious disadvantages. One is a bias in favour of power. To ask society what its social concerns are, is to ask those in power. Those in power are not poor, and the poor are not in power. (Ringen, 2007, p 124)

The risk identified by Ringen itself represents a form of exclusion – exerted in this instance by those in positions of power against the poor and others at the receiving end of policy. The latter are in effect given no voice in setting an agenda whose alleged purpose is to improve their ability to participate.

Béland makes a similar point, arguing that:

> ... social exclusion can become a policy paradigm, the centrepiece of influential reform blueprints and a justification discourse.... [It] can become a useful intellectual tool, and perhaps references to this idea could draw the public's attention towards major social problems not associated with traditional concepts such as poverty and the "underclass".... Yet, in the current context, the dominant political discourse about social exclusion has done little more than legitimise modest social programmes that seldom challenge the liberal logic seeking to limit social spending while encouraging citizens to become increasingly dependent on market outcomes. (Béland, 2007, p 134)

In other words, it is not that the concept of exclusion lacks the ability to bring about a more radical social policy agenda, but rather that its subjugation to political control results in an affirmation of the hegemony of current theoretical frameworks and reinforces existing policy priorities.

A spectrum of definitions

The view that social exclusion is a metaphor or discourse used to set broad policy themes contrasts with the academic goal of seeking conceptual clarity within a clearly defined theoretical framework informed by a critical assessment of the literature in the field. It needs to be recognised, however, that an academic definition of this kind may not sit comfortably with those who are confronted with different forms of exclusion, as Richardson and Le Grand (2002) discovered. Despite this, the focus within the academic paradigm (and adopted here) is on comparing how well competing definitions can provide new insights, identify common patterns or highlight important differences that require further reflection, as Millar (2007) has emphasised.

In the spirit of this approach, Levitas and colleagues at the University of Bristol identify 12 separate definitions of social exclusion and note that:

> ... although the definitions may be clear and precise, their level of abstraction means they are not *empirically* precise. While they help to conceptualise social exclusion, this is not the same as providing an

operational definition that is amenable to measurement. Operational definitions are always a compromise between conceptual precision and clarity and what is theoretically and practically measurable. (Levitas et al, 2007, p 22; emphasis in the original)

The spectrum of definitions reviewed by Levitas and her colleagues covers those that seek to identify the central features of exclusion in a few key words, and those that adopt more complex characterisations that identify its main features and provide specific examples.

Examples of the former approach include definitions that focus on inadequate social participation, lack of social integration and lack of power as key features of exclusion (see Room, 1995; Burchardt, 2000). Similarly, Peace (2001) sees the inclusion agenda as seeking to enhance individual and group capacity in three dimensions: opportunity, reciprocity and participation. An even simpler approach is proposed by researchers at the Centre for the Analysis of Social Exclusion (CASE) at the London School of Economics and Political Science (LSE), who define an individual as socially excluded:

> ... if he or she does not participate in key activities in the society in which he or she lives. (Burchardt et al, 2002b, p 30)

This definition overcomes the ambiguities contained within the definition originally proposed by the UK Social Exclusion Unit (SEU, 2001), which identified social exclusion as:

> A short-hand term for what can happen when people or areas suffer from a combination of linked problems such as unemployment, poor skills, low incomes, poor housing, high crime environment, bad health and family breakdown. (SEU, 2001, p 10)

As Levitas (2000) has observed, the Social Exclusion Unit definition refers to 'what *can* happen' as a result of exclusion but does not specify what actually *does* happen. This is an example of the kind of ambiguity that researchers are uncomfortable with, yet at the same time it reinforces the uncertainties that underlie the processes of exclusion, highlighting the fact that its consequences are conditional, not inevitable. The CASE approach avoids this uncertainty, but leaves open the question of what constitutes 'key activities', thereby introducing another level of ambiguity.

The perceived shortcomings of these simple definitions have resulted in a series of more complex formulations that identify specific instances of exclusion as a way of making its actual manifestations more transparent. One such approach that has been cited favourably in work being conducted by the Australian Social Inclusion Board (ASIB, 2009a) is that proposed by Pierson (2001):

> Social exclusion is a process that deprives individuals and families, and groups and neighbourhoods, of the resources required for participation

in the social, economic and political activity of society as a whole. This process is primarily a consequence of poverty and low income, but other factors such as discrimination, low educational attainment and depleted living environments also underpin it. Through this process, people are cut off for a significant period in their lives from institutions and services, social networks and developmental opportunities that the great majority of society enjoys. (Pierson, 2001, cited in ASIB, 2009a, p viii)

This formulation has many similarities with the 'composite working definition' adopted by Levitas et al that expands on the CASE definition and 'encapsulates many of the factors reflected in the literature':

Social exclusion is a complex and multi-dimensional process. It involves the lack or denial of resources, rights, goods and services, and the inability to participate in the normal relationships and activities, available to the majority of people in society, whether in economic, social, cultural, or political arenas. It affects both the quality of life of individuals and the equity and cohesion of society as a whole. (Levitas et al, 2007, p 9)

These two definitions have much in common with that adopted by the European Commission, which identifies social exclusion as:

... a process whereby certain individuals are pushed to the edge of society and prevented from participating fully by virtue of their poverty, or lack of basic competencies and lifelong learning opportunities, or as a result of discrimination. This distances them from job, income and education opportunities as well as social and economic networks and activities. They have little access to power and decision-making bodies and thus often feel powerless and unable to take control over the decisions that affect their day to day lives. (European Commission, 2004, cited in Böhnke, 2008, p 305)

All three definitions provide practical examples of exclusion and its consequences and importantly, by introducing a time dimension explicitly, they each emphasise that exclusion is a *process*. This feature provides a clear differentiation between exclusion and other aspects of social disadvantage such as poverty (defined in terms of a lack of income) and deprivation (which reflects an inability to afford perceived necessities), while noting that exclusion and poverty will often be closely connected.

Most formulations include poverty as a specific form of exclusion and poverty rates, gaps and persistence measures (defined using low-income benchmarks) are often included among the indicators of exclusion. There are, however, more deep-seated differences between concepts like poverty and deprivation – both of which reflect a lack of access to economic resources – and the emphasis given to the role of societal structures and relationships in contributing to exclusion. This point is made forcefully by Saraceno (2002), who suggests that the relationship between poverty and exclusion is complex and raises important conceptual and theoretical issues. Thus:

> The concept of social exclusion seems to have at least two different genealogies of linked terms and phenomena, which keep surfacing in a quite unresolved alliance in social exclusion discourse. There are poverty and material deprivation on the one hand, reviewed in the light of social rights thinking: and social disintegration, marginality, un-belonging, and uprootedness on the other hand. One level of analysis points to the social conditions by which individuals and groups are included or excluded from relevant resources and social rights; the other points to processes by which individuals and social groups belong to, or are detached from, relevant and meaningful social networks, and share in values and identifications within a given community. (Saraceno, 2002, p 42)

Saraceno goes on to argue that few studies attempt to pursue both avenues of enquiry, with the result that the exclusion literature is fragmented, advancing along parallel trajectories. Empirical evidence showing a lack of overlap between statistical measures of exclusion and poverty compound this problem by failing to examine the interactions between the underlying causes or identify how they play out in specific circumstances, or for specific social groups.

Unlike the more complex formulations cited above, the CASE definition of social exclusion captures the simple idea that exclusion is about not participating, without prejudging what kinds of activity are relevant, or being definitive about the underlying causes or the consequences of non-participation. These are left open as separate avenues of inquiry, but do not appear in specific form in the definition itself.

Use of the term 'activities' in the CASE definition should be interpreted broadly to include the processes that often precede a specific form of engagement or participation. There are often more willing participants in an activity than it is possible to accommodate (for example, in sporting events or a community choir) so it becomes necessary to have some kind of selection process. However, those who miss out because they are not selected have participated in the *process* of selection and have thus not been socially excluded. This distinction mirrors that between capability (what one values and has the capacity to achieve) and functioning (the levels of achievement actually realised) identified by Sen (1985, 1999).

The distinction between participating in a process and participating in a specific event or activity can be accommodated by amending the CASE definition to replace the phrase 'does not participate in key activities' by 'does not *have the opportunity to* participate in key activities'. This adjustment highlights the idea that in many instances it is the denial of opportunity that represents exclusion, not the lack of participation itself.

This is not always the case, however. Those people who face exclusion as a result of unemployment have participated (and thus been included in) the labour market, but have failed to find (and thus been excluded from) employment. Their exclusion has flow-on consequences, not only in terms of income, but also in terms of the loss of status and self-respect that are a consequence of being unemployed. These adverse effects do not arise to anything like the same degree when people fail to be selected for the local football team or community choir. The nature of the activity itself can thus be as important as the process when it comes to identifying exclusion.

The modified CASE approach introduces further complexity into the challenge of identifying social exclusion, since it implies that one cannot determine if exclusion exists simply by observing patterns of participation and non-participation. It also becomes necessary to understand the nature of the underlying determinants and the processes that link them to outcomes. This introduces the role of aspirations into the picture, and this in turn raises questions about issues of choice and agency: does social exclusion exist if the decision not to participate was chosen by non-participants? The answer is clearly no if the amended CASE definition is adopted, since exercising the option to choose not to participate presupposes that the opportunity to participate was available. However, there is no simple way of distinguishing between options that are 'chosen' and those that are 'imposed', particularly bearing in mind that people can choose to exclude themselves from certain activities for many reasons, and that the list of current choices is often constrained by choices made in the past (Burchardt et al, 2002a, Figure 1.2; Sen, 2000).

Related to this is the difficulty of distinguishing between exclusion and diversity. People are different and one would expect them to choose different forms of participation from the menu of options available. Many instances of non-participation will thus reflect personal preferences (we are not all interested in sport, or see ourselves as budding sopranos) but it is difficult to distinguish between these situations and genuine cases of exclusion by observing participation patterns alone. One should certainly be wary of drawing conclusions about whether or not someone is excluded solely on the basis of their non-participation in specific activities. However, as the number of instances of non-participation increases, so will the likelihood that they signify exclusion, although even this cannot be established with certainty without further examination of the context within which decisions are made.

Another aspect of exclusion that is absent from the above definitions relates to the *level* at which participation takes place. Individuals engage in activities at many different levels: within families, neighbourhoods, communities, and on a regional, national and in some instances, international basis. Is the benchmark for identifying exclusion the expectation that everyone should be an active participant at each of these levels, or are there trade-offs between them? Many members of minority ethnic groups, for example, lead very active social lives within their own group, but have little or no links with other groups in the broader community. Does the inclusion implied by the former offset the exclusion implied by the latter?

With the focus of the social inclusion policy agenda on the role of government, there is a natural tendency to concentrate on those forms of exclusion that are amenable to policy intervention. This suggests that participation in national structures like the welfare state, the labour market and the political process assume greater significance than participation in local activities and social networks that government has little direct control over. Yet one clear message to emerge from the social capital literature is that strong communities are built on high levels of local engagement and this in turn creates an environment that makes it easier to achieve effective governance (Putnam, 1993). Social inclusion must thus involve being connected with *national* structures and being an active and engaged citizen at a *local* level.

The importance of this latter issue has increased along with the growing awareness of the role of place in the determination of personal disadvantage and participation. As noted earlier, Vinson (2009b) has observed that:

> ... it has been found that when social disadvantage becomes entrenched within a limited number of localities a disabling social climate can develop that is more than the sum of individual and household disadvantages and the prospect is increased of disadvantage being passed from one generation to the next. (Vinson, 2009b, p 2)

These concerns are reflected in the prominence given to community in social indicator frameworks, as well as in the emphasis given to neighbourhood issues in the social inclusion policy agenda. One way of encouraging participation at the local level is through the provision of local facilities and infrastructure that allow residents to interact in community settings and become included. Government also has a major role to play in maintaining adequate employment opportunities in disadvantaged communities, where joblessness is often the underlying cause of place-based disadvantage.

The idea that people are excluded when they are denied the opportunity to participate across a range of activities that are customary in their society makes explicit the idea that exclusion is the end result of institutional failings in the economic, social and political spheres, or is a direct consequence of the actions (or inactions) of others. This sharpens the distinction between exclusion and poverty, while acknowledging the role that poverty can play in creating the conditions that result in exclusion. It also leads naturally to a focus on the factors that drive the exclusion process. Vinson (2009a) draws on the literature to group these factors into five broad areas: poverty and lack of economic resources; lack of access to the job market; limited social supports and networks; the effect of local neighbourhood; and exclusion from services.

Such classifications provide a useful framework for examining the nature and drivers of exclusion, although it is also possible to adopt a framework that identifies how exclusion affects different vulnerable groups rather than its different spheres of influence. One potential danger with adopting the 'drivers' approach is that it may miss the important interconnections that exist between the identified domains (Bradshaw et al, 2004). Against this, although the 'vulnerable groups' approach is more likely to identify the interconnected nature of exclusionary processes, it runs the risk of individualising the problem and paying insufficient attention to the structural forces that create and perpetuate different forms of exclusion.

In practice, governments have tended to focus their efforts on specific groups like the homeless, those with a mental illness or the long-term unemployed when framing the social inclusion agenda, particularly in its early stages. This was true in South Australia and is equally true of the social inclusion agenda being pursued in the federal sphere in Australia. This approach provides scope to experiment with new forms of policy integration and build on existing knowledge and can be more easily sold to the electorate than more radical interventions. It also is focused on addressing 'real problems' in areas where the likelihood of achievement ('runs on the board') is high. Over time, as the policy becomes embedded in new administrative structures, attention can turn to addressing the deeper structural problems that reflect institutional failings – at least in theory. The danger is that these more intractable problems never make it onto an agenda that 'legitimises modest policy reforms' (see the earlier quote from Béland) without addressing the underlying causes.

Exclusion and poverty

The emergence of social exclusion in Europe reflected deep dissatisfaction with other measures of disadvantage used to inform social policy analysis. However, although poverty research foundered over disagreement over measurement, it was the limitations of the *concept* of poverty rather than its *measurement* problems that led to the emergence of social exclusion as an alternative policy paradigm (Berghmann, 1997). This is apparent from the writings of some of the early proponents of the exclusion approach, including the French sociologist Serge Paugam, who has argued that:

> [T]he "poor" do not form a very homogenous social entity; that is to say, there are several strata within this population ... *poverty is a multidimensional phenomenon, which today corresponds less to a state, than to a process*. Consequently, any static definition of poverty tends to lump together, within the same overall category, sections of the population whose situation is heterogeneous, and to obscure the basic question as to the process by which the problems of individuals or of households progressively accumulate, from its origins to its effects in the medium to long term. (Paugam, 1995, pp 49-50; emphasis added)

The two key words in this description are 'multidimensional' and 'process', both of which challenge an approach that identifies poverty as a snapshot characterised by a lack of income. Social exclusion raises issues that a poverty approach is incapable of addressing, not because of the strictures imposed when measuring poverty using a poverty line, but because of its aggregation of 'the poor' into a single group that share a common characteristic: low income (relative to need).

As many critics have pointed out, this one-dimensional approach leads to the self-evident proposition that poverty can be 'solved' through income transfers, without the need to address (or even identify) its underlying causes. The limitations of the approach were recognised in Australia over three decades ago by the Poverty Commission, which prefaced all of its reports with the statement that:

> If poverty is seen as a result of structural inequality within society, any serious attempt to eliminate poverty must seek to change those conditions which produce it. (Commission of inquiry into Poverty, 1975, p viii)

Unfortunately, the Commission did not take up this challenge, nor did it attempt to elucidate what was meant by 'structural inequality within society', or explore its role in creating the conditions that result in poverty. Instead, it focused on reforms that did not seek to change the existing structures of inequality but redistributed resources within them. This approach ignores the possibility that efforts to reduce poverty will have limited impact unless the underlying structural inequalities are addressed. In light of this, it is ironic that the Commission's own recommendations were swept off the policy agenda by the transformative economic changes brought about by the 1970s oil shocks that were emerging as its work was being completed (Manning, 1998).

The relationship between poverty and social exclusion is best viewed from the perspective suggested by Ruth Lister, who argues that:

> [P]rovided it is not used to camouflage poverty and inequality, social exclusion can usefully be understood and used as a lens that illuminates aspects of poverty ... it is a way of looking at the concept of poverty rather than an alternative to it. (Lister, 2004, p 74)

This approach has much to recommend it, although there is the danger that the two concepts can become blurred, particularly if poverty measures (for example, the proportion of the population with incomes below half the median) are included as indicators of exclusion. This has the effect of re-defining poverty as a form of exclusion rather than as an independent phenomenon that can be viewed through an exclusion lens. It also makes it difficult to examine the similarities and differences between poverty and exclusion using overlap analysis like that conducted in the previous (and following) chapters. Against this, the decision to include the poverty rate among the indicators of exclusion provides a vehicle for ensuring that poverty does not slip off the policy radar screen. Poverty also becomes less of a moral imperative when it is included as one among many indicators, taking the pressure off the tools used to measure it.

The social exclusion paradigm reflects an underlying shift of focus, away from income onto other factors that contribute to different forms of social disadvantage.

The emergence of multi-dimensionality as a key feature of contemporary disadvantage reflects studies showing that those affected by one problem often experience a number of others that constrain their choices and block opportunities. This adds to the task of finding solutions that have the capacity to address in an integrated way the complex realities that shape people's lives.

The social exclusion/inclusion perspective has also generated a shift of focus onto broader inequalities and the structures and processes that underpin them. As indicated earlier, the view adopted by Giddens (1998) equates inequality with exclusion and equality with inclusion, but only where inequality is interpreted in a broad sense to cover all forms of political and social rights and obligations. At a more specific level, Atkinson (1998) has drawn together many of the main themes that define social exclusion into three underlying ideas: *relativity* – the idea that exclusion can only be judged by comparing the circumstances of individuals, groups or communities with others, in a given place and at a given time; *dynamics* – the idea that the effects of exclusion need to be traced through time to be understood; and *agency* – the idea that people are excluded through choices of their own, or by the acts of others. The emphasis on the relational nature of exclusion is also seen as important by Sen (2000), who argues that the key contribution of social exclusion 'lies in emphasising the role of relational features in the deprivation of capability and thus in the experience of poverty' (Sen, 2000, p 6).

The features identified by Atkinson highlight the idea that exclusion is the result of certain *processes*. It follows that exclusion studies must seek to identify these, and this shifts the focus away from merely identifying who is excluded onto questions relating to who is responsible, and what are the contributing factors (Saunders, 2005c). These are important questions that shape the policy (and other) responses to exclusion and help to define the 'inclusion' that such responses seek to achieve (Donnison, 1998).

Language plays an important role in influencing which perspective attracts most attention, as Peace (2001) has observed. She notes that the semantic process of nominalisation converts verbs into nouns, the effect being in this case that:

> ... agency disappears – whoever or whatever was "doing the thing" becomes either abstract or invisible.... The action turns into a thing in its own right. Thus, a commentary that discusses the active act of "excluding" someone or something from somewhere involves an identification of agency.... But "exclusion", as a verb ... has been turned into a noun [that] signifies a "thing" rather than an "action". (Peace, 2001, p 21)

Through this process, how a concept like exclusion is described or labelled exerts a powerful effect on how it is perceived, the methods used to examine it and the kinds of actions needed to address it.

Language has also been an important factor behind the emerging importance of social exclusion among policy makers. As noted in Chapter Two, the word 'poverty' carries with it the moral imperative for action, and this puts great strain on the methods used to define and measure it. In contrast, social exclusion does not have the same moral connotations as poverty, and has proved to be more adaptable in a variety of policy settings. The shifting language of disadvantage used in the European anti-poverty programmes spanning 1975 to 1994 has been described in the following terms:

> Within this succession of programmes, there has been a varied vocabulary of disadvantage. "Poverty" was at the heart of … the first and second programmes…. The third programme, in contrast, was concerned with the integration of the "least privileged" – we are all privileged but some are less privileged that others. By the time this programme was actually launched, "social exclusion" became fashionable terminology. (Room, 1995, p 3)

Use of the word 'fashionable' suggests that these terminological shifts are temporary and social exclusion will eventually be replaced by another term. Against this, recent trends suggest that the concept is sufficiently flexible to allow it to be re-defined to encompass new issues as they emerge onto the policy agenda.

Reflecting these subtle but pervasive terminological shifts, much of the empirical literature on social exclusion has focused on the characteristics and conditions of those who have been excluded from various domains of economic and social life. Relatively little attention has been paid to identifying the acts of exclusion themselves, and even less to identifying those individuals, institutions, structures or conventions that implicitly endorse and are thus responsible for accommodating various acts of exclusion. In order to gain an understanding of the *processes* of exclusion, it is necessary to identify those whose actions exclude others, as well as those who are at the receiving end.

This discussion has highlighted some of the features that explain the rise to prominence of social exclusion as a new organising theme for social policy. The overriding focus in the exclusion approach on understanding the processes that prevent people from realising their full potential is consistent with 'Third Way' ideas about the roles and obligations (or rights and responsibilities) that determine how a modern welfare state interacts with the citizens that support it as taxpayers and rely on it when needed. This flexibility has allowed researchers and policy makers to engage in a productive dialogue that has resolved (or avoided) the definitional ambiguities and offered practical solutions to policy problems.

Above all, its success has relied on the willingness of government to acknowledge that social exclusion takes many forms and exists across a broad range of areas, but is often concentrated in particular individuals and/or specific locations. This has shifted the focus away from issues of poverty and low income, and led to the development of government-wide solutions that address the complexities that exist. This in turn has reinforced the need for actions to promote inclusion to be based on the evidence generated by research.

The role and nature of indicators

The emergence of social exclusion as a focus of the social policy reform agenda has been accompanied by a revitalisation of the role and importance of indicators. The use of indicators is inevitable where the underlying concept is both multi-dimensional and elusive, both of which are features of social exclusion, as the discussion so far has demonstrated. Indicators are signposts or pointers that represent things that are not amenable to measurement, but they do not represent the thing itself, as Spicker (2004, p 432) has emphasised. The more agreement there is among the indicators about the nature of the issue being examined, the more confidence one can have that the indicators are capturing what is going on, but such agreement will not always exist and there will be instances where different indicators suggest different, perhaps contradictory, conclusions.

Experience overseas and in Australia has shown that indicators can play an important role in shaping the social inclusion policy agenda and creating the conditions for action. They have provided a practical impetus to a debate about identification, measurement and change that might otherwise have become bogged down in definitional and statistical issues. They have given practical expression to what governments are seeking to achieve and provided a self-imposed benchmark against which to monitor trends and judge performance. Governments have generally been wary of developing and publishing indicators that provide concrete evidence of their performance, for fear that it will be shown to lag behind what was promised. Even though the large number of indicators provides adequate scope to establish at least some areas of success, the fact that indicators are being developed and published highlights the impact of the social inclusion agenda on what kinds of data are collected, how they are disseminated and what kinds of debate this generates.

However, developing indicators and collecting the data required to compare outcomes with implied targets does not, of itself, imply that the benchmarks set are appropriate. This also requires that the indicators are relevant to the task, have a clear interpretation in terms of directions of change and are supported by relevant and timely data. There is a risk – confirmed by some of the early UK developments according to Levitas (2006) – that the indicators produced are constrained by the available data rather than allowing the indicators to drive the collection of new data where there are gaps. Or that the data that are used, while relevant to the topic, may not adequately capture what is intended when using an indicator to capture a particular aspect of inclusion. Millar (2007, p 5) cites the examples of using the amount of contact with neighbours as an indicator of social isolation 'with little regard for the nature and quality of the contact' or measuring political participation 'simply by voting or membership of political parties'.

To the extent that the data used to construct indicators of exclusion and inclusion reflect what is available nationally, this may also prevent cross-national comparisons of social exclusion, where a uniform approach to measurement is required. This issue has particular relevance in the EU context where member states are committed to a common set of inclusion objectives, and has led to the development of agreed indicators and the collection of comparative data (EU-SILC) that allows countries to be compared.

The indicators adopted by the EU (the Laeken indicators) reflect the analysis and advice provided in a report prepared for the Council of the European Union by Atkinson et al (2002). Before specifying the *content* of the list of indicators, the report argued that each indicator should satisfy the following *principles*:

- clarity and lack of ambiguity;
- robustness and validation;
- policy responsiveness (and lack of manipulation);
- comparability (within and between countries) and consistency (with established national and international standards);
- timeliness (but subject to revision);
- avoidance of unnecessary informational burden on states, enterprises and citizens.

The authors also argued that the portfolio of indicators as a whole should be:

- balanced across its different dimensions;
- mutually consistent and appropriately weighted;
- transparent and accessible to citizens.

These principles have much in common with those used by the ABS to develop the indicators selected for inclusion in its reports on *Measures of Australia's progress* (MAP) (for example, ABS, 2002c, 2010). The MAP indicators are designed to inform decisions about Australia's progress in three broad dimensions – economic, social and environmental. The ABS has identified the following criteria as defining what constitutes a 'good' headline indicator (ABS, 2002c, Appendix 1):

- relevance (to a particular aspect of progress);
- outcome-focused (as opposed to input- or process-focused);
- unambiguous in interpretation (in relation to progress);
- supported by timely and good quality data;
- availability as a time series;
- sensitivity (to changes in underlying conditions);
- be summary in nature;
- capable of disaggregation (by population groups or regions);
- be intelligible and interpretable by the general reader.

These criteria bear many similarities to the principles embedded in the Laeken indicators. Although the purpose of the MAP indicators is to assess the direction (and magnitude) of progress across a broader range of areas than just social inclusion, they include several that have direct relevance to social exclusion, including in the areas of education and training, work, economic disadvantage and inequality, housing, crime and social attachment.

Combining the indicators: an overall index?

Implicit in the above discussion is the idea that social exclusion is multi-dimensional, with the different indicators capturing its different dimensions. This raises the question of whether or not to combine the indicators into a single summary index and if so, how. The main argument in favour of aggregation relates to the ease of disseminating information about a single (or small set of) headline indicators, compared with a complex and unwieldy set of disaggregated indicators.

One argument for maintaining the disaggregated approach relates to the fact that social exclusion is experienced in degrees rather than in all-or-nothing terms, and that there are substantial differences in the way that the different forms of exclusion are experienced. Exclusion normally exists across several domains (see below) and the specific manifestations differ widely in terms of their impact and how they are measured. Some forms of exclusion (for example, living in a jobless household, or not having access to appropriate transportation) will create greater problems for those affected and raise important policy issues, while others (for example, being lonely or socially disconnected) may be more open to interpretation and less amenable to policy action. The links between the separate indicators can also provide valuable information on the interconnections that often drive exclusion.

These features are an integral part of exclusion (and are reflected in the definitional disagreements discussed earlier), and have led some researchers to argue that the different dimensions of social exclusion should not be 'amalgamated into a single category of the "social excluded"' (Burchardt et al, 1999, p 241). To combine the different dimensions of exclusion into a single 'headline indicator' is not only at odds with the underlying diversity and interrelated nature of the concept itself, but also risks providing information that can be misleading or meaningless: what can it mean to say that the Australian community is X% more (or less) excluded this year than last year?

It also needs to be remembered that one of the most important insights provided by a list of indicators of exclusion relates to the circumstances of different demographic groups, identified on the basis of such variables as age, gender, family status, location and ethnicity. If, for example, the indicators reveal that lone-parent families face exclusion in more dimensions than couple families, or that those living in regional areas or the suburbs are more excluded than those living in inner metropolitan areas, there is no need for a summary measure to reinforce the point. But if the group rankings differ across the different forms of exclusion, this important information will be lost if an overall index is used. A summary index may thus be unnecessary in some instances and undesirable in others.

Against this, a case for aggregation can be made on the basis that the use of a summary index forces decisions to be taken about the relative importance of the different dimensions of the problem. In addition, because summary indicators are more easily disseminated they are more likely to generate pressure to address the issue. These are important considerations, but they are only claims and there is no hard evidence that summary measures are more easily disseminated, or are more likely to spur action. Although some composite indicators like the Human Development Index (HDI) produced by the United Nations Development Programme (UNDP, 2009) have contributed to international debate about how countries compare in terms of the well-being of their populations, others have been beset by controversy over the methods used to derive them. Thus, recent Australian efforts to compare and publish the relative performance of schools that rank similarly using an Index of Community Socio-Educational Advantage (ICSEA) has shown that the debate can become bogged down (at least initially) in the properties of the summary index rather than on what the performance comparisons themselves reveal.

Composite headline indicators may provide good media copy, but when there is community interest in the underlying issues, the public want to see the details so that they can assess for themselves what the figures mean. The ABS has acknowledged that the main problem with the single indicator approach is that 'any composite indicator is based on some judgement regarding the relative weights to be applied to the components' (ABS, 2009c, p 7). This implies that it may be preferable to adopt a suite of indicators approach and leave it to others to make their own judgements about what the indicators together imply.

A more compelling case for aggregation rests on the ability to identify who is experiencing deep (multi-faceted) exclusion. One simple way of doing this is to follow the procedure adopted when measuring deprivation in Chapter Five and calculate a score by adding up the number of different forms of exclusion experienced. Attention then focuses on those who are in deep exclusion that have index scores above some threshold. This kind of analysis (presented in the next chapter) can be used to identify which specific forms of exclusion are most pronounced among those who face the severest levels of multiple (deep) exclusion. This information is important for policy makers, who are keen to identify where to direct their actions in order to alleviate the problems faced by those who are most disadvantaged as a whole, although a disaggregated approach is also needed to identify the actions needed to address specific forms of exclusion.

If the case for aggregation is accepted, there remains the problem of whether the indicators should be simply added up, or if some form of weighting scheme should be applied and if so, what weights should be used. Studies conducted by researchers at the Melbourne Institute have addressed this issue in the context of developing new multi-dimensional estimates of poverty and social exclusion (Scutella et al, 2008, 2009). The latter study presents estimates of social exclusion based on 29 indicators across seven domains using data from the first seven waves of data from the HILDA Survey. A range of alternative weighting schemes is examined, including simple aggregation (to produce what they refer to as a sum-score), and schemes that assign higher or lower weights to certain indicators or domains. The authors acknowledge the limitations of the sum-score, noting that:

'The nature of an individual's exclusion is not communicated by the score, and so it is not immediately informative on the appropriate policy response', although they reinforce the point made above by noting that 'a priority for future work is to describe the domains of exclusion of the most severely excluded individuals' and this obviously requires the use of a summary measure (Scutella et al, 2009, p 63).

The Melbourne Institute research shows that estimates of the extent and severity of exclusion are affected by the weighting scheme used, and the (downward) trend in exclusion also becomes less pronounced when greater weight is given to the income ranking of individuals. Use of more complex statistical techniques for identifying the weights finds (as others have done; see Capellari and Jenkins, 2008) that the ranking of exclusion across individuals is similar to that produced using the simple sum-score approach. Even so, the weighting issue is sufficiently important to warrant further examination, because:

> This sensitivity of our findings to the weighting regime would suggest that further research into the most appropriate weighting regime, or research into methods by which the most appropriate regime could be identified, would be beneficial. (Scutella et al, 2009, p 42)

This makes good sense, although it is also important to relate the weights in some way to independent evidence about the importance attached to each dimension of exclusion (for example, what proportion of the community regards the activity as essential, or what proportion actually participates in each activity). Such analysis can make the measurement of exclusion better grounded in community norms, making the findings more relevant to current experience.

Domains of exclusion

Most academic studies of social exclusion specify a number of broad areas or domains of exclusion and within each, develop a series of indicators. In contrast, government efforts to identify exclusion have tended to avoid the use of domains, preferring instead to compare indicator values across population sub-groups (including communities) as a way of highlighting where improvements are needed. Both dimensions are important, and it is possible to develop a matrix that compares the incidence and severity of exclusion across the identified domains, and between different demographic groups, helping policy makers to target their policies in the right areas, and on the right groups.

If the indicators are chosen on the basis of data availability, it is important to identify existing data gaps so that steps can be taken to fill them. Insufficient attention has been paid in most exclusion studies to identifying the 'key activities' from which people are excluded, including the vexed question of whether the indicators should be generally applicable across the whole population, or reflect the diverse practises that define different age, ethnic or cultural groups in society (Saunders, 2008). This raises the issue of whether exclusion should be identified at the individual level, or whether it should also be identified at the group or community level. As noted earlier, some groups may be extremely active *within* the group, but have few connections with the wider community, so that individual-level indicators may show that group members are included, but conceal the exclusion faced by the group as a whole.

These limitations introduce a degree or arbitrariness into the coverage of the indicators that can distort the resulting patterns and divert attention away from needed responses. More fundamentally, there is a danger that lists of indicators lead to a disjointed assessment of exclusion that fails to address the connections between different forms of exclusion that lead to its concentration within specific groups or areas. Uncovering these connections requires detailed qualitative studies of how the forces that drive exclusion play out in specific instances. Indicators can help to identify where different dimensions of exclusion co-exist, but in-depth studies are needed to better understand the motivations and processes that affect what is happening.

One of the overriding limitations of the indicators approach (however the indicators are structured and/or combined) is that it tends to place the focus on the *outcomes* associated with different forms of exclusion rather than on the *processes* that produce those outcomes. Unless the approach is capable of capturing the individual and structural determinants of exclusion, there is the risk that policy will be directed at the symptoms rather than the underlying causes, leading to interventions that address problems once they arise rather than adopting a preventative approach. The inclusion agenda must not only identify existing forms of exclusion, but also seek to change the assumptions and attitudes that prevent people from participating and being included.

The development of social exclusion indicator frameworks using a small number of domains has been shaped by the work undertaken by the EU referred to earlier. That work led to the commitment by all EU member states to monitor progress in tackling poverty and social exclusion using the Laeken indictors (European Commission, 2002). The original list of 18 indicators covered dimensions of income inequality, the level, variation and persistence in poverty (measured using a poverty line set at 60% of median income), changes in poverty anchored at a point in time, poverty before and after the receipt of income transfers, regional variation in employment rates, rates of long-term (more than 12 months) and very long-term (more than 24 months) unemployment, and the share of the population aged 18-24 not in education or training. The original list focused primarily on economic factors, although subsequent revisions have broadened the scope to reflect improved data on the social dimensions of inclusion and exclusion.

Another influential development has taken place in the UK, where the *Opportunity for all* suite of indicators referred to earlier has produced important new information on levels and trends in exclusion and inclusion. The 2007 *Opportunity for all* report, for example, reports on 59 indicators, of which 41 are identified as main indicators, that cover income levels, inequality, regional cohesion (measured by differences in employment rates), life expectancy at birth, poverty risks, unemployment, joblessness, poverty traps, employment gaps of immigrants, material deprivation, housing deprivation, unmet needs for medical care, child well-being, homelessness, education (literacy and numeracy), births to young mothers, smoking rates and fear of crime (DWP, 2007). The indicators are disaggregated using a life cycle framework that distinguishes three broad life cycle groups – children and young people, people of working age and people in later life – plus a cross-cutting category that relates to communities.

The two frameworks that have been influential in shaping the UK social exclusion research agenda have emanated from research conducted at CASE and by researchers associated with the PSE Survey based at the Universities of Bristol, Loughborough and York. Studies undertaken by CASE have relied on existing data sets (mainly the British Household Panel Survey, BHPS) to map the exclusion landscape, supplemented by information from detailed qualitative case studies to provide a better understanding of the processes at play (Hills et al, 2002; Richardson and Le Grand, 2002). In contrast, the PSE group has used the PSE Survey (and its predecessors) to collect new data to fill the existing gaps in order to shed new light on the nature of exclusion and its impact on different groups (Pantazis et al, 2006a).

The CASE framework identifies the following four broad dimensions of exclusion:

- *Consumption exclusion* – defined as having an income below one half of median equivalised income.
- *Production exclusion* – defined as not being either employed, self-employed, in education or training, or looking after a family member (that is, being jobless because of unemployment, long-term sickness or disability, or forced early retirement).
- *Political engagement* – defined as not voting or being a member of a campaigning organisation (for example, a political party, trade union or tenants/residents association).
- *Social interaction* – lacking someone who will offer support in one of five areas: listen, comfort, help in crisis, relax with and 'really appreciates you'.

All four indicators are expressed in terms of not having or engaging in activities that active citizens have access to or undertake, and the incidence of exclusion, changes over time and persistence measures are estimated using the BHPS data.

Researchers associated with the different versions of the PSE Survey have identified the following four main dimensions of social exclusion:

- *Impoverishment, or exclusion from adequate resources* – defined as being poor in terms of both low income and deprivation.
- *Labour market exclusion* – identified using a range of labour market indicators, including living in a jobless household, but recognising that these are only valid indicators of exclusion when they correlate with exclusion from social relations.

- *Service exclusion* – where services encompass public transport, play facilities and youth clubs, and basic services inside the home (gas, electricity, water, telephone, etc).
- *Exclusion from social relations* – which covers five dimensions: non-participation in common activities (defined as being regarded as essential by a majority of the population); the extent and quality of social networks; support available in normal times and in times of crisis; disengagement from political and civic activity; and confinement, resulting from fear of crime, disability or other factors.

This a more complex listing than that proposed by CASE, and reflects the increased relevance of the data derived from the PSE Survey.

In Australia, the Melbourne Institute work on indicators of poverty and social exclusion discussed earlier has adopted an approach that distinguishes between seven domains (Scutella et al, 2009, Table 2). These are:

- *Material resources* – covering a range of indicators of low economic resources and reported financial stress.
- *Employment* – high levels of unemployment and sustained unemployment and low attachment to the labour market.
- *Education and skills* – low educational performance and qualifications and little or no work experience.
- *Health and disability* – poor general physical or mental health or the presence of disability in the household (including among children).
- *Social* – low levels of social interaction.
- *Community* – poor neighbourhood quality and low levels of participation in community activities.
- *Personal safety* – victim of violence or property crime and low levels of perceived safety.

Although the HILDA Survey that is used to estimate the incidence of exclusion was not designed specifically for this purpose, its coverage has been broadened to allow a richer array of dimensions of exclusion to be identified and estimated. Importantly, HILDA (like the BHPS) is a panel survey and thus allows the persistence of exclusion to be examined, contributing to a better understanding of the dynamics of exclusion/inclusion and the factors and events that help determine pathways in and out.

There is a strong emphasis in the CASE and PSE approaches on identifying aspects of exclusion that relate to the labour market and economic aspects of exclusion (including poverty). This can provide a limited understanding of exclusion because, as Levitas (2006, p 155) has noted, 'without appropriate indicators, the complex relationships between different dimensions of social exclusion cannot be explored'. Another limitation of the two UK frameworks is their failure to adequately address the question of *agency* and its impact on the indicators used to identify and measure exclusion. As the CASE team itself has noted:

> Perhaps the most significant gap between the concept and measurement tools available is the question of agency. Social exclusion is almost invariably framed in terms of the *opportunity* to participate, yet existing indicators measure actual participation or non-participation. We neither know whether the (non) participation is regarded as problematic by the individual, nor whether he or she has other options. (Burchardt et al, 2002b, p 41; emphasis in the original)

This raises the important issue that whereas social exclusion relates to things that people do not (or cannot) do, most of the data used to study it describe what people actually do (and can) do. This creates a major methodological challenge in drawing inferences about the existence of exclusion by observing participation behaviour as reported in social surveys.

There are additional problems associated with differentiating between the risk of exclusion and its actual incidence, and in drawing conclusions about the presence of exclusion from indicators. Those who live alone, for example, may be at risk of becoming excluded and it may thus be appropriate to include the variable 'living alone' as a *risk factor* when analysing exclusion. But it may not be appropriate to include it as an *indicator* of exclusion unless it can also be demonstrated that those who are living by themselves are actually experiencing some degree of exclusion as a consequence. Similarly, low income restricts people's ability to participate and is thus an exclusion risk factor, but it is also used (as noted earlier) as an indicator of exclusion, and will also be an important consequence of the joblessness that represents exclusion from the labour market.

It is also important to differentiate between those situations that reflect externally imposed exclusion and those that reflect people's choices, or to distinguish between what Sen (2000) refers to as active and passive exclusion. Individuals should not be labelled as 'excluded' simply because they happen to prefer circumstances (for example, to live by themselves) that others have decided are indicative of the condition. However, this raises the difficulties associated with distinguishing between the roles of choice and constraint, an issue that warrants further examination in the exclusion context.

One possible way of untangling these effects (examined in Chapter Nine) involves examining independent measures of subjective well-being as a way of providing additional evidence that the exclusion observed is imposed, not chosen. Such evidence will be suggestive rather than definitive, but can serve to filter out those whose apparent exclusion is not associated with a low level of well-being and thus serve a similar role to the affordability filter used to identify deprivation (see Chapter Six).

The Australian social inclusion agenda

Reference was made earlier to recent developments in the social inclusion agenda in Australia. Among the more significant of these was the release by the federal government, in 2008, of a set of social inclusion principles for Australia covering the new policy's ends (or aspirational principles) and means (or principles of approach) (Australian Government, 2008, 2009). The report *A stronger, fairer Australia. National statement on social inclusion* identifies the following eight principles as underlying the government's approach:

* building on individual and community strengths;
* building partnerships with key stakeholders;
* developing tailored services;
* giving a high priority to early intervention and prevention;
* building joined-up services and whole of government(s) solutions;
* using evidence and integrated data to inform policy;
* reducing disadvantage; and
* planning for sustainability.

These principles reflect current thinking about the design and implementation of social policy and are desirable features of any policy, irrespective of whether or not it forms part of the social inclusion agenda. They have existed in one form or another for many years, but the hope is that the inclusion agenda will allow them to exert a coordinated influence over how policy evolves by giving greater emphasis to addressing the clustering of disadvantage (in individuals and communities) in ways that will promote policies (and generate the resources) that can address this reality.

Government support for the adoption of a social inclusion strategy was reaffirmed, and the report opened by noting that:

> Social inclusion means building a nation in which all Australians have the opportunity and support they need to participate fully in the nation's economic and community life, develop their own potential and be treated with dignity and respect. Achieving this vision means tackling the most entrenched forms of disadvantage in Australia today, expanding the range of opportunities available to everyone and strengthening resilience and responsibility. (Australian Government, 2009, p 2)

The report sets out government plans to reduce social disadvantage while increasing national prosperity and identifies the following six early priorities:

* targeting jobless families;
* improving the life chances of children at risk;
* reducing homelessness;

- improving outcomes for people with a disability or mental illness and their carers;
- closing the gap for Indigenous Australians; and
- breaking the cycle of entrenched, multiple disadvantage.

The approach will be guided by the eight social inclusion principles and informed by the compendium indicator framework that comprises headline and supplementary indicators grouped into 12 domains. The resources needed to produce these documents and the political capital embodied within them illustrates how far the Australian social inclusion agenda has progressed since its muted impact on, and narrow focus in, the welfare reform report *Participation support for a more equitable society* that was released over a decade ago (Reference Group on Welfare Reform, 2000).

The indicators included in the compendium are based on the list of EU indicators developed in 2001, although that list has been extended, specifically in the areas of social, political and cultural exclusion and inclusion. As Table 8.1 shows, the 33 indicators are arranged into six domains (and two contextual factors) and include 20 of the EU indicators (indicated with an asterisk). The overlap between the Australian and EU lists allows Australia's performance to be compared with, and judged against, that of EU countries. The divergence between the Australian and EU lists is greatest for the third, fourth and fifth domains shown in Table 8.1, where nine of the 15 Australian indicators are not included in the EU set. This difference is important, since it is in these areas of exclusion that many have argued that the Europeans have taken a narrowly economic focus, ignoring some of the more socially oriented aspects of inclusion that are being given greater prominence in Australia.

The compendium is an important sign that the government takes seriously the need to address the challenges associated with tackling poverty and social exclusion in Australia, while the use of EU benchmarks signifies a willingness to acknowledge where progress has been (comparatively) poor and where greater effort is needed. There is, however, still an over-emphasis on the economic dimensions of exclusion, with little attempt to include indicators that reflect the degree of social participation and community engagement, or identify areas of alienation or disempowerment.

The inclusion of access to services is a welcome attempt to assess the outreach of existing provisions, although the only two indicators included relate to the difficulty experienced in accessing transport and services generally. The latter generic term needs to be made more specific if it is to provide any guidance to where policy change is needed. Although some of the specific areas where service deficiencies are most pressing (homelessness, disability support and mental illness) have become policy priorities in their own right, the unbalanced composition of the indicator list suggests that there is a role for greater community input into its further development.

Of greater immediate significance are the 'recurring themes' that emerge from the estimates presented in the compendium about which groups are

Table 8.1: Compendium of social inclusion indicators for Australia

1 Poverty and low income
At-risk of poverty rate after social transfers*
Depth of deficient income*
Income distribution*
Income inequality*
Persistent risk of poverty rate*
More stringent risk of poverty rate*
Relative incomes of people aged 65 and over*
Housing affordability

2 Lack of access to the job market
Participation in the labour market*
Employment rate*
Employment rate of older workers*
Long-term unemployment rate*
Persons living in jobless households*
People with a mild or moderate disability who are working
Regional disparity in employment rates*

3 Limited social supports
Assistance given and received
Influencing decision makers

4 Effect of the local neighbourhood
Fear and actual experience of violence
Neighbourhood, community involvement and communal relations

5 Exclusion from services
Early school leavers not in education or training*
Adults with low educational attainment*
Adult literacy rate
Academic progress of Year 3 and Year 7 students
Access to the internet and information technology
Homelessness
Access to services
Teenage mothers

6 Health
Life expectancy at birth*
Healthy life expectancy at birth*
Self-defined health status*
Risk of mental illness

7 Contextual
Total health expenditure per capita*
Total social expenditure per capita*

Note: Indicators marked with an asterisk (*) are included in the current list of EU indicators.

Source: Australian Social Inclusion Board (2009a)

experiencing the greatest degree of exclusion, and in which dimensions. Five groups are identified as experiencing above-average rates of exclusion across several indicators: aged persons; public housing renters; Aboriginal and Torres Strait Islander peoples; one-parent families; and people of non-English-speaking backgrounds. One specific area of exclusion that shows up as relevant for several of these groups is poverty, identified using either the current risk (poverty rate), its stringency (assessed using a lower poverty line) or its persistence over a three-year period (ASIB, 2009a, Section 1).

If the inclusion indicators are published regularly, they will provide important new information about changes in Australia's economic and social fabric, and help to identify the gaps that need filling (including in data availability). Public debate will be greatly enhanced by the availability of the indicators, and this has the potential to give people a greater voice in influencing the social inclusion agenda as it evolves. As noted earlier, efforts are already under way to collect new data on social exclusion as part of the 2010 General Social Survey (GSS), and this will fill some of the existing data gaps. This process of incremental improvement illustrates how indicator lists can have an impact on the policy agenda when they are taken seriously by those with the power to set policy. Although it is still in its infancy, the Australian social inclusion agenda is a good example of how an evidence-based approach can work to improve the scope and quality of the research evidence and of the policies that build on it.

Summary and implications

The social inclusion agenda being developed in Australia has drawn on the British and European experience, which demonstrates that government must play a leadership role if efforts to combat exclusion and promote inclusion are to be successful. Governments must see a need for evidence before they will commit the resources required to collect the data and fund the research needed to support better policy. It is encouraging to note that efforts are underway to expand the scope and make greater use of existing surveys like HILDA and the GSS in order to shed new light on the extent and nature of social exclusion in Australia.

Research based on these surveys will help to set boundaries around the extent of social exclusion and identify its different components. However, the nature of social exclusion is such that large quantitative studies must be accompanied by qualitative surveys that have the capacity to explore the processes, relationships, motivations, expectations and barriers that produce exclusion and prevent inclusion. It is important to identify not just who is being excluded, but who or what is excluding them, and how these processes operate and are legitimised.

For several years, the Brotherhood of St Laurence has been using an exclusion approach to examine the circumstances of refugees (Taylor, 2004; Taylor and Stanovic, 2005), and this work illustrates how small-scale studies can illuminate how exclusionary processes evolve in specific circumstances. Another important non-governmental organisation (NGO), Anglicare Sydney, that delivers a range of community and aged care services, has recently released a report focusing on several dimensions of disadvantage, including economic exclusion and social disconnection among its clients. It justifies the use of a social exclusion approach by arguing that:

> Social exclusion provides an additional focus on subjective and relational issues such as participation, civic engagement, power and opportunity rather than the more easily quantifiable measures such as income and its distribution. (King et al, 2010, p 5)

These studies help to turn the spotlight onto factors that have not been traditionally linked with research on social disadvantage (for example, examples of covert discrimination, or practices that lead to the exclusion of children in school settings). One of the factors that emerged as a major barrier for many people who participated in the focus groups described in Chapter Four was the demeaning treatment that many low-income Australians experience when dealing with welfare bureaucracies and front-line service provision and delivery mechanisms. These frictions at the client–provider interface foster attitudes of resentment and mistrust that can prolong episodes of exclusion by failing to attune service delivery to the needs of users.

More research is also needed into the dynamics of exclusion, focusing on identifying the key pathways into and out of exclusion, the barriers that promote or impede such transitions and the associated triggers. Some of these questions may be capable of being answered with HILDA and other longitudinal surveys, but others will require qualitative panel data to unearth the dynamics of the underlying motivations and processes. In addition, area and community studies are needed to better understand the impact of location on exclusion, particularly in culturally diverse, remote and under-serviced communities. This kind of information has a crucial role to play in identifying how the effects of different forms of multiple exclusion cumulate and reinforce each other over time.

These examples illustrate that much more information is needed about the nature of social exclusion before a comprehensive evidence base will be available to inform action. The fact that social exclusion covers such a myriad of events – actions, inactions, processes, decisions, relationships, motivations, choices and responses – should be seen as a strength, not a weakness, because it reflects the complexity that characterises the realities of social disadvantage.

CASE director John Hills' reflections on the UK experience are relevant here. He notes that:

> ... in practice, the emergence of the language of exclusion and inclusion into the UK policy debate since the late 1990s, has, at least, not damaged more traditional concerns. In the most optimistic interpretation, embracing both an anti-poverty and anti-exclusion agenda has led to a much richer policy mix, with a much greater chance of long-run success. (Hills, 2002, p 243)

Social policy has been neglected for far too long in Australia, where attention has focused on generating economic prosperity and developing 'practical' solutions to social problems (whatever that means) as a kind of palliative for those who are down and out. The failure of Australian policy makers to put serious effort into better understanding issues surrounding social exclusion is now being redressed. This development can learn from the UK experience, which suggests that, in the right circumstances, the fruits of such effort can enrich the policy debate and generate better outcomes. Social exclusion can open up a constructive, problem-focused dialogue between researchers and policy makers that has the potential, in conjunction with research on other aspects of social disadvantage (including poverty studies), to form the basis of a new social policy agenda.

NINE

Identifying social exclusion

Introduction

With interest in social exclusion increasing in Australia and social inclusion emerging as a major focus of social policy, examining the extent of the problem has become increasingly important. Estimating the incidence and severity of exclusion can help to identify high-risk groups and guide where action is needed, what form(s) it should take and allow its effects to be monitored. It is particularly important to highlight instances where exclusion exists among members of the population that do not fall into the conventional categories associated with social disadvantage.

There can be no presumption that exclusion is concentrated on those with limited access to economic resources and thus only affects the 'usual suspects' identified in poverty line studies. One of the advantages of exclusion-focused research is its ability to draw the attention of policy makers to issues (and their interconnections) that had previously gone unnoticed. Research must support this effort by taking a broad approach that is capable of uncovering forms of exclusion that were previously hidden.

The CUPSE Survey has generated the data needed to undertake this latter task. It includes information on different forms of social and community participation, and on the incidence of events that are indicative of exclusion. The data also make it possible to identify what Australians regard as the 'key activities' that can be used to identify who is excluded, and from what. This information allows Australian exclusion to be mapped using a set of indicators that are grounded in everyday experience and reflect community attitudes and practices. Once exclusion has been mapped in this way, it becomes possible to examine its relation to other forms of social disadvantage, including poverty.

Recent research

Until recently, Australian research on social exclusion has focused on issues associated with housing (Arthurson and Jacobs, 2003) or location (Randolph, 2004; Vinson, 2007; Daly et al, 2008), or has examined how exclusion affects vulnerable groups such as the homeless (Australian Government, 2010) and refugees (Taylor and Stanovic, 2005), who are particularly prone to being excluded. These reports and research studies have highlighted important aspects of exclusion, including how its effects unfold in specific instances, but do not provide a national picture of its scale and patterns.

This limitation has been addressed in two recent national studies undertaken by the Australian Social Inclusion Board (ASIB, 2009a) and the Melbourne Institute (Scutella, Wilkins and Kostenko, 2009). The Australian Social Inclusion Board study utilises data from a range of sources – primarily from ABS household surveys conducted between 2000 and 2008 – to estimate the incidence of 33 indicators of exclusion. The Melbourne Institute study uses data from the first seven waves (2001-07) of the HILDA Survey to estimate the incidence of up to 29 indicators. Both studies group the indicators into a smaller number of domains that capture different forms of exclusion: restricted access to income or material resources; exclusion from the labour market; restricted access to services; poor health or disability; and limited access to, or participation in, social supports, neighbourhood and community life.

Despite some differences, the picture revealed by both studies is broadly the same. Thus, for example, the Social Inclusion Board study shows that, across all of the indicators examined, the following groups are most often among those with above-average rates of exclusion:

- older people (aged 65 and over);
- public housing tenants;
- Aboriginal and Torres Strait Islander people;
- lone-parent families; and
- people of non-English-speaking backgrounds.

Some of the estimates presented in the Melbourne Institute study are summarised in Table 9.1. The estimates are based on two separate measures of the severity of exclusion: the percentage that experience at least one form of exclusion (sum-score ≥ 1) and the percentage that experience at least two forms of exclusion (sum-score ≥ 2).

The groups most susceptible to exclusion can be identified by comparing the group-specific incidence rates shown in the columns of Table 9.1 with the overall incidence rates shown in the final row. Comparisons based on the first index reveals that exclusion is most common among the following groups:

- older (aged 65 and over) and younger (aged under 25) people;
- lone-parent families;
- people living in regional areas;
- people born in non-English-speaking countries;
- public and private renters;
- Indigenous Australians; and
- people with a long-term health condition.

Use of the harsher index produces similar results, although these suggest that those aged between 55 and 64 are more susceptible to multiple exclusion than those aged 65 and over (reflecting the high incidence of unemployment and joblessness

Table 9.1: Rates of exclusion by demographic characteristics in 2001 and 2007

Characteristic	Sum-score ≥ 1		Sum-score ≥ 2	
	2001	2007	2001	2007
Gender				
Male	26.3	19.3	5.5	3.7
Female	31.5	24.0	6.5	4.5
Age				
15-24	31.1	21.3	5.0	3.1
25-34	21.5	13.8	5.4	2.7
35-44	24.2	15.0	6.0	3.5
45-54	21.4	16.9	4.4	4.0
55-64	36.2	26.9	9.2	6.7
65 and over	49.8	42.3	7.2	5.0
Place of residence				
Major city	27.0	19.6	5.4	3.7
Inner regional Australia	31.0	25.6	6.7	4.8
Outer regional Australia	36.4	27.2	7.7	4.9
Remote Australia	25.5	16.7	6.7	3.7
Family type				
Couple	28.3	21.7	4.9	3.4
Couple plus dependent child(ren)	21.8	14.9	3.3	2.3
Lone-parent family	51.1	38.1	17.0	9.2
Lone person	40.5	31.0	10.4	6.7
Place of birth				
Australia	27.8	21.0	5.7	3.7
Overseas – English-speaking country	26.3	22.3	4.8	3.9
Overseas – non-English-speaking country	36.7	25.0	8.2	6.3
Indigenous	49.7	42.4	17.1	14.5
Housing tenure				
Homeowner (outright)	29.4	22.7	4.9	3.3
Home purchaser (with mortgage)	20.0	13.2	3.2	1.8
Private renter	37.4	26.9	10.5	5.9
Public housing tenant	67.4	67.9	25.4	28.4
Health status				
Has long-term health condition	56.1	49.2	15.6	12.6
All individuals aged 15 and over	**28.8**	**21.6**	**6.0**	**4.1**

Note: Sum-score is defined as the sum of separate instances of exclusion reported (the maximum varies between 23 and 27 according to the survey wave).

Source: Scutella, Wilkins and Kostenko (2009, Tables 5 and 6)

among older workers). In general, however, the groups identified as most at risk of exclusion are similar in the two studies, although the HILDA data makes it possible to produce more finely-grained estimates despite the low coverage and/ or response rates for some groups.

The Melbourne Institute study also reveals a sharp decline in exclusion between 2001 and 2007. This was primarily a reflection of the strong employment growth that occurred over the period and reflects a narrow focus on the economic dimensions of exclusion. However, this also serves as a reminder that keeping unemployment to a minimum should be an explicit goal of the inclusion agenda – as long as it is not pursued in ways that exacerbate other forms of exclusion (for example, by punitive treatment of jobseekers reliant on the welfare system).

It is also notable that the decline identified by the Melbourne Institute study was less marked – in some instances not even apparent – among some of the groups identified as most excluded in the initial year. Thus, exclusion *increased* between 2001 and 2007 for public housing tenants and declined only marginally for Indigenous Australians and those with a long-term health condition. The overall picture of declining exclusion thus conceals a tendency for exclusion to become relatively more severe among some groups and, by implication, for inequality in exclusion rates to increase in some dimensions.

The final point noted in the Melbourne Institute study is that for many, the experience of exclusion is often short-lived. Drawing on the longitudinal component of the HILDA data, the study shows that long-term (persistent) exclusion is relatively rare, although it is noted that 5% of the population face deep exclusion (a sum-score of two or more in at least three of the seven years analysed), with many children affected by persistent exclusion.

These findings suggest that economic policy alone is not capable of addressing the many forms of social exclusion that exist in Australia. The authors of the Melbourne Institute study note that HILDA 'is not the appropriate information source' from which to study exclusion among groups like the homeless, new immigrants and people living in very remote areas. To fully understand the nature of exclusion faced by these groups, studies designed to identify specific examples of social exclusion are needed to flesh out the details.

Three domains of exclusion

In presenting new results on social exclusion in Australia, a framework similar to that used in the two studies reviewed above and in overseas studies has been adopted. Indicators have been specified and arranged into a small number of domains and a simple summary measure (an unweighted sum-score index that corresponds to the deprivation scores presented and discussed in Chapter Six) has been used to describe and compare the degree of exclusion experienced in different domains and by different socioeconomic groups.

As noted in Chapter Eight, this kind of index has its limitations, but is useful for identifying those groups that suffer from deep exclusion that extends across several dimensions, while the use of domains to segment the different forms of exclusion can help to identify possible causes. However, as noted earlier, the approach conceals the interconnections between the different forms of exclusion that is often an important factor for those who are most excluded. Use of this approach can thus be justified when the focus is mainly on producing *evidence* on the incidence of exclusion and comparing its incidence, nature and severity across different groups in the population. But when it comes to better understanding the underlying *causes* and the *policies* that are needed to promote inclusion, it is vitally important to look beyond the summary measures and identify the individual factors driving particular forms of exclusion, including how they combine and accumulate in specific circumstances or locations.

Social exclusion has been examined using 27 indicators grouped into three broad domains: disengagement; service exclusion; and economic exclusion. Disengagement refers to a lack of participation in the kinds of social activities and events that are customary and widely practised by members of the community. Service exclusion focuses on restricted access to the kinds of services that meet basic needs, whether they are mainly provided publicly and subsidised by government (for example, healthcare, disability, mental health and aged care services), or are predominantly provided privately and subject to extensive user charges (for example, dental treatment, childcare, basic household utilities and financial services). Economic exclusion refers to those with low economic capacities and restricted access to economic resources. It covers situations characterised by a range of indicators of economic or financial stress, including inadequate access to savings, credit, assets and lack of access to the labour market.

Although a case can be made for including the poverty rate as an indicator of economic exclusion (as many other studies have done), a clear demarcation has been maintained here between poverty (not having enough income) and economic exclusion (inadequate access to economic resources and limited economic skills and capacities). Even though poverty will be a cause of exclusion for many people, the approach adopted allows the overlap between poverty and exclusion to be examined in a way that is not possible if the poverty rate is included as one of the indicators of exclusion. It is important to establish whether exclusion and poverty *are* different before examining how they are related and what this implies for policy.

The exclusion indicators are shown in Table 9.2, along with (when it was explicitly asked) the percentage of respondents who indicated that they had participated in each activity. These percentages are generally well above 50%, which is the benchmark used to identify key activities. The one instance where the percentage fails (just) to reach the majority benchmark (access to disability support services) probably reflects uncertainty about the availability of this item for those who, when surveyed, did not need it. Several of the items are relevant to only sub-groups and in these instances, the relevant sub-group is identified in square brackets in Table 9.2. The size of these sub-groups was used to calculate the exclusion incidence rate presented below for these indicators. In all other cases, incidence rates are estimated as a percentage of all respondents.

The indicators in Table 9.2 cover a wide variety of forms of exclusion and the underlying issues to which they relate are of differing significance as dimensions of social disadvantage. To be either unemployed or living in a jobless household might, for example, be regarded as more serious than not having a social life, not participating in community activities, or not being able to pay one's way when out with friends. Although it can be argued that only the former variables raise

Table 9.2: Social exclusion domains and indicators[a]

Disengagement (9 indicators)	Service exclusion (10 indicators)	Economic exclusion (8 indicators)
No regular social contact with other people (87.0%)	No medical treatment if needed (97.0%)	Does not have $500 in savings for use in an emergency (76.1%)
Did not participate in any community activities in last 12 months[b]	No access to a local doctor or hospital (95.5%)	Had to pawn or sell something, or borrow money in the last 12 months
Does not have a social life	No access to dental treatment if needed (91.3%)	Could not raise $2,000 in a week
No annual week's holiday away from home (56.3%)	No access to a bulk-billing doctor (73.6%)	Does not have more than $50,000 worth of assets
Children do not participate in school outings or activities (68.9%) [those with school-age children only]	No access to mental health services (75.1%)	Has not spent $100 on a 'special treat' for myself in last 12 months
No hobby or leisure activity for children (74.1%) [those with children only]	No childcare for working parents [working-age parents only]	Does not have enough to get by on
Couldn't get to an important event because of lack of transport in last 12 months	No aged care for frail older people [people aged 70+ only]	Is currently unemployed or looking for work
Could not go out with friends and pay my way in last 12 months	No disability support services when needed (49.8%)	Lives in a jobless household
Unable to attend wedding or funeral in last 12 months	No access to a bank or building society (93.0%)	
	Couldn't keep up with payments for water, electricity, gas or telephone in last 12 months	

Notes: [a] Figures shown in brackets show the percentage that participated in each activity.

[b] The community activities referred to in the survey question are: education or school-based activities, a volunteer in health or community services, church groups or activities (other than attending services), arts, music or cultural groups/activities, sport (participant, volunteer or spectator), neighbourhood groups or activities of any kind, and a political campaign or event of any kind. The last response category was 'None of the above' and those who gave this response were identified as excluded on this indicator.

genuine policy concerns and can be affected by policy interventions, the latter are equally legitimate aspects of exclusion and thus also warrant consideration. It is possible to assign different weights to each indicator to allow for this, but how these weights can capture the importance of different items is unclear, and this has not been attempted in order to keep the focus on the diversity of exclusion.

Table 9.3 compares the incidence of each indicator of exclusion in the community and (2006) client samples. As before (for example, Table 6.1 in Chapter Six), the incidence rates for the community sample are shown on both a raw (unweighted) basis and after the data have been re-weighted to better represent the age structure of the population. The client sample estimates have also been re-weighted to conform to the age structure of the community sample in order to make them more comparable. Such re-weighting has little impact on the broad pattern of results and the following discussion thus focuses (as before) on the unweighted estimates. The patterns of exclusion in each of the three domains of exclusion are illustrated in Figures 9.1, 9.2 and 9.3, which show the contrast between the community and client sample results more starkly.

Looking first across all 27 indicators, the three with the highest incidence in the community sample all relate to a lack of service provision: no childcare for working parents (52.7%); no access to disability support services when needed (50.2%); and no access to aged care services (47.8%). The first two also rank highly among the client sample, where the four most prevalent indicators are: living in a jobless household (75.3%); does not have $500 in savings for an emergency (73.6%); no annual holiday (72.6%); and has less than $50,000 in assets (excluding the family home and any superannuation assets) (72.4%). It is clear that many forms of social exclusion are widespread – even among the general population – with some affecting more than half of those seeking assistance from welfare services.

There are, of course, major differences in the interpretation to be placed on the different indicators, as well as their implications for policy. Governments are likely to be more directly concerned about joblessness and lack of access to healthcare or other public services than about people not having a social life or lacking emergency savings. Against this, these latter items can serve as important buffers in times of crisis that support resilience and prevent people from becoming dependent on state support. This aspect of the results also raises questions about how resources are distributed and the barriers that prevent inclusion for many community members.

The results in Table 9.3 raise questions about the adequacy and accessibility of government service provisions that facilitate people's economic and social participation, including basic medical services as well as childcare, transportation and support for important leisure activities – at school and more generally. The findings also cast doubt on the view that most Australians have active social lives and engage with their communities, and it is clear that many people are on the margins of economic survival with few resources (social as well as economic) to call on in an emergency. There are also likely to be some important interconnections between the different indicators, with lack of transport preventing people from

Table 9.3: The incidence of social exclusion in the community and client samples

Exclusion indicator	Community sample		Client sample	
	Unweighted	Weighted	Unweighted	Weighted
Disengagement				
No regular social contact with other people	13.0	12.5	24.2	22.5
Did not participate in community activities	28.1	26.9	32.8	32.2
Does not have a social life	11.3	10.5	n/a	n/a
No week's holiday away from home each year	43.7	43.9	72.6	71.0
Children do not participate in school activities or outings	6.7	7.0	27.0	24.4
No hobby or leisure activity for children	14.2	15.3	37.4	37.6
Couldn't get to an event due to lack of transport	5.0	5.7	25.6	22.0
Could not go out with friends and pay their way	21.4	24.1	52.0	47.4
Unable to attend a wedding or funeral	3.2	3.1	11.7	11.5
Service exclusion				
No medical treatment if needed	3.0	3.1	11.1	11.5
No access to a local doctor or hospital	4.5	4.4	8.7	8.3
No dental treatment if needed	18.7	19.2	57.0	53.8
No access to a bulk-billing doctor	26.4	25.8	14.3	13.1
No access to mental health services, if needed	24.9	25.0	38.8	39.5
No childcare for working parents	52.7	51.3	60.0	60.1
No aged care for frail older people	47.8	46.7	12.5	12.7
No disability support services, when needed	50.2	50.2	60.2	55.0
No access to a bank or building society	7.0	7.0	10.9	9.8
Couldn't make electricity, water, gas or telephone payments	12.5	13.4	41.4	39.0
Economic exclusion				
Does not have $500 in emergency savings	23.9	26.1	73.6	66.0
Had to pawn or sell something or borrow money	6.5	7.2	30.7	26.8
Could not raise $2,000 in a week	14.2	14.6	53.8	52.1
Does not have $50,000 worth of assets	27.2	27.7	72.4	76.1
Has not spent $100 on a special treat	9.1	8.6	25.3	29.3
Does not have enough to get by on	6.2	6.1	30.3	30.1
Currently unemployed or looking for work	3.9	4.2	38.9	30.7
Lives in a jobless household	20.8	19.9	75.3	76.0
Mean incidence of exclusion	**18.7**	**19.3**	**37.0**	**35.5**

Note: n/a = not available.

participating in social events and also restricting their access to services when they are needed. These linkages have not been explicitly identified and require further study using alternative methods.

The contrast between the overall profiles of exclusion in the two samples once again highlights the precarious economic circumstances of those in the welfare services client sample. However, it is also apparent from a broader review of all of the indicators that economic barriers are not the only factors that contribute to the exclusion of those forced to seek assistance from welfare services. Many forms of exclusion are broad in their incidence, but there are clearly also deep pockets of exclusion that affect specific groups.

In relation to disengagement, Figure 9.1 shows that the incidence rankings of the community and client samples are similar, with the four most common indicators in both cases being: no annual week's holiday away; no hobby or leisure activity for children; could not pay one's way when out with friends; and no participation in community activities. The fact that two of these four items impact on children is of particular concern, while the other two show that many are excluded from the kinds of social and community activities that help to strengthen community networks and build social capital.

There are also significant proportions of both samples who report having no regular social contact with other people and, in the case of the community sample, say that they have no social life (this question was not asked in the client survey). Around 30% of both samples had not participated over the previous 12 months in any form of community activity including volunteering, sporting events (as a participant or spectator), or cultural, political or neighbourhood activities.

Figure 9.2 indicates that service exclusion is widespread in Australia, with a large proportion of both samples excluded from childcare, disability and dental services in particular. There are two cases (access to a bulk-billing doctor, and aged care for frail older people) where the incidence of exclusion is *higher* in the community sample than in the client sample. Although the latter result may reflect the low numbers of older people in the client sample, the high proportion of the community sample who do not have access to a bulk-billing doctor (26.4%) is indicative of the erosion of the universal coverage of the Medicare scheme. Around 11% of the client sample and about one third as many in the community sample are excluded from medical treatment and a significant proportion of welfare service clients (over 40%) faced exclusion from basic domestic services over the past 12 months, as a result of being unable to pay their household utility bills.

It is in relation to the incidence of economic exclusion (Figure 9.3) that exclusion among those in the client sample shows up as much worse than among those in the community sample. The client sample exclusion rate exceeds 50% for four of the eight indicators, and is over 70% in three of these four cases. Over one quarter of those in the community sample do not have more than $50,000 of (non-housing, non-superannuation) assets, while around 15% could not raise $2,000 in a week if they needed to and close to 10% had not spent a modest sum ($100) on a special treat for themselves in the last year. Close to one third (30.7%) of the client sample had been forced to pawn or sell something or borrow money from a money lender over the last year. These findings reinforce the message that although economic prosperity may have been widespread when the survey was conducted in 2006, many faced the risk of economic exclusion and had few resources to call on to avoid it.

Figure 9.1: The incidence of disengagement in the community and client samples

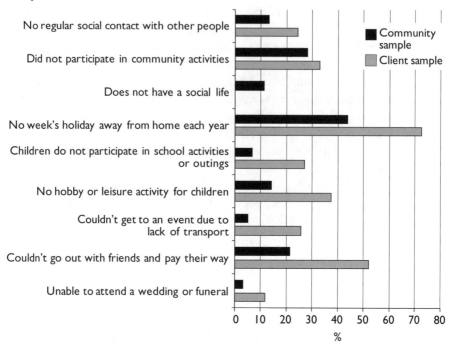

Figure 9.2: The incidence of service exclusion in the community and client samples

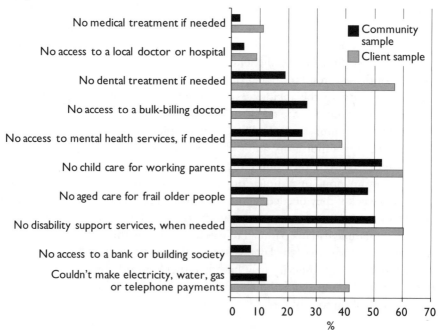

Figure 9.3: The incidence of economic exclusion in the community and client samples

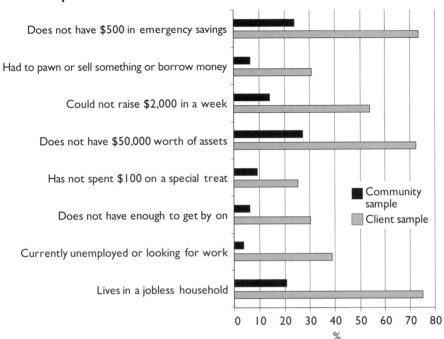

Multiple exclusion

It was noted above that an aggregate index of social exclusion can conceal the interconnections between the different forms of exclusion and can do little to advance our understanding of an issue that takes many different forms. Notwithstanding the validity of these concerns, it is useful to examine the extent to which individuals experience multiple forms of exclusion, since this provides important information about the severity of exclusion, and who is most susceptible to deep exclusion.

The (unweighted) incidence of multiple exclusion (in total and within each domain) is shown in Table 9.4 for the community and client samples. Multiple exclusion has been identified by deriving a sum–score index for each individual that varies between zero (no instances of exclusion) and 27 (excluded in all dimensions identified). The indices for disengagement, service exclusion and economic exclusion are similarly constructed, varying in this case between zero and the maximum number of indicators specified in each domain.

It is evident from Table 9.4 that those in the client sample face a serious level of multiple exclusion, however it is defined. Thus, while close to one quarter (24.0%) of the community sample experience six or more separate instances of exclusion in total, more than two thirds (70.0%) of the client sample fall into this category of deep exclusion. Well over one third of the community sample is not in

Table 9.4: The cumulative incidence of different forms of social exclusion

Number of indicators	All	Domain Disengagement	Service exclusion	Economic exclusion
Community sample				
0	9.9	38.2	29.0	49.8
1 or more	90.1	61.8	71.0	50.2
2 or more	72.9	33.9	42.9	26.0
3 or more	55.5	16.6	22.2	14.2
4 or more	42.4	7.7	9.9	7.5
5 or more	31.3	3.5	4.3	3.8
6 or more	24.0	1.2	1.6	1.3
7 or more	17.9	0.3	0.6	0.6
8 or more	13.3	0.0	0.1	0.0
9 or more	9.8	–	0.0	–
10 or more	7.6	–	–	–
Mean exclusion score	**3.81**	**1.25**	**1.53**	**1.04**
Client sample				
0	1.2	16.2	16.7	6.8
1 or more	98.8	83.8	83.3	93.2
2 or more	95.2	60.2	62.9	84.4
3 or more	90.5	38.3	42.1	72.1
4 or more	84.7	21.2	23.1	57.8
5 or more	77.1	11.0	11.2	40.4
6 or more	70.0	4.2	4.6	23.2
7 or more	62.4	1.8	2.2	8.2
8 or more	53.9	0.4	0.7	0.9
9 or more	45.6	0.0	0.1	0.0
10 or more	37.4	–	0.0	–
Mean exclusion score	**8.30**	**2.21**	**2.30**	**3.80**

any way disengaged, while around 30% and 50% experience no forms of service exclusion and economic exclusion, respectively. Between 8% and 10% (around one in eleven) of the community sample experience four or more examples of disengagement and service exclusion, while closer to 22% (approaching one in four) of the client sample are similarly affected.

However, it is in relation to economic exclusion where the difference between the two samples is again starkest. Thus, while only 7.5% of the community sample experience four or more indicators of economic exclusion, the corresponding percentage for the client sample is *almost eight times higher*, at close to 58%. Almost one quarter (23.2%) of those in the client sample experienced six or more of the eight indicators of economic exclusion, whereas only just over one per cent of those in the community sample are similarly affected. Clearly, if the analysis had been based on the community sample only, the results would not have revealed the severe economic exclusion that exists among many of the most disadvantaged Australians.

Characteristics of those in deep exclusion

Deep exclusion exists when individuals experience a number of different forms of exclusion simultaneously. Since it represents the most serious manifestation of exclusion, addressing deep exclusion is an obvious policy priority. However, before any specific action can be contemplated, it is necessary to know which groups are most prominent among those in deep exclusion and what forms of exclusion they face. The following analysis sheds light on the answer to these questions, using a definition of deep exclusion that covers those in the community sample who face at least seven separate instances of exclusion. (The deep-excluded sub-sample contains 484 individuals or 17.9% of those in the community sample.)

Table 9.5 compares the exclusion incidence rates for the full community sample with that sub-sample that is identified as being in deep exclusion. The estimates provide a point of comparison that allows the forms of exclusion that are most prevalent among those in deep exclusion to be identified. This has been done by calculating the ratio of the incidence rates in the deep-excluded and full samples (shown in the final column of Table 9.5). These ratios need to be interpreted with caution, since they depend to some degree on the size of the exclusion incidence rate in the full sample: if the original incidence rate is high, there is less room for it to increase further, leading to a lower ratio.

A benchmark for comparing the ratios is provided in the final row of Table 9.5, which shows that, on average across all 27 indicators, those in deep exclusion have a mean exclusion score that is 2.29 times higher than those in the full sample. There are 13 items where the incidence rate ratio exceeds three, and these are, in declining order:

- no medical treatment if needed;
- does not have enough to get by on;
- had to pawn or sell something or borrow money;
- could not raise $2,000 in a week;
- couldn't make electricity, water, gas or telephone payments;
- couldn't get to an event due to lack of transport;
- no dental treatment if needed;
- unable to attend a wedding or funeral;
- children could not participate in school activities or outings;
- currently unemployed or looking for work;
- could not go out with friends and pay one's way;
- no regular social contact with other people; and
- does not have $500 in emergency savings.

Table 9.5: Exclusion incidence rates in the full community and deeply excluded samples

Exclusion indicator	Full sample (a)	Deep exclusion sub-sample (b)	Ratio (b)/(a)
Disengagement			
No regular social contact with other people	13.0	41.4	3.18
Did not participate in community activities	28.1	46.8	1.67
Does not have a social life	11.3	31.3	2.77
No week's holiday away from home each year	43.7	86.0	1.98
Children do not participate in school activities or outings	6.7	22.7	3.39
No hobby or leisure activity for children	14.2	38.1	2.68
Couldn't get to an event due to lack of transport	5.0	18.3	3.66
Could not go out with friends and pay their way	21.4	69.1	3.23
Unable to attend a wedding or funeral	3.2	11.3	3.53
Service exclusion			
No medical treatment if needed	3.0	13.2	4.40
No access to a local doctor or hospital	4.5	13.2	2.93
No dental treatment if needed	18.7	67.0	3.58
No access to a bulk-billing doctor	26.4	32.8	1.24
No access to mental health services, if needed	24.9	51.3	2.06
No child care for working parents	52.7	76.5	1.45
No aged care for frail older people	47.8	80.8	1.69
No disability support services, when needed	50.2	70.6	1.41
No access to a bank or building society	7.0	14.9	2.13
Couldn't make electricity, water, gas or telephone payments	12.5	46.0	3.68
Economic exclusion			
Does not have $500 in emergency savings	23.9	75.9	3.18
Had to pawn or sell something or borrow money	6.5	25.8	3.97
Could not raise $2,000 in a week	14.2	54.6	3.85
Does not have $50,000 worth of assets	27.2	66.3	2.44
Has not spent $100 on a special treat	9.1	26.2	2.88
Does not have enough to get by on	6.2	25.1	4.05
Currently unemployed or looking for work	3.9	13.0	3.33
Lives in a jobless household	20.8	39.2	1.88
Mean incidence of exclusion	**18.7**	**42.9**	**2.29**

Of the 13 items that are most commonly associated with those identified as being in deep exclusion, five fall into each of the disengagement and economic exclusion domains, and the remaining three are examples of service exclusion. Three of the top five ranked items represent forms of economic exclusion, while a fourth (unable to pay household utility bills) is also indicative of low economic capacity.

It is clear that those in deep exclusion are also disengaged in several areas, including not being able to get to important events, to interact socially with others more generally, and not being able to send their children on school outings and activities. Some of these latter examples also reflect restricted access to economic resources, further highlighting the role that reduced economic capacity plays in contributing to deep exclusion. Importantly, these results highlight how the social dimensions of exclusion can compound the problems associated with its economic dimension.

The results in Table 9.5 are now supplemented by comparing the socio-demographic characteristics of those in deep exclusion with those in the community sample as a whole. The socioeconomic characteristics on which the comparisons are based are those used to identify the deprivation profile in Chapter Six (see Tables 6.4 and 6.5) and the corresponding exclusion comparisons are presented in Table 9.6.

The final column again shows the ratio of the estimates in columns 2 and 1 and provides an indication of the relative risk of being in deep exclusion faced by different groups. Thus, for example, the first row shows that a person selected at random from among those in deep exclusion is 38% more likely to be aged under 30 than a person selected at random from the total sample. If deep exclusion was distributed randomly among all socioeconomic groups, than the ratios in the final column of Table 9.6 would (aside from sampling errors) all be equal to one. The difference between the calculated ratio and one is thus indicative of where the risks of deep exclusion are greatest.

There are five groups where the ratio (relative risk) exceeds two. They are (in declining order):

• unemployed people;
• public renters;
• lone parents;
• Indigenous Australians; and
• private renters.

These are the same five groups that were shown earlier (Table 6.3 in Chapter Six) to experience the highest levels of deprivation. There is also considerable overlap between these groups and those identified as most at risk of exclusion in the studies conducted by the Australian Social Inclusion Board and the Melbourne Institute described earlier. The evidence thus confirms that both forms of disadvantage – deprivation and social exclusion – are heavily concentrated among these groups.

The two groups with the next highest risk of facing deep exclusion are those caring for children or an adult with a disability, and those who themselves have an ongoing disability. Again, both groups were shown earlier (in Table 6.4, Chapter Six) to also experience above-average levels of deprivation. The fact that some of these groups are over-lapping (for example, lone parents living in public rental

Table 9.6: Comparing the socioeconomic characteristics of the full community sample and those in deep exclusion

Characteristic[a]	Full sample (a)	Deep exclusion sub-sample (b)	Ratio (b)/(a)
Age			
Under 30	12.5	17.3	1.38
30-64	65.8	71.9	1.09
65 and over	21.7	10.9	0.50
Family type[b]			
Single, working age	7.8	13.7	1.76
Single, older person	6.0	4.1	0.68
Working-age couple, no children	19.9	13.2	0.66
Older couple	12.1	4.5	0.37
Working-age couple, with children	42.1	40.9	0.97
Lone parent	6.3	16.2	2.57
Main activity[c]			
Employed	63.8	57.9	0.91
Unemployed	2.9	11.8	4.07
Retired	25.9	18.5	0.71
Caring for children or adults	4.4	8.5	1.93
Principal source of income			
Wages, salaries or interest	74.0	55.0	0.74
Social security payment	25.6	44.6	1.74
Education			
Degree/higher degree	30.5	13.4	0.44
High school or less	69.5	86.6	1.24
Housing tenure			
Owner/purchaser	80.8	53.7	0.66
Private renter	14.7	33.4	2.27
Public renter	4.4	12.9	2.93
Country of birth			
Australia	75.9	75.6	1.00
Another English-speaking country	13.3	9.8	0.74
Another non-English-speaking country	10.8	14.7	1.36
Indigenous (ATSI)			
No	98.4	96.2	0.98
Yes	1.6	3.8	2.38
Has an ongoing disability			
No	80.7	67.7	0.84
Yes	19.3	32.3	1.67

Notes: [a] Not all of the categories shown are exhaustive, but the excluded categories contain a diverse range of groups and often contain small numbers of cases.

[b] Single working-age people are aged between 18 and 64; older people are aged 65 or over; older couples are those where the respondent is aged 65 or over; children include only dependent children, aged under 18.

[c] Main activity refers to the respondent only and excludes those who provided multiple responses.

housing, or unemployed private renters) further highlights the severity of the problems faced by those experiencing multiple manifestations of disadvantage.

Overlap between exclusion and poverty

The analysis of the overlap between poverty and deprivation reported in Chapter Seven confirmed overseas studies by showing that the overlap between the two indicators of social disadvantage is rather low in Australia. However, it is also clear that there is considerably greater overlap among the more disadvantaged welfare service client sample than among the community at large, which suggests that the degree of overlap itself is indicative of the degree of disadvantage experienced.

This section examines whether a similar pattern exists for the overlap between poverty and social exclusion. One might expect an even lower degree of overlap in this case because the focus of exclusion is shifted away from the constraints imposed by restricted access to economic resources. Against this, it has already been demonstrated that low economic capacity is an important determinant of exclusion, particularly for those in deep exclusion.

Table 9.7 examines the overlaps between social exclusion and poverty using the definition of deep exclusion applied earlier, that is, being excluded in at least seven dimensions. This definition not only allows the results to be compared with those presented earlier, but also produces an overall rate of deep exclusion that is very close to the estimated poverty rate of 17.7% (see Saunders et al, 2007b, Chapter 7, 2008). (The poverty estimates used in the overlap analysis are based on gross income for both community and client samples in order to maximise their comparability – as noted earlier, disposable income is not available for the client sample, but this approximation is unlikely to affect the conclusions drawn from the overlap analysis.)

Table 9.7: Overlap between poverty and social exclusion

	Community sample	Client sample	
		Unweighted	Weighted
Poverty rate	17.7	61.9	54.7
Social exclusion rate (overall)	17.9	62.4	57.3
Percentage of poor who are also excluded	36.6	71.0	65.6
Percentage of poor who are also disengaged	29.5	42.9	39.2
Percentage of poor who also face service exclusion	29.7	44.0	39.8
Percentage of poor who also face economic exclusion	35.1	84.8	82.7
Percentage of poor who are also excluded *and* deprived	28.7	60.9	56.3

Source: Saunders et al (2007b; Table 13)

The approach used (as before) has the advantage that the results are (approximately) independent of the base on which the overlaps are expressed (that is, as a percentage of those identified as poor, or as a percentage of those identified as excluded). For the same reason, exclusion in each of the three domains has been identified as experiencing at least three forms of exclusion within each domain.

The results in Table 9.7 show that the overlap between overall exclusion and poverty is in fact quite similar to that between deprivation and poverty shown in Figures 7.2 and 7.3. As before, the degree of overlap is considerably higher among the client sample than among the community sample. However, contrary to expectations, the overlap between economic exclusion and poverty in the community sample is only slightly greater than that for the other domains of exclusion. This difference is, however, far more marked among the client sample, where around five out of six of those with incomes below the poverty line face economic exclusion.

The final row of Table 9.7 shows how many in each sample who are in poverty are also experiencing both exclusion and deprivation. This is a stringent indicator of social disadvantage that identifies what can be referred to as core poverty, or the core of the problem of social disadvantage. These estimates imply that 5.1% of those in the community sample face all three forms of disadvantage simultaneously ($17.7 \times 0.287 = 5.1$) and are in core poverty, while the corresponding (weighted) figure for the client sample is over six times higher, at 30.8%. This again highlights the fact that the existence of overlapping conditions is itself an important marker of disadvantage.

Exclusion and subjective well-being

The estimates presented so far in this chapter demonstrate that social exclusion is a varied and multi-layered form of social disadvantage that affects a broad spectrum of Australians. What the evidence does not reveal is the impact of the different forms of exclusion on those affected, nor even if the experience of exclusion is associated with adverse outcomes. The discussion in Chapter Eight highlighted the need for greater scrutiny of the exclusion evidence in order to establish that exclusion reflects an undesirable outcome *from the perspective of those identified as excluded*. Unless this is done, it will not be possible to establish whether instances of identified exclusion reflect the diversity of people's own choices and actions, or are indicative of blocked opportunities and constrained options.

Not everyone wants to participate in all of the activities that most Australians engage in, and the failure to participate in customary activities so defined cannot be automatically assumed to be evidence of exclusion. Some of those identified as being excluded will have had the opportunity to participate but decided not to, for a range of reasons that may have nothing to do with externally imposed barriers. Caution should thus be applied when interpreting any *single* event as evidence of exclusion. It is also important to remember that the evidence is based on *indicators* that will not always have a single, unchallengeable interpretation. This criticism will have less force as the number of instances of exclusion increases and the likelihood that those in deep exclusion have chosen the observed outcomes is likely to be inversely related to the number of conditions experienced.

But there is still a need to provide *independent* evidence that those identified as excluded have been denied the opportunity to participate. One approach to this issue involves comparing the well-being of individuals categorised by their social exclusion status. If those identified as excluded have in fact chosen the situations that have led to that identification, one should expect to find that their well-being is no different from those who are not identified as excluded. In contrast, if their exclusion has been forced on them (or self-imposed, reluctantly), they should on average experience a lower level of well-being as a consequence.

Evidence on expressed levels of subjective well-being can thus be used to test whether or not the indicators used to identify exclusion have actually done so. In adopting this approach, it is important to acknowledge the difficulty (discussed earlier) of distinguishing between outcomes that are a consequence of internal choices and those that reflect external constraints. The choices made always reflect the options available (as they are perceived by those making the decision) and current choices will often be constrained by those made in the past. As a consequence, the method will not always produce definitive conclusions, although it may provide further evidence that the indicators used are capturing the problem.

The use of well-being indicators to validate evidence of a restricted range of exclusion indicators has been applied to families with children using the CUPSE data by Saunders and Zhu (2009), and the following analysis extends the scope of that work by refining the method and applying it to a broader range of well-being indicators and household types. This involves comparing the values of several well-being indicators for those experiencing different degrees of exclusion and for those facing the different combinations of poverty and social exclusion identified earlier.

The well-being indicators used in the analysis are defined in Table 9.8, which explains how they have been derived from the survey questions and responses. The dimensions of well-being overlap with those used earlier (in Table 7.4, Chapter Seven) to examine the impact of poverty and deprivation on well-being. In this instance, they cover people's assessment of their standard of living, their satisfaction with it, their reported level of happiness and the degree to which they feel they have choice and control in their lives. All four indicators are defined so that a higher value implies a higher level of well-being.

Although the first three indicators capture the impact of a broader range of determinants than just exclusion, the patterns revealed should make it possible to determine whether there is a systematic relationship between exclusion and well-being. The final indicator (choice and control) relates more directly to the role of choice in influencing observed outcomes (and thus the loss of agency that is associated with being excluded), and here the patterns might be expected to be stronger.

Table 9.8: Survey questions and well-being indicators

Indicator/question	Response categories	Indicator definition
Assessed living standard		
The things people buy and do – their housing, furniture, food, cars, recreation, travel – make up their standard of living and determine how well off they are. How would you rate your current standard of living?	Very high (score = 5), fairly high (4) medium (3), fairly low (2) and very low (1).	Mean value
Satisfaction with living standard		
How satisfied or dissatisfied do you feel about your overall standard of living at present?	Very satisfied(score = 5), fairly satisfied (4), neither satisfied nor dissatisfied (3), fairly dissatisfied (2), very dissatisfied (1)	Mean value
Happiness		
Overall, in terms of how you feel generally, would you say you are:	Very happy (score = 4), fairly happy (3), fairly unhappy (2) and very unhappy (1)	Mean value
Choice and control		
How much choice and control do you believe you have over your own life and the things that happen to you?	A ten-point scale ranging from none at all (score = 1-2), some control (4-6) to a great degree of control (9-10)	Mean value

Table 9.9 compares the mean values of the four well-being indicators for individuals differentiated by the depth of their social exclusion (measured as before, by the number of indicators experienced), while Tables 9.10, 9.11 and 9.12 provide the corresponding comparisons separately for each of the three domains of exclusion. For convenience, the comparisons only apply to those experiencing up to 16 indicators of overall exclusion and up to seven indicators in each domain, but this truncation removes very small numbers and does not affect the pattern of results.

The results in Table 9.9 show that there is a clear gradient linking the degree of exclusion and each of the four indicators of well-being. The more prevalent exclusion is, the lower the level of reported well-being, although there is some variability once the number of exclusion conditions reaches around 10 due to the smaller numbers in the higher categories. The first two (living standards-related) well-being indicators decline by just over 40% as the number of exclusion conditions experienced increases from zero to 16, while the corresponding decline in the happiness and choice and control indicators are 35% and over 50%, respectively. These gradients suggest that the exclusion indicators are capturing the loss of agency that they are intended to capture, and are not simply reflecting the diversity of individual preferences.

Table 9.9: Mean subjective well-being scores by number of social exclusion indicators

	Indicator of subjective well-being			
Number of exclusion indicators	Assessed living standard	Satisfaction with living standard	Happiness	Choice and control
0	3.67	4.25	3.28	7.76
1	3.46	4.10	3.22	7.49
2	3.42	3.95	3.17	7.25
3	3.32	3.80	3.14	7.20
4	3.11	3.69	3.03	6.89
5	3.07	3.57	2.99	6.43
6	2.99	3.32	2.87	6.40
7	2.70	3.14	2.75	5.76
8	2.62	2.90	2.75	5.46
9	2.47	2.81	2.67	5.64
10	2.45	2.79	2.76	5.64
11	2.31	2.38	2.56	5.02
12	2.28	2.45	2.41	5.04
13	2.52	2.57	2.61	4.96
14	2.00	2.25	2.60	5.11
15	2.50	1.90	2.11	4.80
16	2.14	2.43	2.14	3.75
Ratio of final to initial value	0.583	0.572	0.652	0.483

The general patterns revealed by the corresponding results for each of the three domains of exclusion are broadly similar to those for exclusion overall. Table 9.10 reveals downward sloping well-being gradients as disengagement becomes more concentrated. However, all four of the ratios in the final row are above the corresponding (based on seven indicators) ratios based on Table 9.9, which suggests (albeit guardedly) that the relationship between disengagement and the perceived level of (and satisfaction with) the standard of living is not as close as for the other domains of exclusion.

The well-being gradients implied by the results in Table 9.11 suggest that an inverse relationship exists between the depth of service exclusion and subjective well-being across all four dimensions. In this case, the ratios in the final row are considerably above those in the other two domain-specific tables, suggesting that those who face multiple forms of exclusion from services are nevertheless still able to maintain their well-being.

The results in Table 9.12 reveal clearly that those who face deep economic exclusion also regard their standard of living, their satisfaction with it, their happiness and the degree to which they have control over their lives as much lower than those who face a similar level of exclusion in the other two domains. This

Table 9.10: Mean subjective well-being scores by number of disengagement indicators

Number of exclusion indicators	Indicator of subjective well-being			
	Assessed living standard	Satisfaction with living standard	Happiness	Choice and control
0	3.51	4.07	3.21	7.48
1	3.21	3.77	3.12	7.06
2	2.99	3.41	2.93	6.40
3	2.74	3.13	2.82	5.90
4	2.65	2.89	2.63	5.63
5	2.26	2.49	2.35	4.65
6	2.00	1.87	2.09	3.95
7	2.13	2.13	2.00	3.75
Ratio of final to initial value	0.607	0.523	0.623	0.501

Table 9.11: Mean subjective well-being scores by number of service exclusion indicators

Number of exclusion indicators	Indicator of subjective well-being			
	Assessed living standard	Satisfaction with living standard	Happiness	Choice and control
0	3.37	3.94	3.18	7.24
1	3.25	3.78	3.08	7.06
2	3.15	3.65	3.03	6.81
3	2.97	3.38	2.89	6.20
4	2.85	3.15	2.89	6.17
5	2.76	2.93	2.72	6.00
6	2.76	3.16	2.79	5.68
7	2.69	2.54	2.54	4.92
Ratio of final to initial value	0.798	0.645	0.799	0.680

finding is consistent with earlier results and reinforces the finding that economic exclusion is a major contributor to social disadvantage.

Having examined the relationships between the severity of different forms of exclusion and perceived levels of well-being, attention now focuses on whether similar well-being gradients exist for those experiencing different combinations of exclusion and poverty. Table 9.13 compares the mean well-being scores using the four indicators defined in Table 9.8 for those in the different combinations of poverty and exclusion status identified in Table 9.7.

As before, care must be taken when comparing the (row) values shown in Table 9.13 because of differences in the response scales from which the well-

Table 9.12: Mean subjective well-being scores by number of economic exclusion indicators

	Indicator of subjective well-being			
Number of exclusion indicators	Assessed living standard	Satisfaction with living standard	Happiness	Choice and control
0	3.45	4.03	3.17	7.36
1	3.21	3.70	3.05	6.89
2	2.94	3.33	2.94	6.43
3	2.73	3.00	2.81	5.83
4	2.29	2.59	2.67	5.18
5	2.17	2.40	2.52	5.03
6	1.62	2.29	2.33	4.52
7	1.71	1.79	1.93	3.29
Ratio of final to initial value	0.496	0.444	0.609	0.447

being indicators have been constructed. However, interest focuses on comparing how the values of a *given* well-being indicator vary within the columns, that is, with differences in the poverty and exclusion status of households. The first point to note is that, for overall exclusion and all three exclusion domains, all four indicators show that well-being is lower among those who are either poor or excluded than among those who experience neither condition. It is also the case that, for all four well-being indicators and for all three forms of exclusion, those who experience both poverty and exclusion together have lower levels of well-being than those who face only one of these two conditions.

Thus, for example, the mean assessed living standard of those who are neither excluded on the overall definition or poor is equal to 3.40 (on a scale of 1 to 5). It declines by 24% (to 2.60) if they are excluded but not poor, by 12% (to 2.98) if they are poor but not excluded, and by 33% (to 2.28) if they are both excluded and poor. Similar patterns are evident across all three domains of exclusion and for all four indicators of well-being. It is also the case that, except for service exclusion (where the scores are very close), the mean level of well-being is *lower* for those who are excluded but not poor than it is for those who are poor but not excluded.

This again suggests that exclusion as identified in this analysis is capturing something that has adverse effects on the well-being of those affected and does not simply reflect differences in choices about lifestyle and participation patterns. The fact that the above pattern also exists for economic exclusion reinforces this point, while suggesting that those dimensions of economic adversity other than income that are embodied in the definition of economic exclusion also have negative impacts on those that experience them.

Service exclusion appears to have a different impact on well-being than either disengagement or economic exclusion. In this case, those who are excluded but

Table 9.13: Mean subjective well-being scores by exclusion and poverty status

Exclusion and poverty status	Indicator of subjective well-being			
	Assessed living standard	Satisfaction with living standard	Happiness	Choice and control
Overall exclusion				
Neither excluded nor poor	3.40	3.94	3.15	7.25
Excluded but not poor	2.60	2.84	2.69	5.55
Poor but not excluded	2.98	3.54	3.01	6.67
Excluded and poor	2.28	2.60	2.56	5.04
All households	2.49	2.76	2.65	5.38
Disengagement				
Neither excluded nor poor	3.38	3.90	3.15	7.22
Excluded but not poor	2.71	3.00	2.70	5.69
Poor but not excluded	2.89	3.43	2.97	6.51
Excluded and poor	2.33	2.63	2.55	5.02
All households	2.59	2.90	2.65	5.51
Service exclusion				
Neither excluded nor poor	3.35	3.89	3.13	7.18
Excluded but not poor	3.03	3.37	2.92	6.38
Poor but not excluded	2.84	3.37	2.93	6.42
Excluded and poor	2.45	2.78	2.64	5.23
All households	2.90	3.23	2.85	6.11
Economic exclusion				
Neither excluded nor poor	3.38	3.90	3.13	7.18
Excluded but not poor	2.46	2.73	2.69	5.48
Poor but not excluded	2.95	3.52	2.99	6.59
Excluded and poor	2.30	2.60	2.59	5.12
All households	2.42	2.70	2.67	5.36

not poor face a much smaller decline in well-being than is the case for the other two forms of exclusion, and even those who are excluded and poor end up with a higher level of well-being than those in this situation in the other two domains of exclusion. One possible explanation may relate to the fact that several of the service exclusion indicators refer to needs that apply to only specific sub-sets of the population (mental health, childcare, aged care and disability services), so that some of those identified as excluded are classified as unable to access services that they do not currently need, with no consequent impact on their well-being.

Summary

This chapter provides a comprehensive picture of the extent of social exclusion in Australia. Social exclusion has been defined to exist when people do not participate in key activities that the majority of the population engage in. The diversity of exclusion has been captured in three dimensions: disengagement (non-participation in or withdrawal from, different forms of social interaction), service exclusion (a lack of access to access key health care and other services) and economic exclusion (restricted access to economic resources and a low capacity to generate them).

All three forms of exclusion deny people the benefits and opportunities associated with different forms of social and economic participation. The findings provide a disturbing picture of widespread exclusion in the community sample as a whole, and a heavy concentration of its different forms among the welfare client sample in particular.

The analysis has produced estimates of the overall incidence of different forms of exclusion, examined the extent of multiple exclusion and the distribution of its severity, identified which forms of exclusion and which socioeconomic groups are most affected by deep exclusion and estimated the overlap between the three domains of exclusion and poverty. Special attention has been given to the impact of different forms of exclusion, and different combinations of exclusion and poverty, on levels of well-being using four indicators of subjective well-being. These latter results are designed to establish whether people are forced to endure exclusion, or whether the situations identified as representing exclusion are a reflection of choices that reflect people's preferences for different forms of social, economic and civic participation.

The results reveal that social exclusion is a major problem that affects significant numbers of Australians. For example, the exclusion incidence rates of many of the separate indicators exceed 40%, while a severe level of overall multi-dimensional deep exclusion (experiencing seven or more separate indictors simultaneously) affects almost one fifth (18%) of those in the community sample and more than three times as many (62%) of those in the client sample. A severe level of exclusion (defined as experiencing at least three separate forms of exclusion within each domain) affects over 16% of the community sample in the case of disengagement, over 22% in the case of service exclusion, and over 14% in the case of economic exclusion. The corresponding estimates of deep exclusion in the client sample are 38%, 42% and 72%, respectively – between two and five times higher.

The areas where exclusion is most pronounced relate to economic conditions, including joblessness and lack of emergency savings, but large proportions of vulnerable groups (with the notable exception, in some instances, of Indigenous Australians, although these results have not been presented) also face exclusion from a number of social activities, including having no regular social contact with other people, not participating in community activities and being unable to pay one's way when out with friends. These latter forms of exclusion have obvious spill-over effects on other people, as well as on social cohesiveness more generally. Focusing on those who face deep overall exclusion, the evidence shows that those in this situation are most often excluded from access to medical treatment when needed, from transportation and from accessing dental treatment. Those in deep exclusion also often face multiple forms of economic exclusion.

Overall, the results illustrate the diverse nature of exclusion, but also highlight how its different forms cluster together among those most exposed to exclusion overall. The groups that are most vulnerable to deep exclusion are the unemployed, public renters, lone parents, Indigenous Australians and private renters. Next most affected are those with a disability or caring for a family member affected by a disability. All of these groups were shown in Chapter Six to be also facing the most extreme levels of deprivation, adding to their overall level of social disadvantage.

In the final section, evidence on reported levels of well-being was used as a way of differentiating between those whose exclusion was a choice not to participate, and those for whom it reflects an undesirable consequence of external processes or actions. This evidence shows consistently across different well-being indicators, different domains of exclusion and different combinations of exclusion and poverty, that exclusion has a negative impact on well-being. This suggests that exclusion as identified by the indicators used here is generally imposed on people, not chosen by them. In fact, the evidence suggests that (aside from service exclusion) the existence of exclusion has a bigger adverse impact on well-being than having an income below the poverty line.

Together, the findings in this chapter support the increased priority that has been given to addressing social exclusion through a social policy agenda designed to promote inclusion. Social exclusion has been shown to be both widespread across the community and concentrated among specific groups and in specific forms. It is also an issue that takes many diverse forms and thus requires coordinated action across a broad range of areas. In developing policies to promote inclusion, the indicators used here to capture that diversity must be unpacked so that the causes of specific instances of exclusion can be identified and addressed.

TEN

Conclusions and implications

Introduction

Social disadvantage has many manifestations and can only be adequately captured using multi-dimensional indicators. This is the central message to emerge from recent research on poverty and disadvantage and has shaped the research reported in previous chapters. Why not dispense with quantification altogether? If the problems are so difficult, yet so fundamental, would it not be better to avoid measurement and focus instead on understanding how examples of disadvantage arise and are perpetuated in specific instances and deal with them in ways that are appropriate to the circumstance? These questions raise important issues about the nature of social science research and its relation to policy that are the focus of this concluding chapter.

Discussion begins with a brief overview of the main findings reported earlier. This is followed by a discussion of some of the implications for policy, and for future research on aspects of social disadvantage, including the ways in which research findings are reported and disseminated, as well as for data collection and for how researchers and policy makers can better communicate with each other. Much of the discussion focuses on the key issue of communication – how can research findings be conveyed to the right audiences in ways that promote understanding of their relevance and value to potential users. Central to this task is ensuring that research not only has the academic qualities and content that make it relevant to policy and practice, but also that it can encourage a dialogue between researchers, practitioners and policy makers that can influence action.

This book started by citing the problems facing Leah/Lucky, a young woman who was facing many forms of disadvantage that had overwhelmed her, left her alienated and marginalised and prevented her from participating fully in her society. Although the oppression that she faced resulted from factors that are specific to that society, the underlying idea that people face similarly debilitating obstacles has universal applicability. In the Australian context, many people are still denied the resources needed to live a decent life or face discrimination or other barriers that restrict their ability to participate and constrain their opportunities to develop and flourish. Research has a central role to play in exposing instances where this occurs, but unless it has credibility among those with the power to act and is used to bring pressure for such action, its potential to contribute to better outcomes will not be realised.

Summary of the main findings

The early chapters of this book spelt out the limitations of equating social disadvantage in rich countries like Australia with poverty, and conceiving of poverty narrowly, in terms of a lack of income. Even when poverty is conceived as a relative concept and measured using a poverty line that varies with overall living standards, the approach fails to connect with the reality of disadvantage and thus provides a limited (and limiting) perspective that undermines its credibility. These problems are reinforced by the moral imperative view that puts poverty on a pedestal above all other social problems, calling for action not only to alleviate it but to eliminate it. In the face of such pressure, it is no surprise that governments have been wary of the poverty statistics and cautious about their implications for policy.

When poverty is conceived and measured in terms of income alone (or conceived more broadly but measured using a poverty line), the measurement problems assume a significance that provide governments with many reasons for inaction: the poverty line is arbitrary or simply too high; it is a moving target that can never be reached; the equivalence adjustment is arbitrary, but can exert a powerful impact on the estimates; many people on low income have access to other economic resources; the incomes reported in social surveys (even when conducted by official statistical agencies) are inaccurate and lead to an over-estimation of the poverty rate – one could go on.

Overriding these technical concerns is a more fundamental issue about the kind of evidence that is needed to demonstrate that poverty (and other forms of social disadvantage) actually exists. It is not sufficient to presume that poverty is an automatic consequence of low income; instead, the unacceptability of the standard of living achieved by those below the poverty line must be demonstrated if the estimates generated by poverty research are to be taken seriously and not dismissed as an artefact of a specific set of assumptions or technical procedures.

From this, it follows that research must move beyond the poverty statistics to examine actual living conditions in order to assess whether or not they are consistent with prevailing standards of acceptability. Either that, or poverty must be viewed through a lens that is capable of focusing on the factors that exclude people not only from the resources needed to function as economic agents (workers, consumers and investors), but also from the cohesive social and political activities and networks that define citizenship and bond individuals together in civil society.

These latter perspectives have resulted in the emergence of deprivation and social exclusion as concepts embedded in a living standards framework that offers a genuine alternative to conventional poverty research. By focusing on whether people miss out on the items needed to achieve widely approved norms in their society, or are denied the opportunity to participate in customary activities, both approaches locate the experience of disadvantage within a broader social context, not only conceptually but also empirically. At the same time, by highlighting the relative and relational aspects of disadvantage, they emphasise that the disadvantage endured by some is directly linked to the advantages enjoyed by others.

Despite the criticism levelled at how poverty is measured, and the important insights provided by the deprivation and exclusion perspectives, poverty line studies help to identify an important dimension of social disadvantage and cannot be allowed to disappear. Particularly in a country like Australia, with its heavy reliance on means-tested social benefits and a wage-fixing system designed to provide and protect an adequate minimum wage, there is intense interest in issues of income adequacy, income distribution and redistribution. Popular conceptions of these topics are captured in the 'gap between rich and poor' – a phrase which testifies to the enduring importance of poverty as a concept that resonates with public opinion and is a key (if imprecise) dimension of economic inequality more generally.

With so much redistribution achieved through income transfers and social security spending absorbing a large proportion of their budget, governments should have an intense interest in assessing the impact of their income transfer programmes on inequality in general, and on poverty in particular. The fact that they appear not to is in part a reflection of changing attitudes to inequality under the neoliberal policy agenda, but is also an acknowledgement of the frailties of poverty research. Even so, it is important to establish how many households are below the poverty line and how this has changed, if only as a way of assessing the impact of social change and the effectiveness of past and existing policies.

Poverty research generates estimates that are subject to the normal range of limitations, and is incapable of producing definitive statistics that are unchallengeable. This fact sits uncomfortably with the requirements of the moral imperative view. This is not to deny the importance of drawing on estimates of poverty to crusade on behalf of the poor, but rather to accompany this with other research that addresses the weaknesses of the poverty statistics. One way to help bring about this realignment is to regard income-based estimates as capturing poverty risks rather than poverty as such. Low income is a risk factor that increases the likelihood of poverty, but further evidence on the consequences is needed before it can be concluded that poverty actually exists.

When conceived in this way, poverty research not only plays an important role in identifying income as a key factor that puts individuals at risk, but leads naturally to further studies that examine whether or not that risk translates into an unacceptable outcome. Poverty research is thus the first stage in a process that requires other evidence to be examined before any conclusions can be drawn. And that other evidence can be collected in ways that strengthen the robustness of the research and grounds it in the living standards of those who are most disadvantaged.

This was the motivation underlying the research reported in Chapters Two and Three. That analysis began by using income data and poverty lines to estimate poverty rates, and then went on to explore the use of other data (on consumption spending, wealth ownership and the experience of financial stress) to assess whether those with incomes below the poverty line have the capacity to escape poverty, or display the financial stresses thought to accompany it.

One message that emerged from the analysis was that a significant proportion of those below the poverty line have levels of spending or wealth which suggested that they may not be poor, or do not face the financial stress expected to be a consequence of poverty. Using a poverty line set at 50% of median income – the kind of measure most commonly used when studying poverty in affluent countries like Australia – adjusting the estimates to reflect the removal of those households with high levels of spending or wealth or low levels of financial stress results in a reduction in the poverty rate of about 30%, from around 10% to between 7% and 7.5%. This is a significant reduction, but is far smaller than the impact of moving the poverty line 10 percentage points up the income distribution (from 50% to 60% of the median), which causes the poverty rate to double from 10% to almost 20%.

There is, of course, no scientific basis for choosing whether to set the poverty line at 50% or 60% of the median. Nor is it possible to determine exactly how to adjust the poverty estimates to reflect information on spending, wealth or financial stress. Judgements are required and in one sense this inevitably introduces an element of subjectivity that is inconsistent with describing the estimates as objective or scientific. However, it is still possible to refine the estimates so that they embody advances in social science knowledge and practice, and in this sense they can be legitimately regarded as the best available in current circumstances.

The fact that no serious discussion has yet taken place of the methods used to generate the extended poverty estimates presented in Chapters Two and Three means that they are best regarded as experimental at this stage. Their aim is to show that it is possible to use existing data to refine poverty estimates in ways that address some of the criticisms that have been levelled at poverty line studies. They do this in a way that is illustrative of the potential of the approach, while also producing new information about the extent of the biases that currently exist and about the sensitivity of the estimates more generally.

Chapters Four to Six present the results from the first national study of deprivation in Australia, while Chapter Seven shows how these estimates can build on, and be linked with, those produced by the conventional approach to estimating poverty. This analysis shows clearly that the deprivation approach is capable of generating sensible and robust results that shed important new light on this aspect of social disadvantage. The survey instrument itself reflects the input provided by low-income Australians and the responses confirm that there is a high level of agreement in Australia about what constitutes the essential of life – things that no one should have to go without. Deprivation rates vary across the 25 items identified as essential although around 14% (one in seven) of those surveyed were deprived of at least four items. This figure rises fourfold among those in the smaller survey of clients of selected welfare services, confirming that many members of this group face extreme economic adversity.

The deprivation approach was also shown to provide a better way of identifying disadvantage than an approach based on comparing income with a poverty line. There is a clearer delineation between deprived and not-deprived groups than between those identified as poor or not poor in terms of both the susceptibility to specific instances of deprivation, and in terms of expressed levels of subjective well-being. Regression modelling indicates that there is a closer relationship between variables expected to be markers of disadvantage and people's deprivation status than between those same markers and their poverty status. These findings are all robust and not sensitive to variations in how deprivation or poverty are empirically defined and measured.

Confirming overseas studies, the Australian results show that the overlap between poverty and deprivation is relatively low, with only just over one third of those identified as deprived having incomes below the poverty line and a similar percentage of the poor identified as deprived. Importantly, however, the overlap is much higher (at around 60%) for those in the more disadvantaged welfare clients sample, which suggests that the size of the overlap itself is an important indicator of disadvantage.

Following European developments, a measure of consistent poverty was developed in Chapter Seven to include those who have incomes below the poverty line and are experiencing a specified degree of deprivation. On this measure, the Australian consistent poverty rate is just below 12% compared with a conventional (income-based) poverty rate of almost 20%. The consistent poverty approach thus results in a decline in measured poverty of about 40%, which is slightly higher than the 30% reduction that was caused by the adjustments described in Chapter Three. The consistent poverty measure was then shown to be associated with the same set of socioeconomic variables identified in the earlier separate analyses of poverty and deprivation.

In Chapters Eight and Nine, the focus shifted from poverty and deprivation to a third dimension of social disadvantage – social exclusion. Because the concept is relatively new (particularly in the Australian research and policy context) the definition and meaning of social exclusion was given a thorough examination. This discussion highlighted the ambiguities of many definitions, although one common thread is that exclusion signifies the denial of the opportunity to participate in customary activities.

The discussion in Chapter Eight revealed that precise articulations of social exclusion vary in their ability to identify specific instances of exclusion and are constrained by data availability. However, most researchers have been content to work within a flexible and evolving framework rather than getting bogged down in endless debate over definition and measurement. This is largely a reflection of the interest that policy makers have shown in the concept, an interest that makes research on the topic subject to the fluctuating imperatives that drive political and policy debate.

There is, however, concern expressed by some that the social exclusion/inclusion research agenda has been too strongly influenced (and controlled) by government, and this has led to a narrow perspective that has failed to acknowledge and address those aspects of the problem such as inequality that sit uncomfortably with a policy approach that is still dominated by neoliberal thinking. This concern reflects an underlying tension between the goals of researchers and policy makers: the former want their work to be taken seriously by other scholars, which requires an open and critical assessment that will inevitably leave key issues unresolved and contested; the latter want an evidence base for their actions that is unsullied by the disagreement and lack of resolution that are often features of healthy academic debate. Finding the intersection between these competing perspectives can be very difficult.

Despite these differences, there is a high degree of similarity between the indicators used to identify social exclusion by researchers and government agencies, and in the domains that are used to organise the indicators into key themes. The main criticism directed at the approaches employed to date has been that they focus too much on the economic aspects of inclusion/exclusion (particularly the role of the welfare system and labour market in contributing to joblessness) and too little on the structural aspects, and the social and political dimensions of exclusion. Against this, where the use of social exclusion indicators to monitor progress has received official endorsement by government, the scope of the indicators has expanded to include issues of poverty and inequality that had previously failed to make it onto the policy agenda.

Chapter Nine presents new estimates of the extent of social exclusion in Australia using an indicator framework that comprises 27 indicators across three broad domains. The results reveal that many forms of exclusion are widespread, affecting large proportions of those in the general community as well as the clients of welfare services. It is also the case that many of the differences in the exclusion incidence rates between the two groups are smaller than those that relate to deprivation, reinforcing the wide reach of some forms of exclusion. Service exclusion in particular affects many Australians, with large numbers unable to access dental treatment if needed, services that meet specific needs such as mental illness and disability (although lack of information about availability may be a factor here) and unable to pay for domestic services such as electricity, gas and water.

The one domain where the incidence of exclusion among those in the welfare client sample is far above that in the community generally is economic exclusion, defined to cover limited access to economic resources and restricted economic capacity. Over 70% of those in the client sample were identified as excluded using three indicators in this domain: does not have $500 in emergency savings; does not own at least $50,000 in assets; and lives in a jobless household. Using as the indicator missing out on at least four items, over 42% of those in the community sample and 85% of those in the client sample are excluded overall – reinforcing the message about the high level of exclusion.

The poverty rate was not included as an indicator of economic exclusion so that the overlap between poverty and exclusion could be examined. When this is done, the degree of overlap is broadly similar to that between poverty and deprivation reported in Chapter Seven, despite the fact that lack of economic resources is not used to identify exclusion. Again, however, the degree of overlap is far higher among those in the client sample, and the overlap between all three aspects of social disadvantage (that is, those who are poor, deprived and excluded) is around 5% for the community sample but is far higher at almost 31% in the client sample.

Finally, it was shown that there is a clear gradient linking the severity of exclusion – identified by the number of indicators experienced – and four indicators of subjective well-being. These results suggest that exclusion is a situation that people have, in one way or another, forced on them and is not a consequence of choices freely entered into. Comparisons of subjective well-being across those in different combinations of poverty and exclusion (as identified in the overlap analysis) confirms this impression, showing that the experience of exclusion has more marked negative impact on subjective well-being than having an income below the poverty line. Social exclusion is thus an important element of social disadvantage that can add new insights to the pictures revealed by those identified as poor or deprived.

Most of the refinements to poverty line studies discussed throughout the book result in a decline in the estimated poverty rate. This is true for the resource exclusions and validation approaches discussed in Chapter Three, for the consistent poverty approach discussed in Chapter Seven and for the overlap between poverty, deprivation and exclusion ('core poverty') presented in Chapter Nine. However, on even the most restrictive of the approaches used (the three-way overlap measure of core poverty presented in Table 9.7), the poverty rate still exceeds 5%. This implies that at a minimum, over one million Australians do not have the resources to buy the items and undertake the activities that are needed to achieve an acceptable standard of living. Given the stringency of the measure, it is difficult to justify the failure to address this core of the problem of social disadvantage, particularly as it affects the children involved.

Implications for policy

No explicit attempt has been made to examine the impact of policy on the indicators of social disadvantage, although it is clear that policies do exert an influence on many of the outcomes observed. In highlighting some of these impacts, the aim is not to identify specific policy failings since this would require a systematic and rigorous assessment of pre- and post-policy outcomes. Instead, the aim is to identify some of the broad policy themes that emerge from the findings and draw out the overall implications for policy change and reform.

An obvious starting point for this discussion is the role and impact of the income support system, which has been shown in several places to play a major role in supporting the living standards of vulnerable Australians. This is most evident in the poverty estimates presented in Chapters Two and Three and in the discussion of pension adequacy in Chapter Six, although the effects are pervasive and are embedded in many of the other findings. Although it has been argued that the causes and manifestations of social disadvantage extend beyond a lack of money income, the primary role that income plays in providing a platform on which people can construct a decent and acceptable standard of living has also been acknowledged.

The role of the social security system is to provide such a platform in a way that does not prevent or discourage people from seeking to generate an adequate income from their own efforts. It is clear that the Australian system has not achieved this goal – at least for some groups – and that its provisions have left others at risk or on the margins of poverty. One consistent finding is that lone parents face a high poverty risk and are also subject to above-average levels of deprivation and exclusion. Other groups that are prominent among those most susceptible to social disadvantage across several indicators are Indigenous Australians, unemployed and jobless people, people with a disability, carers and those in rental accommodation.

The detailed analysis of deprivation by income source in Chapter Six reinforced many of these findings, while also highlighting the perilous circumstances of age pensioners living alone and/or in rented accommodation. These results provide clear guidance to where additional income support is needed to achieve adequacy objectives, but also highlight the need to reform the housing sector so that it is better able to supply a range of low-cost housing options to those whose limited resources prevent them from achieving the Australian home ownership dream. The discussions with low-income Australians in Chapter Four highlighted the difficult choices that those with few resources are often forced to make when deciding where to live and how much of their limited budgets to allocate to housing.

The sensitivity analysis of poverty rates highlighted how the income-tested nature of the Australian social security system leads to a bunching of incomes at and just above prevailing payment rates. The fact that the bunching occurs at around one half of median income explains why Australia often performs badly on international comparisons of poverty rates like those presented in Table 2.4 in Chapter Two. One consequence of this is that it is unwise to rely on a single estimate to establish the severity of Australia's poverty problem. Another, more sanguine implication, is that it would require only a modest increase in payments to shift Australia a long way up the international poverty league table.

Any such increase should be targeted where the need is greatest (particularly when, as in Australia, the system as a whole is heavily targeted) yet in practice the demands for improved benefits are often most frequently voiced by, or on behalf of, those who are currently relatively well treated. The politics of welfare reform and concern over minimising disincentive effects for those of working age have tended to take precedence over the adequacy of their benefits and the overall equity of the system, although the social inclusion agenda provides an opportunity to reverse this trend.

Mention has already been made of the importance of housing issues. The role of housing costs in contributing to poverty has been highlighted in previous Australian studies, which have shown that generous tax concessions and other policies that promote home ownership have given many an effective protection against poverty, particularly in later life. The importance of housing is further highlighted by the fact that five of the 25 essential items identified in Chapter Four relate specifically to dwelling quality, while a further three items relate to the quality of accommodation in relation to such aspects as heating and furnishings. Location is also highlighted as an important determinant of disengagement and service exclusion, and many are excluded from domestic services because they are unable to pay household bills on time.

The issue of housing affordability has attracted considerable attention since the global financial crisis struck in 2008 – even though Australia managed to avoid the worse of its effects by acting decisively to support demand through fiscal stimulus measures. However, much of that attention has focused on the problems facing those purchasing their homes on a mortgage, where variations in interest rates have an immediate impact on living standards, while the prospect of falling house prices can have more profound longer-term consequences. Far less attention has been paid to the flow-on effects on the rental market and thus on the living standards of those unable to own their own home. These groups must take the short-run pain inflicted by rising housing costs without enjoying the longer-term capital gains that accrue to the vast majority of home owners. High housing costs and inadequate housing facilities are a major cause of social disadvantage that require greater attention from policy makers in both federal and state governments.

A third general policy-related theme that emerges from the findings relates to the inadequate provision of services, particularly health services. Access to health services when needed accounts for four of the 25 essential items and seven of the nine indicators of service exclusion. The failings of the dental system were highlighted by several participants in the interviews reported in Chapter Four and although there is some evidence of recent improvement, this remains an area where further reform is urgently needed. Another distressing finding relates to the inability of many to afford the medications prescribed by a doctor. This is not only an inefficient use of scarce health resources, but represents a waste of the resources spent on the initial consultation. The fact that people are unable to take recommended medications, like having to endure the pain and ignominy of bad teeth, are clear signs of social disadvantage that should not exist or be tolerated in an affluent country like Australia.

Some of the other items used as indicators of disadvantage have implications for policy in specific areas. These include the importance of ensuring that children at school have access to all aspects of the schooling experience and are not excluded from hobbies, activities and excursions because they are unaffordable, or must face the scorn of their peers because of the poor quality of their clothing or study materials. There is obvious scope here for education authorities to address these shortcomings. Pricing policy more generally appears to prevent people from accessing key essentials related to home and car insurance, adequate heating and domestic services more generally, holidays and social activities. Low income is obviously a factor here, but this is reinforced by the lack of price subsidies that might assist those with few resources to access items that others have, and most regard as essential.

The final area where the results highlight policy failings is perhaps so obvious that it is easy to overlook. This relates to the extreme and multi-dimensional disadvantage experienced by those forced to rely on the assistance provided by non-government welfare agencies. It is important to emphasise that these groups were recruited specifically to ensure that information was collected on those most susceptible to disadvantage and it is thus not surprising that those in the welfare client sample are more disadvantaged than those in the general community. What is alarming is the size of the disadvantage gap that separates the two groups. On virtually all of the indicators examined, those in the client sample not only have lower incomes, but are also more deprived and excluded than those in the community generally – and it is important to recall that the indicators used to establish this reflect community views, not the views of the clients themselves.

The mere existence of the client sample indicates that there are large numbers of Australians who are forced to seek assistance from non-government agencies, either because they are not eligible for government support or because that support is not adequate to meet their needs. Yet even after receiving agency support, they face rates of deprivation and exclusion that place them far above the norm in terms of the degree of social disadvantage experienced. This is evidence of systemic failure that requires urgent attention across a broad range of policy areas.

Implications for research

The importance of dissemination

It is self-evident that in order for research to have an impact, its results must be disseminated. Despite this, those working on policy issues often pay too little attention to how best to ensure that their findings reach those who are most likely to want to use them. This applies mainly to researcher-initiated, curiosity-driven research and is generally not an issue for research that is commissioned by potential users, since they have open access to the findings (and often exert an important influence on how they are produced). But the identification of appropriate research dissemination channels is an important task for those researchers whose ideas, arguments and findings might otherwise not find their way onto the desks (and into the minds) of policy makers.

The main dissemination outlet for most academic researchers is publication in professional, peer-reviewed journals since it is here that academic reputations are established and career trajectories advanced. But policy makers rarely read the academic literature and if they do, the time lags involved in getting published are likely to mean that many useful ideas are likely to be well past their use-by date. In order for research to have an impact on policy, researchers must seek other avenues through which to engage with policy makers, as Edwards (2001, 2004) has emphasised.

This involves identifying options for an effective interchange and communicating effectively in order to maximise the resulting returns. As former British politician David Blunkett (2000) argued in a speech to the ESRC:

> For researchers to maximise the potential impact of their work, they must ensure that politicians and civil servants are aware of their findings. This means learning how to communicate effectively with government, and discovering the entry points into the policy-making process.

This process must not be a one-way street. The onus should not be entirely on researchers to identify the entry points into the policy process, but policy makers must also make them more apparent and open to researchers. From a researcher perspective, this can be achieved in several ways, as Saunders and Walter (2005) have argued, by developing dissemination strategies that target the different audiences through which research can exert an influence on policy and practice.

In this context, it is difficult to disagree with Blunkett's emphasis on the need for researchers to communicate more effectively. Most researchers are unfamiliar with the demands of non-scholarly outlets and public media, both of which present very different challenges from those involved in publishing in academic journals. The emphasis is on brevity and clarity of exposition, and in getting the message across in a way that does justice to the underlying ideas without dwelling on the technicalities and reservations. Researchers are often uncomfortable working in this terrain because these demands are seen as compromising the professional integrity of their work, but this is an inevitable consequence of stepping outside of the ivory tower of scholarship.

The evidence-based policy movement has given new impetus to the need to ensure that policy is based on, or at least consistent with, research findings. This ought to bring about a closer relationship between researchers and policy makers, who have a common interest in producing policy-relevant evidence through research. Against this, current trends within the tertiary sector are making it less attractive for academic researchers to acquire and use the skills needed to communicate effectively with a wider audience. With funding increasingly tied to demonstrated performance that is measured by metrics that are heavily weighted towards peer-reviewed academic publications, the incentive to write for a broader audience is becoming less attractive for all but a small pool of talented academic communicators and public intellectuals.

Despite these trends, there is a high level of interest in Australia in the issues of social disadvantage addressed in this book and the need to communicate the findings to a broad audience was an explicit aim of the Left Out and Missing Out Project from the outset. This was achieved by ensuring that the NGO research collaborators had, through their engagement in the research process, ownership of the research and were committed to making its results public through their own networks. In practice, this involved the production of a series of brief (four-page) pamphlets that used everyday language to describe different aspects of the research and its main findings. Four such pamphlets were produced, covering: identification of the essentials of life; the deprivation profile in Australia; the nature and extent of social exclusion; and social exclusion and children.

All four were produced under the joint authorship of all contributors to the project and were released simultaneously under the headings of the five collaborating institutions in hard copy and on the websites of each institution. This process allowed the research to become widely disseminated throughout the community sector and led in part to the demand from the sector to conduct the second client survey in 2008. Growing public awareness of the research, particularly within government, also led to the replication of the community survey in 2010, this time with cash and in-kind support provided by the Australian and two state government social inclusion units, as well as several new community sector NGOs. Presentations of findings at a number of community sector (as well as academic) conferences also promoted awareness of the research and stimulated interest in its methods, findings and implications.

This emphasis on dissemination is a logical extension of one of the original ideas that motivated the research – the need to ground poverty research in the experience of disadvantage. This goal would not have been fulfilled if the findings had only been delivered to an academic audience. It required that the voices of disadvantage were not only incorporated into the research instruments, but also that they were transmitted through those instruments back to the wider population in a form that all could understand and relate to.

Data collection

Mention has been made at several places of the lack of data on those aspects of social disadvantage that are necessary inputs into the development of indicators of deprivation and exclusion. In fact, this situation is changing rapidly in Australia as improvements are made to existing household survey data, and as the social inclusion agenda gathers pace, some of the other data gaps have been (or soon will be) filled. Extensions to two major national surveys – the HILDA Survey and the General Social Survey – have been introduced specifically to provide a better picture of social exclusion in Australia and the studies by the Melbourne Institute and the Australian Social Inclusion Board discussed in Chapter Nine are testimony to the value of these developments. Results from the 2010 GSS have not yet been made publicly available but when they are, this will generate additional studies that will flesh out the picture and provide a benchmark against which to assess progress.

However, even with this new data, Australia will still lack a comprehensive, large-scale national survey designed to identify the essentials of life that can form the basis for estimating deprivation and hence consistent poverty. This is unfortunate given the emphasis placed by the 2020 Summit on developing poverty reduction targets as the basis for establishing a national poverty reduction strategy. Without the resources that only a body like the ABS can mobilise, studies of deprivation like this one will not have the capacity to document the national picture, or achieve the coverage that is necessary to allow the circumstances of small groups to be examined and compared. Yet it is often these groups (Indigenous Australians, refugees, people affected by mental illness) that are most vulnerable to the forces that create and perpetuate deprivation. Without the data to document their plight, the prospects for doing anything to relieve it remain poor.

Deprivation is a close cousin of exclusion, as the results presented earlier attest. If the Australian government is to maintain social inclusion as a social policy priority, it is difficult to see how this can be achieved without a major reduction in deprivation. It is therefore vitally important that further data be collected to allow the nature and incidence of deprivation to be estimated on a regular basis. This can be achieved by asking a relatively limited number of questions because, as shown in Chapters Six and Seven, restricting the number of deprivation items does not have a major impact on the nature of the problem, or who is affected by it.

If these advances in data availability are achieved, they will go a long way towards providing a national picture of social disadvantage in Australia at the end of the first decade of the 21st century – just over a century after the pioneering work on family needs that led to the establishment of the basic wage. However, that data must be complemented by information gathered in small-scale studies using in-depth interviews to explore the processes that give rise to deprivation and (particularly) to the different forms of social exclusion. The nature of both issues is such that quantitative data alone will not capture all aspects, and qualitative research is needed to flesh out the picture, fill the gaps and promote better understanding of causes and consequences.

Particularly in relation to social exclusion, there can be no presumption that the factors that operate to exclude some people are the same for others, or operate through the same mechanisms on all occasions. There is a degree of specificity about the concept of exclusion (revealed to some extent in the debate over definitions reviewed in Chapter Eight) that requires instances of exclusion to be studied in context. The combination of factors that interact to create the exclusion of group A living in community B of items identified in domain C cannot be assumed to apply universally. In-depth studies are needed to help identify the constellation of factors that give rise to a particular outcome in situation X but not in situation Y. Only when we have access to an appropriate combination of quantitative data and qualitative information will it be possible to answer such questions in ways that can help guide policy makers to develop effective responses.

The research–policy interface

The above discussion has already strayed at several points into issues surrounding the interface between research and policy. Although the usefulness of the moral imperative position on poverty has been questioned, this does not mean that the need to tackle social disadvantage is any less pressing. The main motivation for examining the incidence of poverty, deprivation and social exclusion is to build up an evidence base that can support action to address existing problems.

This process does not stop when the manuscript is completed, only when those actions are implemented. This means that it is important to explore the interface between research and policy in order to better understand its role in the processes of dissemination, debate and implementation. The fact that this discussion comes last should not be taken to imply that it is unimportant: on the contrary, it lies at the heart of the problem because it provides the key that can unlock the door to action.

It has already been noted that policy makers are keen to demonstrate that their actions are supported by research, and politicians are eager to show that they are 'open to ideas' and that their policies are based on evidence. However, the relationship between research and policy is an uneasy one that reflects the underlying differences in role and expectation alluded to earlier (Edwards, 2004). The points of contact are increasing but more action is required from both sides to narrow the divide that separates the research and policy communities. As Young et al (2002, p 223) have argued in the UK context: 'Bridges need to be built [that are] capable of carrying the weight of traffic in both directions'. This traffic should include not just a flow of ideas and arguments, but also a flow of personnel between research institutes, service providers and policy agencies. Such exchanges would contribute greatly to an improved understanding of the pressures faced by those who sit on either side of the research–policy divide.

Harvard academic Carol Weiss (1986) has argued that research can be utilised in many different ways: as a process of enlightenment that fills the 'well of knowledge' from which all may draw; as a way of lubricating the machinery of policy development by solving problems; and as a way of raising awareness and exerting pressure for action. She has emphasised the importance of ideas, arguing that:

> More often, it is the ideas and general notions coming from research which have had an impact … [they] are picked up in diverse ways and percolate through to office-holders in many offices who deal with the issues.… Because research provides powerful labels for previously inchoate and unorganised experience, it helps to mould officials' thinking into categories derived from social science. (Weiss, 1986, p 218)

These observations suggest that it is difficult to establish where and how – or even whether – research has influenced policy. This is likely to be just as difficult to pinpoint when policy makers are asked as when researchers themselves are: most policy researchers (the current author included) stare blankly into space when asked which of their ideas has had the biggest impact on policy. Such ignorance provides an evocative example of existing deficiencies.

Two main points have emerged from reflections on the relationship between research and policy. The first is the importance of the conventional hallmarks of research quality – independence of thought, conceptual sophistication and methodological rigour – as 'critical ingredients' in determining what gets used (Weiss, 1986, p 234). The second is the need, emphasised earlier, for researchers to make the effort to ensure that their work is disseminated effectively to those engaged in formulating policy and implementing practice. This means that researchers must not only understand the nature of the policy-making process that they seek to influence, but also that they must learn how to disseminate their findings effectively by identifying better ways of connecting with policy makers and practitioners.

The changing nature of the relationship between the bureaucracy and politicians has affected the kinds of research that government is prepared to fund. The attractiveness of the concept of social exclusion to policy makers is based in part on the implication that social disadvantage is not just about a lack of money and that complex problems like exclusion require multi-faceted ('joined-up') solutions. Governments have been willing to fund research and data collection on social exclusion because they are committed to an agenda that places inclusion, in the sense of promoting opportunity, at its centre. This has opened up a productive dialogue between policy makers and researchers about what kinds of data are needed, and what key research questions need answering. Similar developments have not yet emerged in relation to other aspects of social disadvantage, although even here the issue of poverty (measured using a consistent poverty approach that includes deprivation) is emerging onto the policy agenda as a form of exclusion that must be addressed.

Is it too much to hope that a future government will commit itself to a sustained attack on all forms of social disadvantage or must that remain an idealist dream? Research on poverty and other aspects of social disadvantage help to keep the pressure on by identifying existing problems and highlighting who is most affected. The ultimate test of success must, however, rest on how effective that research is in bringing about policies that address the underlying problems. Without that action, research on social disadvantage will never fulfil its full potential.

References

Abe, A. (2006) 'Sotai-teki Hakudatsu no Jittai to Bunseki' ('Analysis of relative deprivation – an empirical study using Japanese micro-data'), *Shakai Seisaku Gakkaishi (Journal of Social Policy)*, vol 16, pp 251-75.

ABS (Australian Bureau of Statistics) (2000) *Household Expenditure Survey Australia. User guide 1998-99*, Catalogue No 6527.0, Canberra: ABS.

ABS (2002a) 'Upgrading household income distribution statistics', *Australian economic indicators*, April, Catalogue No 1350.0, Canberra: ABS, pp 3-8.

ABS (2002b) 'Expenditure: households in financial stress', in *Australian social trends 2002*, Catalogue No 4102.0, Canberra: ABS, pp 170-4.

ABS (2002c) *Measures of Australia's Progress 2002*, Catalogue No. 1370.0, Canberra: ABS.

ABS (2003) 'Revised household income distribution statistics', in *Australian economic indicators, June*, Catalogue No 1350.0, Canberra: ABS, pp 3-15.

ABS (2006a) *Household Expenditure Survey Australia 2003-04. Summary of results (re-issue)*, Catalogue No 6530.0, Canberra: ABS.

ABS (2006b) *Population by age and sex, Australian states and territories*, Catalogue No 3201.0, Canberra: ABS.

ABS (2007a) 'Low income low wealth households', in *Australian social trends 2007*, Catalogue No 4102.0, Canberra: ABS, pp 164-9.

ABS (2007b) *Household income and income distribution, Australia 2003-04 (re-issue)*, Catalogue No 6523.0, Canberra: ABS.

ABS (2009a) 'Report on low consumption possibilities research project', in *Methodological News*, June, Canberra: ABS, pp 2-3.

ABS (2009b) *Household income and income distribution, Australia, 2007-08*, Catalogue No 6523.0, Canberra: ABS, Appendix 4, pp 60-4.

ABS (2009c) *Measures of Australia's progress: Summary indicators, 2009*, Catalogue No 1383.0.55.001, Canberra: ABS.

ABS (2010) *Measures of Australia's progress 2010*, Catalogue No 1370.0, Canberra: ABS.

ACOSS (Australian Council of Social Service) (2003) *The bare necessities: Poverty and deprivation in Australia today. Submission to the Senate Inquiry into poverty and financial hardship*, Paper 127, Sydney: ACOSS.

ACOSS (2007a) *A fair go for all Australians. International comparisons, 2007 – 10 essentials*, Sydney: ACOSS.

ACOSS (2007b) *Towards a fairer Australia – ACOSS 2007 election statement*, Sydney: ACOSS.

Adelman, L., Middleton, S. and Ashworth, K. (2003) *Britain's poorest children: Severe and persistent poverty and social exclusion*, London: Save the Children.

AIHW (Australian Institute of Health and Welfare) (2007) *Australia's welfare 2007*, Canberra: AIHW.

Alber, J., Fahey, T. and Saraceno, C. (2007) 'Introduction: EU enlargement and quality of life. The context and purpose of this book', in J. Alber, T. Fahey and C. Saraceno (eds) *Handbook of quality of life in the enlarged European Union*, Abingdon: Routledge, pp 1-24.

Allardt, E. (1992) 'Having, loving, being: an alternative to the Swedish model of welfare research', in M.C. Nussbaum and A.K. Sen (eds) *The quality of life*, Oxford: Clarendon Press, pp 88-94.

Arthurson, K. and Jacobs, K. (2003) *Social exclusion and housing*, Melbourne: Australian Housing and Urban Research Institute.

Arthurson, K. and Jacobs, K. (2004) 'A critique of the concept of social exclusion and its utility for Australian social housing policy', *Australian Journal of Social Issues*, vol 39, no 1, pp 25-40.

ASIB (Australian Social Inclusion Board) (2009a) *A compendium of social inclusion indicators. How's Australia faring?*, Canberra: Department of Prime Minister and Cabinet.

ASIB (2009b) *Social inclusion in Australia. How Australia is faring*, Canberra: Department of Prime Minister and Cabinet.

Atkinson, A.B. (1989) 'How should we measure poverty? Some conceptual issues', in A.B. Atkinson, *Poverty and social security*, London: Harvester Wheatsheaf, pp 7-24.

Atkinson, A.B. (1998) 'Social exclusion, poverty and unemployment', in A.B. Atkinson and J. Hills (eds) *Exclusion, employment and opportunity*, CASEpaper 4, London: Centre for the Analysis of Social Exclusion, London School of Economics and Political Science, pp 1-20.

Atkinson, A.B. (2004) 'The Luxembourg income study (LIS): past, present and future', *Socio-Economic Review*, vol 2, no 4, pp 165-90.

Atkinson, A.B. (2007) 'EU social policy, the Lisbon agenda and re-imagining social policy', Henderson Oration, 21 February, University of Melbourne.

Atkinson, A.B., Rainwater, L. and Smeeding, T.M. (1995) *Income distribution in OECD countries: The evidence from the Luxembourg income study (LIS)*, Paris: Organisation for Economic Co-operation and Development.

Atkinson, A.B., Cantillon, B., Marlier, E. and Nolan, B. (2002) *Social indicators. The EU and social inclusion*, Oxford: Oxford University Press.

Australian Fair Pay Commission (2006) *AFPC 2006 wage-setting review*, Melbourne: Australian Fair Pay Commission.

Australian Government (2008) *Social inclusion principles for Australia*, Canberra: Department of Prime Minister and Cabinet.

Australian Government (2009) *A stronger, fairer Australia. National statement on social inclusion*, Canberra: Department of Prime Minister and Cabinet.

Australian Government (2010) *The road home – Homelessness White Paper*, Canberra: Department of Families, Housing, Community Services and Indigenous Affairs.

Barnes, H. (2009) *Child poverty in South Africa: A socially perceived necessities approach*, Measures of Child Poverty Project Key Report 2, Pretoria: Department of Social Development, Republic of South Africa.

Bartlett, D. (2008) 'Message from the premier', in *A social inclusion strategy for Tasmania*, Hobart: Department of Premier and Cabinet, p 3.

Béland, D. (2007) 'The social exclusion discourse: ideas and policy change', *Policy & Politics*, vol 35, no 1, pp 123-39.

Berghman, J. (1997) 'The resurgence of poverty and the struggle against exclusion: a new challenge for social security', *International Social Security Review*, vol 50, no 1, pp 3-21.

Berthoud, R. and Bryan, M. (2008) 'Deprivation indicators', in R. Berthoud and F. Zantomio (eds) *Measuring poverty: Seven key issues*, Colchester: Institute for Economic and Social Research, University of Essex, pp 14-15.

Berthoud, R., Blekesaune, M. and Hancock, R. (2006) *Are poor pensioners deprived?*, Research Report No 364, London: Department for Work and Pensions.

Berthoud, R., Bryan, M. and Bardarsi, E. (2004) *The dynamics of deprivation: The relationship between income and material deprivation over time*, Research Report No 219, London: Department for Work and Pensions.

Billing, J., Kindermann, B., McColl, B. and Rolfe, N. (2010) 'Improving our understanding and measures of economic hardship: Australia's development of a low consumption possibilities framework', Presented to the 31st General Conference of the International Association for Research on Income and Wealth, St Gallen, Switzerland, 22-28 August.

Blunkett, D. (2000) 'Influence or irrelevance: can social science improve government?', Secretary of State's ESRC Lecture Speech, London: Department for Education and Employment.

Boarini, R. and d'Ercole, M.M. (2006) *Measures of material deprivation in OECD countries*, Working Paper No 37, Paris: Directorate for Employment, Labour and Social Affairs, Organisation for Economic Co-operation and Development.

Böhnke, P. (2008) 'Feeling left out: patterns of social integration and exclusion', in J. Alber, T. Fahey and C. Saraceno (eds) *Handbook of quality of life in the enlarged European Union*, Abingdon: Routledge, pp 304-27.

Borooah, V. (2007) 'Measuring economic inequality: deprivation, economising and possessing', *Social Policy and Society*, vol 6, no 1, pp 99-109.

Bradbury, B. (1996) *Are the low income self-employed poor?*, Discussion Paper No 73, Sydney: Social Policy Research Centre, University of New South Wales.

Bradbury, B. (2003) *Child poverty: A review*, Policy Research Paper Number 20, Canberra: Department of Families, Housing, Community Services and Indigenous Affairs.

Bradbury, B. and Jäntti, M. (1999) *Child poverty across industrialized nations*, Innocenti Occasional Paper No 71, Florence: UNICEF International Child Development Centre.

Bradbury, B., Rossiter, C. and Vipond, J. (1986) *Poverty, before and after paying for housing*, Reports and Proceedings No 26, Sydney: Social Welfare Research Centre, University of New South Wales.

Bradshaw, J. (ed) (1993) *Budget standards for the United Kingdom*, Aldershot: Avebury.

Bradshaw, J. (2004) 'How has the notion of social exclusion developed in the European discourse?', *Economic and Labour Relations Review*, vol 14, no 2, pp 168-86.

Bradshaw, J. and Finch, N. (2002) *A comparison of child benefit packages in 22 countries*, Research Report No 174, Leeds: Department for Work and Pensions.

Bradshaw, J. and Finch, N. (2003) 'Overlaps in dimensions of poverty', *Journal of Social Policy*, vol 32, no 4, pp 513-25.

Bradshaw, J. and Sainsbury, R. (eds) (1999) *Researching poverty*, Aldershot: Ashgate.

Bradshaw, J., Hoelscher, P. and Richardson, D. (2006) *Comparing child well-being in OECD countries: Concepts and methods*, Innocenti Working Paper IWP-2006-03, Florence: Innocenti Research Centre.

Bradshaw, J., Kemp, P., Baldwin, S. and Rowe, A. (2004) *The drivers of social exclusion. A review of the literature for the Social Exclusion Unit in the Breaking the Cycle series*, London: Office of the Deputy Prime Minister.

Bray, J.R. (2001) *Hardship in Australia. An analysis of financial stress indicators in the 1998-99 Australian Bureau of Statistics Household Expenditure Survey*, Occasional Paper No 4, Canberra: Department of Families, Housing, Community Services and Indigenous Affairs.

Breunig R. and Cobb-Clark, D. (2006) 'Understanding the factors associated with financial stress in Australian households', *Australian Social Policy 2005*, pp 13-64.

Breunig, R., Cobb-Clark, D.A., Gong, X. and Venn, D. (2005) *Disagreement in partners' reports of financial difficulty*, Discussion paper No 1624, Bonn: Institute for the Study of Labour (IZA).

Brewer, M., Muriel, A., Phillips, D. and Sibieta, L. (2008) *Poverty and inequality in the UK: 2008*, London: Institute for Fiscal Studies.

Brooks-Gunn, J. and Duncan, G. (1997) 'The effects of poverty on children', *The Future of Children*, vol 7, no 2, pp 55-71.

Brumby, J. (2008) 'Message from the premier', in *A fairer Victoria. Strong people, strong communities*, Melbourne: Department of Planning and Community Development.

Buddelmeyer, H. and Verick, S. (2008) 'Understanding the drivers of poverty dynamics in Australian households', *Economic Record*, vol 84, no 266, pp 310-21.

Buhmann, B., Rainwater, L., Schmaus, G. and Smeeding, T.M. (1988) 'Equivalence scales, well-being, inequality and poverty: sensitivity estimates across ten countries using the Luxembourg income study (LIS) database', *Review of Income and Wealth*, vol 34, no 1, pp 115-42.

Burchardt, T. (2000) 'Social exclusion: concepts and evidence', in D. Gordon and P. Townsend (eds) *Breadline Europe. The measurement of poverty*, Bristol: The Policy Press, pp 385-405.

Burchardt, T., Le Grand, J. and Piachaud, D. (1999) 'Social exclusion in Britain 1991-1995', *Social Policy and Administration*, vol 33, no 3, pp 227-44.

Burchardt, T., Le Grand, J. and Piachaud, D. (2002a) 'Introduction', in J. Hills, J. Le Grand and D. Piachaud (eds) *Understanding social exclusion*, Oxford: Oxford University Press, pp 1-12.

Burchardt, T., Le Grand, J. and Piachaud, D. (2002b) 'Degrees of exclusion: developing a dynamic, multidimensional measure', in J. Hills, J. Le Grand and D. Piachaud (eds) *Understanding social exclusion*, Oxford: Oxford University Press, pp 30-43.

Butterworth, P. and Crosier, T. (2006) 'Deriving a measure of financial hardship from the HILDA Survey', *Australian Social Policy 2005*, pp 1-12.

Calandrino, M. (2003) *Low income and deprivation in British families*, DWP Working Paper No 10, London: Department for Work and Pensions.

Callan, T. and Nolan, B. (1991) 'Concepts of poverty and the poverty line: a critical survey of approaches to measuring poverty', *Journal of Economic Surveys*, vol 5, no 3, pp 243-62.

Callan, T. and Nolan, B. (1993) 'Resources, deprivation and the measurement of poverty', *Journal of Social Policy*, vol 22, no 2, pp 141-72.

Cappellari, L. and Jenkins, S.P. (2007) 'Summarising multiple depriviation indicators', in S.P. Jenkins and J. Micklewright (eds) *Inequality and poverty re-examined*, Oxford: Oxford University Press, pp 166-84.

Cappo, D. (2002) 'Social inclusion initiative. Social inclusion, participation and empowerment', Address to the ACOSS National Congress, Adelaide: Social Inclusion Board.

CARC (Community Affairs References Committee) (2004) *A hand up not a hand out: Renewing the fight against poverty. Report on poverty and financial hardship*, Canberra: The Senate, Parliament House.

Castles, F.G. (1985) *The working class and welfare. Reflections on the political development of the welfare state in Australia and New Zealand, 1890-1980*, Sydney: Allen & Unwin.

Castles, F.G. (1994) 'The wage earners' welfare state revisited: refurbishing the established model of Australian social protection, 1893-93', *Australian Journal of Social Issues*, vol 29, no 2, pp 120-45.

Catholic Social Services Australia (2010) *The social inclusion agenda. Where it comes from, what it means, and why it matters*, Canberra: Catholic Social Services Australia.

Chow, N.S.N. (1983) *The extent and nature of poverty in Hong Kong*, Hong Kong: Department of Social Work, University of Hong Kong.

Combat Poverty Agency (2004) *What is poverty?*, Dublin: Combat Poverty Agency.

Commission of Inquiry into Poverty (1975) *First main report. Poverty in Australia*, Canberra: Australian Government Publishing Service.

Couch, K., Smeeding, T.M. and Waldfogel, J. (2010) 'Fighting poverty: attentive policy can make a huge difference', *Journal of Policy Analysis and Management*, vol 29, no 2, pp 401-7.

Daly, A., McNamara, J., Tanton, R., Harding, A. and Yap, M. (2008) 'Indicators of risk of social exclusion for children in Australian households: an analysis by state and age group', *Australasian Journal of Regional Studies*, vol 14, no 2, pp 133-54.

Dennis, I. and Guio, A.-C. (2003) 'Poverty and social exclusion in the EU after Laeken – part 1', *Statistics in Focus: Population and Social Conditions*, Theme 3 – 8/2003, Luxembourg: Eurostat, pp 1-7.

Department of Prime Minister and Cabinet (2008a) *Australia 2020 summit. Initial summit report*, Canberra: Department of Prime Minister and Cabinet.

Department of Prime Minister and Cabinet (2008b) *Australia 2020 summit. Final report*, Canberra: Department of Prime Minister and Cabinet.

Dillman, D. (1978) *Mail and telephone surveys: The total design method*, New York: Wiley.

Donnison, D. (1998) *Policy for a just society*, London: Macmillan.

DSS (Department of Social Security) (1995) *Developing a framework for benchmarks of adequacy for social security payments*, Policy Discussion Paper No 6, Canberra: DSS.

DWP (Department for Work and Pensions) (2002) *Measuring child poverty. A consultation document*, London: DWP.

DWP (2003a) *Measuring child poverty consultation. Preliminary conclusions*, London: DWP.

DWP (2003b) *Measuring child poverty consultation: Final conclusions*, London: DWP.

DWP (2006) *UK national action plan 2006-2008*, London: DWP.

DWP (2007) *Opportunity for all: Indicators update 2007*, London: DWP.

DWP (2008) *Working together. UK National Action Plan on social inclusion*, London: DWP.

Eardley, T. and Bradbury, B. (1997) 'Not waving but drowning? Low incomes and poverty amongst the self-employed', in M. Bittman (ed) *Poverty in Australia: Dimensions and policies*, Reports and Proceedings No 135, Sydney: Social Policy Research Centre, University of New South Wales, pp 39-65.

Edwards, M. (2001) *Social policy, public policy: From problem to practice*, Sydney: Allen & Unwin.

Edwards, M. (2004) *Social science research and public policy: Narrowing the divide*, Policy Paper No 2, Canberra: Academy of the Social Sciences in Australia.

Esping-Andersen, G. (1990) *The three worlds of welfare capitalism*, Cambridge: Polity Press.

Esping-Andersen, G. (1999) *Social foundations of postindustrial economies*, Oxford: Oxford University Press.

ESRC (Economic and Social Research Council) (1997) *Thematic priorities. Update 1997*, Swindon: ESRC.

European Commission (2002) *Joint report on social inclusion*, Luxembourg: Office for Official Publications of the European Commission.

European Commission (2004) *Joint report on social inclusion*, Brussels: European Commission.

FaHCSIA (Department of Families, Housing, Community Services and Indigenous Affairs) (2003) *Inquiry into poverty and financial hardship. Commonwealth Department of Families, Housing, Community Services and Indigenous Affairs submission to the Senate Community Affairs References Committee*, Occasional Paper No 9, Canberra: FaHCSIA.

Fincher, R. and Wulff, M. (1998) 'The locations of poverty and disadvantage', in R. Fincher and J. Nieuwenhuysen (eds) *Australian poverty: Then and now*, Melbourne: Melbourne University Press, pp 144-64.

Förster, M.F. and d'Ercole, M.M. (2005) *Income distribution and poverty in OECD countries in the second half of the 1990s*, Working Paper No 22, Paris: Directorate for Employment, Labour and Social Affairs, Organisation for Economic Co-operation and Development.

Förster, M.F. and Pearson, M. (2002) 'Income distribution and poverty in the OECD area: trends and driving forces', *OECD Economic Studies*, no 34, pp 7-39.

Förster, M.F. and Vleminckx, K. (2004) 'International comparisons of income inequality and poverty: findings from the Luxembourg Income Study', *Socio-Economic Review*, vol 2, no 4, pp 191-212.

Giddens, A. (1998) *The third way. The renewal of social democracy*, Cambridge: Polity Press.

Giddens, A. (2000) *The third way and its critics*, Cambridge: Polity Press.

Gillard, J. (2008a) 'Speech. National ACOSS Congress', Canberra: Office of the Minister for Social Inclusion.

Gillard, J. (2008b) 'Media release by the Minister for Education, Minister for Employment and Workplace Relations, Minister for Social Inclusion and Deputy Prime Minister: Australian Social Inclusion Board', Canberra: Department of Education, Employment and Workplace Relations.

Goodin, R.E. (2001) 'False principles of welfare reform', *Australian Journal of Social Issues*, vol 36, no 3, pp 189-206.

Gordon, D. (2000) 'The scientific measurement of poverty: recent theoretical advances', in J. Bradshaw and R. Sainsbury (eds) *Researching poverty*, Aldershot: Ashgate, pp 37-58.

Gordon, D. (2006) 'The concept and measurement of poverty', in C. Pantazis, D. Gordon and R. Levitas (eds) *Poverty and social exclusion in Britain. The Millennium Survey*, Bristol: The Policy Press pp 29-69.

Gordon, D. and Pantazis C. (eds) (1997a) *Breadline Britain in the 1990s*, Aldershot: Ashgate.

Gordon, D. and Pantazis, C. (1997b) 'Measuring poverty: breadline Britain in the 1990s', in D. Gordon and C. Pantazis (eds) *Breadline Britain in the 1990s*, Aldershot: Ashgate, pp 5-47.

Gordon, D. and Townsend, P. (eds) (2000) *Breadline Europe. The measurement of poverty*, Bristol: The Policy Press.

Gottschalk, P. and Smeeding, T.M. (2000) 'Empirical evidence on income inequality in industrialized countries', in A.B. Atkinson and F. Bourguignon (eds) *Handbook of income distribution, Volume 1*, Amsterdam: North Holland, pp 261-308.

Government of Ireland (2007) *National plan for social inclusion 2007-2016*, Dublin.

Government of South Australia (2004) *Social inclusion initiative*, vol 1, issue 1, Adelaide: Department of the Premier.

Guio, A-C. (2005) 'Income poverty and social exclusion in the EU25', *Statistics in Focus 13/2005*, Brussels: Eurostat.

Hahn, M. and Wilkins, R. (2008) *A muitidimensional approach to investigation of living standards of the low-paid: Income, wealth, financial stress and consumption*, Research Report No 5/09, Melbourne: Australian Fair Pay Commission.

Halleröd, B. (1994) *A new approach to direct consensual measurement of poverty*, Discussion Paper No 50, Sydney: Social Policy Research Centre, University of New South Wales.

Halleröd, B. (1995) 'The truly poor: indirect and direct measurement of consensual poverty in Sweden', *Journal of European Social Policy*, vol 5, no 1, pp 111-29.

Halleröd, B. (2006) 'Sour grapes: relative deprivation, adaptive preferences and the measurement of poverty', *Journal of Social Policy*, vol 35, no 3, pp 371-90.

Halleröd, B., Bradshaw J. and Holmes, H. (1997) 'Adapting the consensual definition of poverty', in D. Gordon and C. Pantazis (eds) *Breadline Britain in the 1990s*, Aldershot: Ashgate, pp 213-34.

Halleröd, B., Larsson, D., Gordon, D. and Ritakallio, V.-M. (2006), 'Relative deprivation: a comparative analysis of Britain, Finland and Sweden', *Journal of European Social Policy*, vol 16, no 4, pp 328-45.

Hamilton, C. and Denniss, R. (2005) *Affluenza. When too much is never enough*, Sydney: Allen & Unwin.

Harding, A. and Szukalska, A. (2000) *Financial disadvantage in Australia – 1999. The unlucky Australians?*, Sydney: The Smith Family.

Harding, A., Lloyd, R. and Greenwell, H. (2001) *Financial disadvantage in Australia 1990 to 2000. The persistence of poverty in a decade of growth*, Sydney: The Smith Family.

Harmer, J. (2008) *Pension review background paper*, Canberra: Department of Families, Housing, Community Services and Indigenous Affairs.

Harmer, J. (2009) *Pension review report*, Canberra: Department of Families, Housing, Community Services and Indigenous Affairs.

Hayes, A., Gray, M. and Edwards, B. (2008) *Social inclusion. Origins, concepts and key themes*, Canberra: Social Inclusion Unit, Department of Prime Minister and Cabinet.

Headey, B. (2006) *A framework for assessing poverty, disadvantage and low capabilities in Australia*, Melbourne Institute Report No 6, Melbourne: Melbourne Institute of Applied Economic and Social Research, University of Melbourne.

Headey, B. (2007) 'Financial poverty in Australia. Developing a valid measure based on wealth, income and consumption for use by Commonwealth and State governments', Presented to the HILDA Survey Research Conference, Melbourne: Melbourne Institute of Applied Economic and Social Research.

Headey, B. and Warren, D. (2007) *Families, incomes and jobs, Volume 2: A statistical report on waves 1 to 4 of the HILDA Survey*, Melbourne: Melbourne Institute of Applied Economic and Social Research, University of Melbourne.

Headey, B. and Warren, D. (2008) *Families, incomes and jobs, volume 3: A statistical report on waves 1 to 5 of the HILDA Survey*, Melbourne: Melbourne Institute of Applied Economic and Social Research, University of Melbourne.

Headey, B., Marks, G. and Wooden, M. (2005) 'The dynamics of income poverty in Australia: evidence from the first three waves of the HILDA survey', *Australian Journal of Social Issues*, vol 40, no 4, pp 541-52.

Henderson, R.F., Harcourt, A. and Harper, R.J.A. (1970) *People in poverty. A Melbourne survey*, Melbourne: Cheshire for the Institute of Applied Economic and Social Research.

Hills, J. (2002) 'Does a focus on "social exclusion" change the policy response?', in J. Hills, J. Le Grand and D. Piachaud (eds) (*Understanding social exclusion*, Oxford: Oxford University Press, pp 226-43.

Hills, J. (2004) *Inequality and the state*, Oxford: Oxford University Press.

Hills, J., Le Grand, J. and Piachaud, D. (eds) (2002) *Understanding social exclusion*, Oxford: Oxford University Press.

Hong Kong Council of Social Service (2010) *A pilot study of deprivation in Hong Kong*, Hong Kong: Hong Kong Council of Social Service.

Jensen, J., Krishnan, V., Spittal, M. and Sathiyandra, S. (2003) 'New Zealand living standards: their measurement and variation, with an application to policy', *Social Policy Journal of New Zealand*, vol 20, pp 72-97.

Jensen, J., Spittal, M., Crichton, S., Sathiyandra, S. and Krishnan, V. (2002) *Direct measurement of living standards: The New Zealand ELSI scale*, Wellington: Ministry of Social Development.

Jensen, J., Krishnan, V., Hodgson, R., Sathiyandra, S., Templeton, R., Jones, D., Goldstein-Hawes, R. and Beynon, P. (2006) *New Zealand living standards 2004*, Wellington: Ministry of Social Development.

Kangas, O. and Ritakallio, V.-M. (1998) 'Different methods – different results? Approaches to multidimensional poverty', in H.-J. Andreß (ed) *Empirical poverty research in comparative perspective*, Aldershot: Ashgate, pp 167-203.

Kenworthy, L. (2004) *Egalitarian capitalism. Jobs, incomes and growth in affluent countries*, New York: Russell Sage Foundation.

King, A. (1998) 'Income poverty since the 1970s', in R. Fincher and J. Niewenhuysen (eds) *Australian poverty: Then and now*, Melbourne: Melbourne University Press, pp 71-102.

King, S., Bellamy, J., Swann, N., Gavarotto, R. and Coller, P. (2009) *Social exclusion – The Sydney experience*, Sydney: Anglicare, Diocese of Sydney.

Krishnan, V., Jensen, J. and Ballantyne, S. (2002) *New Zealand living standards 2000*, Wellington: Ministry of Social Development.

Layte, R., Nolan, B. and Whelan, C. (2000) 'Targeting poverty: lessons from monitoring Ireland's national anti-poverty strategy', *Journal of Social Policy*, vol 29, no 4, pp 553-75.

Levitas, R. (2000) 'What Is social exclusion?', in D. Gordon and P. Townsend (eds) *Breadline Europe. The measurement of poverty*, Bristol: The Policy Press, pp 357-83.

Levitas, R. (2006) 'The concept and measurement of social exclusion', in C. Pantazis, D. Gordon and R. Levitas (eds) *Poverty and social exclusion in Britain. The Millennium Survey*, Bristol: The Policy Press, pp 123-60.

Levitas, R., Pantazis, C., Fahmy, E., Gordon, D., Lloyd, E. and Patsios, D. (2007) *The multi-dimensional analysis of social exclusion*, Bristol: Department of Sociology and School for Social Policy, University of Bristol.

Lister, R. (2004) *Poverty*, Cambridge: Polity Press.

McCarthy, T. and Wicks, J. (2001) *Two Australias. Addressing inequality and poverty*, Sydney: St Vincent de Paul Society, National Council of Australia.

McColl, R., Pietsch, L. and Gatenby, J. (2001) 'Household income, living standards and financial stress', *Australian economic indicators. June 2001*, Catalogue No 1350.0, Canberra: Australian Bureau of Statistics, pp 13-32.

McKay, S. (2004) 'Poverty or preference: what do "consensual deprivation indicators" really measure?', *Fiscal Studies*, vol 25, no 2, pp 201-23.

McKay, S. and Collard, S. (2003) *Developing deprivation questions for the Family Resources Survey*, Bristol: Personal Finances Research Centre, University of Bristol.

Mack, J. and Lansley, S. (1985) *Poor Britain*, London: George Allen & Unwin.

Maître, B., Nolan, B. and Whelan, C.T. (2006) *Reconfiguring the measurement of deprivation and consistent poverty in Ireland*, Policy Research Series Number 58, Dublin: Economic and Social Research Institute.

Manning, I. (1998) 'Policies: past and present', in R. Fincher and J. Niewenhuysen (eds) *Australian poverty: Then and now*, Melbourne: Melbourne University Press, pp 10-32.

Marks, G.N. (2007) *Income poverty, subjective poverty and financial stress*, Social Policy Research Report No 29, Canberra: Department of Families, Housing, Community Services and Indigenous Affairs.

Marshall, T.P. (1981) *The right to welfare and other essays*, London: Heinemann Educational Books.

Mayer, S. and Jencks, C. (1988) 'Poverty and the distribution of material hardship', *Journal of Human Resources*, vol 24, no 1, pp 88-114.

Melbourne Institute of Applied Economic and Social Research (2009) *Poverty lines, Australia. June quarter 2009*, Melbourne: Melbourne Institute, University of Melbourne.

Millar, J. (2007) 'Social exclusion and social policy research: defining exclusion', in D. Abrams, J. Christian and D. Gordon (eds) *Multidisciplinary handbook of social exclusion research*, Chichester: John Wiley & Sons, pp 1-16.

Muffels, R. and Fourage, D. (2004) 'The role of European welfare states in explaining resources deprivation', *Social Indicators Research*, vol 68, no 3, pp 299-330.

Nicholson, T. (2005) 'Doing things differently. Policies to end persistent poverty', *Brotherhood Comment*, April, Melbourne: Brotherhood of St Laurence, pp 1-2.

Noble, M. W.J., Wright, G.C., Magasela, W.K. and Ratcliffe, A. (2007) 'Developing a democratic definition of poverty in South Africa', *Journal of Poverty*, vol 11, no 4, pp 117-41.

Nolan, B. (2000) 'Targeting poverty – the Irish example', *Australian Social Policy 2000*, no 1, pp 25-41.

Nolan, B. and Marx, I. (2009) 'Economic inequality, poverty, and social exclusion', in W. Salverda, B. Nolan and T.M. Smeeding (eds) *The Oxford handbook of economic inequality*, Oxford: Oxford University Press, pp 315-41.

Nolan, B. and Whelan, C.T. (1996) *Resources, deprivation and poverty*, Oxford: Clarendon Press.

OECD (Organisation for Economic Co-operation and Development) (2007a) *Child poverty in OECD countries: Trends, causes and policy responses*, Document DELSA/ELSA/WP1(2007)17, Paris: OECD.

OECD (2007b) *Babies and bosses: Reconciling work and family Life (Volume 5): A synthesis of findings for OECD countries*, Paris: OECD.

OECD (2008) *Growing unequal? Income distribution and poverty in OECD countries*, Paris: OECD.

OECD (2010) *A framework to measure the progress of societies*, Document STD/DOC(2010)5, Paris: OECD.

Office for Social Inclusion (2004) *What is being done about poverty and social exclusion? Government strategies to combat poverty and social exclusion in Ireland*, Dublin: Office for Social Inclusion, Department for Family and Social Affairs.

Pantazis, C., Gordon, D. and Levitas, R. (eds) (2006a) *Poverty and social exclusion in Britain. The Millennium Survey*, Bristol: The Policy Press.

Pantazis, C., Gordon, D. and Townsend, P. (2006b) 'The necessities of life', in C. Pantazis, D. Gordon and R. Levitas (eds) *Poverty and social exclusion in Britain. The Millennium Survey*, Bristol: The Policy Press, pp 89-122.

Parkinson, M. (2004) *Policy advice and Treasury's wellbeing framework*, Canberra: Department of Treasury.

Paugam, S. (1995) 'The spiral of precariousness: a multidimensional approach to the process of social disqualification in France', in G. Room (ed) *Beyond the threshold. The measurement and analysis of social exclusion*, Bristol: The Policy Press, pp 49-79.

Paugam, S. (1996) 'Poverty and social disqualification: a comparative analysis of cumulative disadvantage in Europe', *Journal of European Social Policy*, vol 6, no 4, pp 166-74.

Peace, R. (2001) 'Social exclusion: a concept in need of definition?', *Social Policy Journal of New Zealand*, issue 16, pp 17-35.

Peel, M. (2003) *The lowest rung. Voices of Australian poverty*, Melbourne: Cambridge University Press.

Perry, B. (2002) 'The mismatch between income measures and direct outcome measures of poverty', *Social Policy Journal of New Zealand*, issue 19, pp 101-26.

Perry, B. (2009) *Non-income measures of material wellbeing and hardship: First results from the 2008 New Zealand Living Standards Survey, with international comparisons*, Wellington: Ministry of Social Development.

Piachaud, D. (1981) 'Peter Townsend and the holy grail', *New Society*, September, pp 419-21.

Piachaud, D. (1988) 'Poverty and inequality: analysis and action', Mimeo, London: Department of Social Policy, London School of Economics and Political Science.

Pierson, J. (2001) *Tackling social exclusion*, London: Routledge.

Pietsch, L., McColl, B. and Saunders, P. (2006) 'The sensitivity of income distribution measures to changes in survey collection tools and estimation techniques in Australia', Presented at the 29th General Conference of the International Association for Research on Income and Wealth, Joensuu, Finland, August.

Putnam, R.D. (1993) *Making democracy work. Civic traditions in modern Italy*, Princeton, NJ: Princeton University Press.

Rainwater, L. (1974) *What money buys. Inequality and the social meanings of income*, New York: Basic Books.

Randolph, B. (2004) 'Social inclusion and place-focused initiatives in western Sydney: a review of current practice', *Australian Journal of Social Issues*, vol 39, no 1, pp 63-78.

Rann, M. (2002), 'News release: Rann announces social inclusion targets – how it will work', Adelaide: Office of the Premier.

Reference Group on Welfare Reform (2000) *Participation support for a more equitable society. Full report*, Canberra: Department of Families, Housing, Community Services and Indigenous Affairs.

Richardson, L. and Le Grand, J. (2002) 'Outsider and insider expertise: the response of residents of deprived neighbourhoods to an academic definition of social exclusion', *Social Policy and Administration*, vol 36, no 5, pp 496-515.

Ringen, S. (1987) *The possibility of politics*, Oxford: Clarendon Press.

Ringen, S. (1988) 'Direct and indirect measures of poverty', *Journal of Social Policy*, vol 17, no 2, pp 351-65.

Ringen, S. (2007) *What democracy is for. On freedom and moral government*, Princeton, NJ: Princeton University Press.

Room, G. (1995) 'Poverty and social exclusion: the new European agenda for policy and research', in G. Room (ed) *Beyond the threshold. The measurement and analysis of social exclusion*, Bristol: The Policy Press, pp 1-9.

Rowntree, B.S. (1901), *Poverty. A study of town life*, London: Macmillan.

Saranceno, C. (2002) 'Social exclusion: cultural roots and variations on a popular concept', in A.J. Kahn and S.B. Kamerman (eds) *Beyond child poverty: The social exclusion of children*, New York: Institute for Child and Family Policy, Columbia University, pp 37-74.

Saunders, P. (1994) *Welfare and inequality: National and international perspectives on the Australian welfare state*, Melbourne: Cambridge University Press.

Saunders, P. (1997) 'Living standards, choice and poverty', *Australian Journal of Labour Economics*, vol 1, pp 49-70.

Saunders, P. (1999) 'Budget standards and the poverty line', *Australian Economic Review*, 1st Quarter, pp 43-61.

Saunders, P. (2001) 'Reflections on social security and the welfare review', *Australian Economic Review*, vol 34, pp 100-8.

Saunders, P. (2002) *The ends and means of welfare. Coping with economic and social change in Australia*, Melbourne: Cambridge University Press.

Saunders, P. (2003a) 'Stability and change in community perceptions of poverty: evidence from Australia', *Journal of Poverty*, vol 7, no 4, pp 1-20.

Saunders, P. (2003b) *The meaning and measurement of poverty: Towards an agenda for action. Submission to the Senate Community Affairs References Committee Inquiry into poverty and financial hardship*, Sydney: Social Policy Research Centre, University of New South Wales.

Saunders, P. (2005a) *The poverty wars: Reconnecting research with reality*, Sydney: University of New South Wales Press.

Saunders, P. (2005b) 'A valuable contribution to research and policy: reviewing four decades of Australian poverty research', *Australian Journal of Social Issues*, vol 40, no 1, pp 13-32.

Saunders, P. (2005c) 'Social exclusion as a new framework for measuring poverty', in P. Smyth, T. Reddell and A. Jones (eds) *Community and local governance*, Sydney: University of New South Wales Press, pp 245-61.

Saunders, P. (2007) 'The costs of disability and the incidence of poverty', *Australian Journal of Social Issues*, vol 42, no 4, pp 461-80.

Saunders, P. (2008) 'Social exclusion: challenges for research and implications for policy', *Economic and Labour Relations Review*, vol 19, no 1, pp 73-91.

Saunders, P. and Abe, A. (2010) 'Poverty and deprivation in young and old: a comparative study of Australia and Japan', *Poverty & Public Policy*, vol 2, no 1, pp 67-97.

Saunders, P. and Adelman, L. (2006) 'Income poverty, deprivation and exclusion: a comparative study of Australia and Britain', *Journal of Social Policy*, vol 35, no 4, pp 559-84.

Saunders, P. and Bradbury, B. (1991) 'Some Australian evidence on the consensual approach to poverty measurement', *Economic Analysis and Policy*, vol 21, no 1, pp 47-78.

Saunders, P. and Bradbury, B. (2006) 'Monitoring trends in poverty and income distribution: data, methodology and measurement', *Economic Record*, vol 82, no 258, pp 341-64.

Saunders, P. and Hill, P. (2008) 'A consistent poverty approach to assessing the sensitivity of income poverty measures and trends', *Australian Economic Review*, vol 41, no 4, pp 371-88.

Saunders, P. and Matheson, G. (1991) 'An ever-rising tide? Poverty in Australia in the eighties', *The Economic and Labour Relations Review*, vol 2, no 2, pp 143-71.

Saunders, P. and Matheson, G. (1992) *Perceptions of poverty, income adequacy and living standards in Australia*, Reports and Proceedings No 99, Sydney: Social Policy Research Centre, University of New South Wales.

Saunders, P. and Naidoo, Y. (2009) 'Poverty, deprivation and consistent poverty', *Economic Record*, vol 85, no 271, pp 417-32.

Saunders P. and Sutherland, K. (2006) *Experiencing poverty: The voices of low-income Australians. Towards new indicators of disadvantage. Project stage 1: Focus group outcomes*, Sydney: Social Policy Research Centre, University of New South Wales.

Saunders, P. and Walter, J. (2005) 'Introduction: reconsidering the policy sciences', in P. Saunders and J. Walter (eds) *Ideas and influence. Social science and public policy in Australia*, Sydney: University of New South Wales Press, pp 1-20.

Saunders, P. and Wong, M. (2008) *Deprivation and other indicators of the living standards of older Australians. Draft report for the Department of Families, Housing, Community Services and Indigenous Affairs*, Sydney: Social Policy Research Centre, University of New South Wales.

Saunders, P. and Wong, M. (2009) *Still doing it tough: An update on deprivation and social exclusion among welfare service clients*, Sydney: Social Policy Research Centre, University of New South Wales.

Saunders, P. and Wong, M. (2011: forthcoming) 'Using deprivation indicators to assess the adequacy of Australian social security payments', *Journal of Poverty and Social Justice*.

Saunders, P. and Zhu, A. (2009) 'Comparing disadvantage and well-being in Australian families', *The Australian Journal of Labour Economics*, vol 12, no 1, pp 21-39.

Saunders, P., Hill, T. and Bradbury, B. (2007a) *Poverty in Australia: Sensitivity analysis and recent trends*, Sydney: Social Policy Research Centre, University of New South Wales.

Saunders, P., Naidoo, Y. and Griffiths, M. (2007b) *Towards new indicators of disadvantage: Deprivation and social exclusion in Australia*, Sydney: Social Policy Research Centre, University of New South Wales.

Saunders, P., Naidoo, Y. and Griffiths, M. (2008) 'Towards new indicators of disadvantage: deprivation and social exclusion in Australia', *Australian Journal of Social Issues*, vol 43, no 2, pp 175-94.

Saunders, P., Thomson, C. and Evans, C. (2001) 'Social change and economic prosperity: attitudes to growth and welfare', *Just Policy*, no 23, pp 4-15.

Saunders, Peter and Tsumori, K. (2002) *Poverty in Australia. Beyond the rhetoric*, Policy Monograph No 57, Sydney: Centre for Independent Studies.

Scutella, R., Wilkins, R. and Horn, M. (2008) *Measuring poverty and social exclusion in Australia*, Melbourne: Melbourne Institute of Applied Economic and Social Research.

Scutella, R., Wilkins, R. and Kostenko, W. (2009) *Estimates of poverty and social exclusion in Australia: A multidimensional approach*, Working Paper No 26/09, Melbourne: Melbourne Institute of Applied Economic and Social Research, University of Melbourne.

Sen, A.K. (1985) *Commodities and capabilities*, Amsterdam: North-Holland.

Sen, A.K. (1992) *Inequality re-examined*, Oxford: Clarendon Press.

Sen, A.K. (1999) *Development as freedom*, New York: Anchor Books.

Sen, A.K. (2000) *Social exclusion: Concept, application and scrutiny*, Social Development Paper No 1, Manila: Asian Development Bank.

SEU (Social Exclusion Unit) (2001) *Preventing social exclusion. Report by the Social Exclusion Unit*, London: The Cabinet Office.

Siminski, P. and Yerokhin, O. (2010) *Is the age gradient in self-reported material hardship explained by resources, needs, behaviours or reporting bias?*, Working Paper 02-10, Wollongong: School of Economics, University of Wollongong.

Simons, R. (2000) 'Preface', in A. Harding and A. Szukalska, *Financial disadvantage in Australia – 1999. The unlucky Australians?*, Sydney: The Smith Family, p v.

Smeeding, T.M. (2004) 'Introduction and overview', *Socio-Economic Review*, vol 2, no 4, pp 149-63.

Smeeding, T.M. (2006) 'Poor people in rich nations: the United States in comparative perspective', *Journal of Economic Perspectives*, vol 20, no 1, pp 69-90.

Smeeding, T.M., O'Higgins, M. and Rainwater, L. (1990) *Poverty, inequality and income distribution in comparative perspective. The Luxembourg Income Study*, Hemel Hempstead: Harvester Wheatsheaf.

Spicker, P. (2004) 'Developing indicators: issues in the use of quantitative data about poverty', *Policy & Politics*, vol 32, no 4, pp 431-40.

Stiglitz, J., Sen, A. and Fitoussi, J.-P. (2009) *Report by the Commission on the Measurement of Economic Performance and Social Progress* (available at www.stiglitz-sen-fitoussi.fr).

Tanton, R., Vidyattama, Y., McNamara, J., Vu, Q.N. and Harding, A. (2009) 'Old, single and poor: using microsimulation and microdata to analyse poverty and the impact of policy change among older Australians', *Economic Papers*, vol 28, no 2 pp 102-20.

Tasmania, Social Inclusion Unit (2008) *A social inclusion strategy for Tasmania: A consultation paper*, Hobart: Department of Premier and Cabinet.

Taylor, J. (2004) 'Refugees and social exclusion: what the literature says', *Migration Action*, vol 26, no 2, pp 16-31.

Taylor, J. and Stanovic, D. (2005) *Refugees and regional settlement. Balancing priorities*, Melbourne: Brotherhood of St Laurence.

The Salvation Army (2010) *Perceptions of poverty: An insight into the nature and impact of poverty in Australia*, Sydney: The Salvation Army.

Tomlinson, M., Walker, R. and Williams, G. (2008) 'Measuring poverty in Britain as a multi-dimensional concept, 1991 to 2003', *Journal of Social Policy*, vol 37, no 4, pp 597-620.

Townsend, P. (1979) *Poverty in the United Kingdom*, Harmondsworth: Penguin Books.

Townsend, P. (1987) 'Deprivation', *Journal of Social Policy*, vol 16, no 2, pp 125-46.

Travers, P. (1996) 'Deprivation among low income DSS Australian families: results from a pilot study', in R. Thanki and C. Thomson (eds) *Mortgaging our future? Families and young people in Australia*, Reports and Proceedings No 129, Sydney: Social Policy Research Centre, University of New South Wales, pp 27-45.

Travers, P. and Robertson, F. (1996) *Relative deprivation among DSS clients. Results of a pilot survey*, Monograph No 2, Adelaide: National Institute of Labour Studies, Flinders University.

UNDP (United Nations Development Programme) (2009) *Human Development Report 2009*, New York: UNDP.

UNICEF (2000) *A league table of child poverty in rich countries,* Innocenti Report Card No 1, Florence: Innocenti Research Centre.

Van den Bosch, K. (2001) *Identifying the poor. Using subjective and consensual measures,* Aldershot: Ashgate.

Van den Bosch, K. (2004) 'Measuring deprivation in the EU: to use or not to use subjective information', Presented to the 28th General Conference of the International Association for Research on Income and Wealth, Cork, Ireland.

Vinson, T. (2004) *Community adversity and resilience: The distribution of social disadvantage in Victoria and New South Wales and the mediating role of social cohesion,* Richmond: Jesuit Social Services.

Vinson, T. (2007) *Dropping off the edge. The distribution of disadvantage in Australia,* Richmond: Jesuit Social Services.

Vinson, T. (2009a) *The origins, meaning, definition and economic implications of the concept of social inclusion/exclusion,* Canberra: Department of Education, Employment and Workplace Relations.

Vinson, T. (2009b) *Markedly socially disadvantaged localities in Australia: Their nature and possible remediation,* Canberra: Department of Education, Employment and Workplace Relations.

Ward, T. (2009) 'Material deprivation', in T. Ward, O. Lelkes, H. Sutherland and I.G. Tóth (eds) *European inequalities. Social inclusion and income distribution in the European Union,* Budapest: TÁRKI Social Research Institute, pp 117-30.

Weiss, C. (1986) 'Research and policy-making: a limited partnership', in F. Heller (ed) *The use and abuse of social science,* London: Sage Publications, pp 214-35.

Welfare Working Group (2010) *Long-term benefit dependency: The issues. Detailed paper,* Wellington: School of Government, Victoria University of Wellington.

Whelan, C.T. and Maître, B. (2007) 'Measuring material deprivation with EU-SILC: lessons from the Irish survey', *European Societies,* vol 9, pp 147-73.

Whelan, C.T. and Maître, B. (2008) 'Poverty, deprivation and economic vulnerability in the enlarged EU', in J. Alber, T. Fahey and C. Saraceno (eds) *Handbook of quality of life in the enlarged European Union,* Abingdon: Routledge, pp 201-17.

Whelan, C.T. and Maître, B. (2009) *Poverty and deprivation in Ireland in comparative perspective,* Research Series No 11, Dublin: Economic and Social Research Institute.

Whelan, C.T. and Nolan, B. (2009) *Poverty and deprivation in Ireland in comparative perspective,* Research Series No 11, Dublin: Economic and Social Research Institute.

Whelan, C.T., Layte, R. and Maître, B. (2003) 'Persistent income poverty and deprivation in the European Union', *Journal of Social Policy,* vol 32, no 1, pp 1-18.

Whelan, C.T., Nolan, B. and Maître, B. (2006) *Measuring consistent poverty in Ireland with EU-SILC data,* Working Paper No 165, Dublin: Economic and Social Research Institute.

Whelan, C.T., Nolan, B. and Maître, B. (2008) *Measuring material deprivation in the enlarged EU*, Working Paper No 249, Dublin: Economic and Social Research Institute.

Whiteford, P. (1997) 'Measuring poverty and income inequality in Australia', *Agenda*, vol 4, pp 39-50.

Whiteford, P. (2001) 'Understanding poverty and social exclusion: situating Australia internationally', in R. Fincher and P. Saunders (eds) *Creating unequal futures? Rethinking poverty, inequality and disadvantage*, Sydney: Allen & Unwin, pp 38-69.

Whiteford, P. and Adema, W. (2007) *What works best in reducing child poverty: A benefit or work strategy?*, OECD Social, Employment and Migration Working Papers No 51, Paris: Organisation for Economic Co-operation and Development.

Wilkins, R. (2008) 'The changing socio-demographic composition of poverty in Australia: 1982 to 2004', *Australian Journal of Social Issues*, vol 42, no 4, pp 481-501.

Wilkins, R., Warren, D., Hahn, M. and Houng, B. (2010) *Families, incomes and jobs, Volume 5: A statistical report on waves 1 to 7 of the household, income and labour dynamics in Australia survey*, Melbourne: Melbourne Institute of Applied Economic and Social Research, University of Melbourne.

Willitts, M. (2006) *Measuring child poverty using material deprivation: Possible approaches*, Working Paper No 28, London: Department for Work and Pensions.

Wilson, S., Meagher, G., Gibson, R., Denemark, D. and Western, M. (2005) *Australian Survey of Social Attitudes. The first report*, Sydney: University of New South Wales Press.

Wolff, J. and de-Shalit, A. (2007) *Disadvantage*, Oxford: Oxford University Press.

Wooden, M. and Watson, N. (2002) 'The HILDA survey: what's in it for economists?', *Australian Journal of Labour Economics*, vol 5, no 3, pp 397-417.

Wright, G. (2008) *Findings from the indicators of poverty and social exclusion project: A profile of poverty using the socially perceived necessities approach*, Key Report 7, Pretoria: Department of Social Development, Republic of South Africa.

Young, K., Ashby, D., Boaz, A. and Grayson, L. (2002) 'Social science and the evidence-based policy movement', *Social Policy and Society*, vol 1, no 3, pp 215-24.

Index

Note: page numbers followed by the letters *f* and *t* refer to information in figures and tables respectively.